D0426621

Collateral Damage

Recent Titles in Contemporary Psychology

Resilience for Today: Gaining Strength from Adversity
Edith Henderson Grotberg, editor

The Destructive Power of Religion: Violence in Judaism, Christianity, and Islam, Volumes I–IV
J. Harold Ellens, editor

Helping Children Cope with the Death of a Parent: A Guide for the First Year
Paddy Greenwall Lewis and Jessica G. Lippman

Martyrdom: The Psychology, Theology, and Politics of Self-Sacrifice
Rona M. Fields, with Contributions from Cóilín Owens, Valérie Rosoux, Michael Berenbaum, and Reuven Firestone

Redressing the Emperor: Improving Our Children's Public Mental Health System
John S. Lyons

Havens: Stories of True Community Healing
Leonard Jason and Martin Perdoux

Psychology of Terrorism, Condensed Edition: Coping with the Continuing Threat
Chris E. Stout, editor

Handbook of International Disaster Psychology, Volumes I–IV
Gilbert Reyes and Gerard A. Jacobs, editors

The Psychology of Resolving Global Conflicts: From War to Peace, Volumes 1–3
Mari Fitzduff and Chris E. Stout, editors

The Myth of Depression as Disease: Limitations and Alternatives to Drug Treatment
Allan M. Leventhal and Christopher R. Martell

Preventing Teen Violence: A Guide for Parents and Professionals
Sherri N. McCarthy and Claudio Simon Hutz

Making Enemies Unwittingly: Humiliation and International Conflict
Evelin Gerda Lindner

Collateral Damage

The Psychological Consequences of America's War on Terrorism

Edited by Paul R. Kimmel and Chris E. Stout

Foreword by Philip G. Zimbardo

Contemporary Psychology

Westport, Connecticut
London

Library of Congress Cataloging-in-Publication Data

Collateral damage : the psychological consequences of America's war on terrorism / edited by Paul R. Kimmel and Chris E. Stout; foreword by Philip G. Zimbardo.

p. cm. — (Contemporary psychology, ISSN 1546–668X)

Includes bibliographical references and index.

ISBN 0–275–98826-0 (alk. paper)

1. Terrorism—United States—Psychological aspects. 2. Terrorism—United States—Prevention. I. Kimmel, Paul R. II. Stout, Chris E. III. Series: Contemporary psychology (Praeger Publishers)

HV6432.C638 2006

973.931—dc22 2006012111

British Library Cataloguing in Publication Data is available.

Library of Congress Catalog Card Number: 2006012111
ISBN: 0–275–98826–0
ISSN: 1546–668X

First published in 2006

Praeger Publishers, 88 Post Road West, Westport, CT 06881
An imprint of Greenwood Publishing Group, Inc.
www.praeger.com

Printed in the United States of America

The paper used in this book complies with the Permanent Paper Standard issued by the National Information Standards Organization (Z39.48–1984).

10 9 8 7 6 5 4 3 2 1

Contents

Foreword: The Political Psychology of Terrorist Alarms

Philip G. Zimbardo

On April 18, 1775, patriot Paul Revere made his famous midnight ride from Boston warning that the British were coming. When the British did arrive the next day, the colonial militia defeated them at Concord, and America's Revolutionary War had its auspicious beginning. Revere's warning was effective because he was a highly credible communicator, his alarm was focused on a specific event, and it called for a concrete set of actions. Contemporary psychological research supports this Paul Revere paradigm for successful public alarms. To be optimally effective, such alarms should arouse only a moderate level of motivation. A level that is too low does not energize action. A level that is too high creates an emotional overload and competing, distracting behaviors. The alarms must be based on reliable evidence and presented clearly by trustworthy sources. They must be about specific dangers or threats that a recommended action may deal with. If the threat is likely to persist over an extended time, debriefing after an alarm is essential. Debriefing corrects misinformation and modifies faulty recommendations. Most of all, debriefing reinforces citizens for heeding the message and reassures them of the value of their collaborative efforts. Finally, if the threat does not materialize, a reputable authority must explain why it did not and then lower or remove the threat alert.

Violations of Effective Psychological Principles

All the color-coded alerts issued by U.S. government officials to warn the public of imminent terrorist dangers violated each of these basic psychological principles. Not one international terrorist attack has occurred on American soil since September 11, 2001. Where are the thousands of terrorists' cells in our country? Where are the debriefings by our authorities to explain why nothing happened? Alerts just silently evaporate until the next alarm is sounded. We know from Aesop's classic story of the Boy Who Cried Wolf that after only three false alarms, people stop believing previously credible messengers. Many false alarms desensitize most Americans to the need to be on high alert. For a few it became normal to be anxiously dreading the worst, given the experience of the first horrific attacks on the World Trade Center and Pentagon. I call this pre-traumatic stress syndrome.

Government officials may feel no need for corrective information because they usually remind the public not to worry and lead normal lives. Nevertheless, false alarms have unintended consequences, and perhaps some intended ones. They frighten us well beyond a realistic nationwide risk level of any new terrorist attacks. These alarms have sustained a heightened sense of anxiety and confusion in the United States for more than four years. They reinforce a public willingness to spend huge sums on the military and homeland security. They also create a climate of hostility and danger that encourages citizens' acceptance of restrictions on their personal freedoms. This climate fosters toleration of human rights violations from the domestic PATRIOT Act to the mistreatment of civilian prisoners at Guantanamo Bay and Abu Ghraib.

Homeland Security planned a nationwide campaign to promote emergency preparedness fashioned after the programs of FEMA for natural disaster readiness and supported by focus-group recommendations. However, it has become apparent that natural disasters and disasters caused by human agents require very different models of response. The impartial laws of nature are very different from the evildoing behind humans' malevolence. Recent experiences in New Orleans and Texas suggest that we are prepared for neither natural nor terrorist disasters.

The Psychology of Terrorism

Terrorism is not about destroying the material resources of an enemy nation and taking over the country. Terrorism is about psychology. Terrorism is about making ordinary people feel vulnerable, anxious, confused, uncertain, and helpless. Terrorism is about imagining the monster under our beds or lurking in dark closets. It is about the faceless, omnipotent enemy who might be the friendly candy man, or neighbor, or some horrible creature of our imagination. The power of terrorism lies precisely in its pervasive ambiguity, its invasion of our minds.

Reactions to feeling personally vulnerable include phobias, triggering of unresolved childhood conflicts, prolonged stress reactions, blindly obeying powerful leaders, and intense feelings of anger. Anger arises from feeling helpless or vulnerable. It is a turning outward of intense and concealed feelings of weakness. Prejudice against out groups is one consequence of such strong negative reactions provoking attacks on safe targets, such as marginalized peoples in our nation. People who feel vulnerable support leaders who are bold, decisive, single-minded, even arrogant men of action. They support leaders who identify an enemy for them and who give it a name, a face, and a location so that they can channel their anger against it as evil. Many Americans have accepted Saddam Hussein as that enemy and Iraq as that location.

The justification to invade Iraq was that Saddam Hussein would supply weapons of mass destruction to al Qaeda and other terrorist groups to use against the United States. Once many Americans accepted that link, they agreed that deposing Hussein was reasonable. They also concluded that we are winning the war against terrorism.

The majority of U.S. citizens believe that Saddam Hussein was partly responsible for the terrorist attacks of September 11, despite the absence of any supporting information. That belief is enough to fuel fires of revenge against him. Calling for deposing the dictator by all means, was the basis for the all-out war against Iraq. Thus, since March 2003, the American public has maintained its high level of anxiety, sustaining its pre-traumatic stress syndrome while keeping before us the image of Saddam and his followers as our collective enemy.

Nevertheless, the terrorists remain faceless, elusive, still able to run and hide and commit their unspeakable horrors in the absence of Saddam. Terrorist attacks escalate in Iraq in retaliation for U.S. invasion and occupation. President Bush's grand vision of creating peace in the entire Middle East region by deposing Iraq's leadership has proven to be a nearsighted, simplistic, and biased view. How can we hope to create a climate of peace in this far-flung region with so many antagonists with disparate interests, needs, and cultural values?

Many other plausible hypotheses about the causes and consequences of these false alarms exist. Even assuming no manipulative intent, we need a serious reevaluation of how to construct future alerts, guide their optimal use, and explain to the public why the events do not materialize when they do not. Of course, we are all relieved when the alarms prove false rather than true. But when officials repeat the alarms over time, they induce a psychic numbing, lulling us to a state of unpreparedness to act constructively and effectively when the foe or Mother Nature does come to our door.

Action Conclusions

There are indeed dangerous individuals and groups who hate some of what America symbolizes to them. These people will try to attack us in various ways, including suicide bombings. Security and preparedness are essential components in countering these individuals, but so are honesty, transparency, and accountability of our leaders. The administration is not listening to the best scientific advice available on how to construct terror alerts, educate the public in this new realm, manage man-made disasters that require different models than traditional natural disasters, evaluate the efficiency and effectiveness of their programs, and evaluate the psychological effects of their efforts to prevent terrorism. High levels of sustained stress have a greater long-term destructive impact on the nation than the consequences of most terrorist attacks. Preparedness would benefit from a wiser appreciation of the behavioral, cognitive, and emotional effects of prevention efforts discussed in this book.

ACKNOWLEDGMENT

We want to express our gratitude to Dr. Arthur J. Kendall for his important contributions to the work of the Task Force on the Psychological Effects of Efforts to Prevent Terrorism and his invaluable assistance in the production of this book. Without his expertise, encouragement, and support our work would not have been as effective. Without his tireless efforts the book you are about to read would not have been possible.

He has dedicated his career to assuring that public policy is based on objective and impartial information. Before retiring, he was senior mathematical statistician at the U.S. General Accountability Office, the oversight and evaluation agency of the U.S. Congress, where he participated in GAO's Terrorism Knowledge Network receiving briefings from flag officers and senior executive branch officials. He is a charter member of the American Statistical Association's section on Statistics in Defense and National Security.

He is also a political/social psychologist, a Fellow of APA and SPSSI. He has been following terrorism issues since the late 70s. More details can be found at www.kingdouglas.com/spss/DiverseCultures/Art/Page01.htm.

Introduction

Paul R. Kimmel

Flight 1586

"The first-class passengers paid a lot of money so that they could have their own bathroom and economy class passengers should not be using it," said the irate flight attendant when I asked why she was confronting me as I exited from the front restroom. She refused to step aside to allow me to return to my seat, loudly insisting that I give her my boarding pass. I told her it was at my seat. She then raised a tray she had in her hands and pushed it into my chest. After regaining my composure, I asked for her name, informing her that I was going to write up this incident. She stopped speaking and pointed at her badge. She then lowered the tray and moved aside and I returned to my seat.

As I was writing down what had occurred, another flight attendant came to my seat. He told me sternly not to come near the other flight attendants and informed me that he could turn the plane around and land it if I caused any more trouble. I gave him my business card. I also requested that he interview the first-class passengers and my colleagues who had witnessed this unfortunate incident. To the best of my knowledge, he did neither.

This was the first time in my 50-plus years of flying that I have ever had a negative contact with any airline personnel in flight. An angry flight attendant using inappropriate language and physical force and an authoritarian one threatening to have me arrested aggravated what should have been at most a benign incident. I was shaken.

Airline Security

Airline security is one of the more visible areas in which our government has made efforts to prevent terrorism. Anyone who has flown since 9/11 is well aware of the additional screening at airports and the flight delays they entail. We are also familiar with the presence of security forces of various kinds at the airports. We may know about proposals to arm airline pilots and have armed plainclothes government personnel on board flights in the future.

Many have welcomed and most tolerated these measures. We are led to believe that the additional security will prevent commercial airliners from being hijacked. But there are other psychological effects of these measures. For example, it is likely my experience with the flight attendants was related to airline efforts to prevent terrorism. Over time these efforts may cause more danger for passengers than security; more negative than positive outcomes for the public.

This book examines some of the effects that current U.S. strategies to prevent terrorism are having on the American public. These strategies may fail or lead to unintended consequences due to a lack of psychological insights. Let's take another look at my airline incident in light of some psychological insights.

Authority and Relationships

Phil Zimbardo at Stanford (see Foreword) found that individuals who have been given more power or new authority tend to depersonalize their subordinates and may harass them. Suppose the Federal Aviation Administration recently gave the personnel on my flight more authority to oversee the passengers. One could hypothesize that this additional authority caused the flight attendants to overreact when their unwritten rule about bathroom use was broken. When they did not get the acquiescence that they expected, they became angry and attacked me. In turn, the incident violated my expectations about airline personnel, which begin with "the customer is always right." The flight attendants undermined my assumptions about my personal well-being, causing stress and apprehension.

This incident illustrates situations that the authors in this book investigated. Their studies evaluate changes in the usual experiences of the people they are studying. These changes produce stress, anxiety, and fear. People need some preparation to help them understand changes in their daily lives and some follow-up to ease anxieties that these changes arouse; otherwise, they will experience negative emotional effects. The current practice of announcing to passengers that the front bathroom is only for first-class passengers, although frustrating, increases awareness. Had such an announcement been made on my flight, the incident would not have occurred.

The incident makes clear that there are many psychological side effects of efforts to prevent terrorism. In setting up security measures, airport and airline authorities may not have considered the changes in relationships between the surveillance personnel and those surveyed. While the government has paid a great deal of attention to the technical side of these security measures, they have paid much less attention to the interpersonal aspects. Giving authority to those not trained to use it in interpersonal situations can lead to conflicts such as mine. If the person given the authority is frustrated or unhappy with a past lack of authority or their current circumstances, they may overreact in their new role. If weapons are added to the mix, training and instruction become even more vital to avert such overreactions.

On the other side, public unwillingness or inability to adapt to the delays and submission required by security measures will increase incidents of conflict escalation. A tired, frustrated passenger who has missed connections and has been ordered about or ignored by airline personnel may become angry. This passenger may cause danger for all on board a flight or in a waiting area. Angry clients and authoritarian security personnel are problematic in any public situation. To prevent conflicts, passengers must learn that the relation between them and the flight crew is no longer only one of provider and consumer. Security personnel must be trained to defuse conflicts without the use of psychological or physical violence.

It is becoming easier to assess the consequences of efforts to prevent terrorism on the public. We have gotten over some of the shock and confusion from 9/11 and the events following. This time lapse makes our psychological reactions easier to assess and relate to specific prevention efforts. This book is the beginning of what we hope will be a long-term effort on the part of behavioral, cognitive, social and organizational scientific and mental health professionals to evaluate the psychological effects of our efforts to prevent terrorism. We should take the lead in assessing the changes that have taken place in the United States since the trauma of 9/11. We can help ameliorate negatively charged relationships related to terrorism prevention.

The Task Force on the Psychological Effects of Efforts To Prevent Terrorism

We undertook the studies in this book at the request of and with support from the Council of Representatives of the American Psychological Association. A report of our work was submitted to the Association's Board of Scientific Affairs in 2005. Each paper in that report showed evidence of negative psychological effects associated with living in a nation "at war." We found that this stressful environment often leads authorities to overestimate the threat and consequences of terrorist activities and to make poor decisions in trying to prevent these activities. The "war on terror," has affected the emotions, beliefs, and behaviors of the American public in ways typical of situations characterized by uncertainty, extreme stress, and fear.

As Zimbardo points out in the Foreword, coping strategies, such as the color-coded alert system of the Homeland Securities Department, without clear explanations of the potential danger during their application or of the reason for their removal, build a sense of apprehension in the American public. Similar misgivings come from unauthorized searches and questioning of the public by government agents. Such unsystematic and unexplained efforts to prevent terrorism increase anxieties and reduce a sense of security in all, but especially in fearful or traumatized individuals.

As many of our studies showed, conformity pressures are stifling international exchange programs and increasing prejudice and stereotyping among Americans. Visitors from other countries, especially from the Middle East, report more fear and persecution since 9/11. Selective government security measures are having an adverse impact on individuals from the Middle East and parts of South Asia. They are also limiting the migration of citizens, visitors, and refugees from other states where there is a great deal of internal and external conflict.

The task force also found that the war in Iraq is affecting individuals who have suffered past traumas, such as combat veterans. Students are becoming more militantly patriotic, and teachers and officials are developing blind spots to situations of domestic conflict. We more easily deny, rationalize, or overlook evidence or ideas contrary to our current decisions and government programs when we are under stress.

Finally, the studies show that personal contact with terrorism is not necessary for the development of the negative emotions, cognitions, and behaviors we found. Rhetorical framing[1] about and media reports of the "war on terror" emphasizing "us" versus "them," loyalty to a central authority, and the belief that our own norms are universal truths also contribute to these psychological effects. They increase fear and prejudicial attitudes, discrimination against others, and curtailment of civil and personal liberties in the United States, independent of any actual terrorist activity. If the American public believes that we are in a war with an evil empire, they will accept restrictions on their freedoms and the killing of civilians in countries said to be part of that empire with no contact with the evil doers. Even if they disagree with the killings and restrictions, they will argue within the frame of reference set by the administration and promoted by the media. To deal constructively with terrorists requires avoiding or getting out of the cognitive and perceptual frames set by our leaders.

There are a number of recommendations in this book. In chapter 1, Fabick divides these recommendations into those that focus on emotional help and those that focus on risk reduction, extending the concepts of emotion-focused and problem-directed coping.[2] Although these two categories overlap in some cases, the suggestions to ameliorate emotional problems are for the most part retrospective recommendations dealing with the effects of terrorism and our efforts to prevent it. The recommendations to promote risk reduction, on the other hand, are more preventative, dealing with the causes of terrorism and their amelioration.

Overall, we recommend that psychologists take the lead in providing impartial and objective information about terrorism and efforts to prevent it. We can use our knowledge about enemy images, stereotyping of other groups, and the processes of group think to open a space for debate, discussion, and interpersonal engagement. If we are to be heard, we must model the kind of critical thinking, problem-solving focus, and tolerance of differing positions that we wish to see in our policymakers. And most important, we must demonstrate that we have ideas to offer that can make a difference.

This book provides an excellent selection of such ideas and information. The Task force on the Psychological Effects of Efforts to Prevent Terrorism was selected in 2003 to cover a broad range of topics that psychologists are qualified to investigate and the methods they can use in those investigations. While we did not begin to contact all the American Psychological Association members who are currently studying terrorism, the Task Force did include social, educational, humanistic, child, medical, mental health, and peace psychologists. The data they gathered came from surveys, interviews, clinical assessments, media analyses, observations, and introspection. They also extensively reviewed the literature in their areas. (The reader is urged to check the works they cite in this book to get details on statistical analyses and methodological considerations.) They have used a variety of psychological perspectives to explain the findings in this book; their recommendations are practical and timely.

In addition to the authors of these incisive chapters, the Task Force included Drs. Leila Dane, Richard Wagner, Margaret Heldring, and Arthur Kendall. We especially want to thank Dr. Kendall—who critiqued and edited many drafts of these chapters—and our authors for their persistence and dedication. Their work will help reduce the **collateral damage** being caused by America's war on terrorism. We want to stop doing the terrorists' work for them.

Notes

1. Rhetorical framing as used in this book refers to how a frame of reference is asserted to evoke particular ideas and to preclude other terms of discussion.

2. R. Gerrig and P. Zimbardo, *Psychology and Life*, 16th ed. (Boston: Allyn and Bacon, 2002).

CHAPTER 1

US & THEM: MODERATING GROUP CONFLICT—A TRACK FOUR DIPLOMACY PROGRAM

Stephen Fabick

> God, give us grace to accept with serenity the things that cannot be changed, courage to change the things that should be changed and the wisdom to distinguish the one from the other.
>
> Rev. Reinhold Niebuhr, 1943

The Task Force on the Psychological Effects of Efforts To Prevent Terrorism was charged with clarifying the psychological effects of efforts to prevent terrorism. (The term "terrorism" in this chapter refers to violence committed by non-state entities—in contrast to "terror," which is used by those in power to maintain it.) The second and related mission was to examine programs that provide alternatives to terrorism—that is, reduce the risk of future terrorism. Thus, there is a focus on dealing with the past (trauma reduction) and a focus on the future (reducing the incidence of terrorism).

Another way to conceptualize that dual focus is to think of two ways of coping with terrorism: emotion-focused coping and problem-directed coping (Gerrig & Zimbardo, 2002). Emotion-focused coping attempts to lessen the traumatic impact of terrorism and its aftermath but does not focus on changing the stressor. This is the type of coping strategy proposed by the Surgeon General. It is also the approach highlighted in the American Psychological Association's (2002) *Road to Resilience* program. Some experts argue that some emotion-focused coping—such as "terror management theory" (Pyszczynski,

Solomon, & Greenberg, 2003)—supports problem-directed coping by inoculating the target population from future trauma, thereby deterring potential terrorists whose ultimate motive is terrorizing the target audience.

Problem-directed coping involves identifying the causes of the stress and eliminating, or more realistically, moderating them. In terms of this definition, the "war on terrorism" is an ineffective problem-directed coping attempt. For example, the justification for the war in Iraq was that "we have to do something. It's better to have tried and failed than to do nothing." We know that to do nothing in the face of threat courts hopelessness and helplessness—that is, depression and, quite possibly, disaster. However, terrorism today is often a response to foreign occupation or domination, and the humiliation, helplessness, and hopelessness it engenders in the populace (Pape, 2003; Wessells, 2004). Too often our leaders see the cause of such terror as the cure—that is, more military control, occupation, and international and domestic intelligence gathering. The research in this book suggests that other problem-directed coping strategies—for example, prioritizing economic interdependence, fostering cultural exchange, and structured intergroup dialogue—are needed.

So, as the Niebuhr prayer at the opening of this chapter indicates, we need both coping approaches to promote peace in our post-9/11 world. Emotion-focused coping can foster acceptance of the reality of terrorism, while lessening its traumatic impact. Problem-directed coping requires Niebuhr's "courage to change what we can," in this case, the incidence of future terrorist attacks. This book provides many recommendations for such changes.

Task Force Recommendations: Emotion-Focused or Problem-Directed Coping?

The work of the task force synthesized by Kimmel in the Task Force Report (2005) plus the specific recommendations of the task force members in this book are discussed below. They will be categorized by the method of coping emphasized, followed by my thoughts on the expansion of terrorism based on experiences in reducing intergroup conflict.

Two of the task force's four main recommendations to the American Psychological Association (Kimmel, 2005) fall into the emotion-focused coping category and two into the problem-directed coping category.

Emotion-Focused Coping Recommendations

The first two recommendations of the task force are examples of emotion-focused coping. The first addresses the stress-inducing effects of the "war on terrorism" metaphor and suggests steps the American Psychological Association (APA) could take to reframe coping with the threat of terrorism in a more "psychologically effective" way. The first task force recommendation states that:

1. The APA should ensure that its members understand the pervasive negative effects that the concept of "the war on terrorism" can have for their patients, students, and other clients.
   A. Examine all APA publications and guides to ensure that they do not reinforce the war on terrorism metaphor. For example, in future editions of the Public Education campaign literature make it clear that the "war" referred to in "a time of war" and "wartime stress" was the war in Iraq, not the "war on terrorism."
   B. Include findings from this report in press releases and ongoing APA public service programs such as the Public Education Campaign and ACT (adults and children together against violence) to point out the problems caused by thinking of our efforts to prevent terrorism as a "war."
   C. Develop more appropriate and thought-provoking metaphors to describe programs that will be more psychologically effective in efforts to prevent terrorism.

The second recommendation, also emotion-focused, encourages the APA to evaluate the success of its various practice guidelines and relevant public education programs in promoting resilience, clearly an emotion-focused approach.

2. The APA should evaluate its own and others' programs for promoting resilience for effectiveness.
   A. Check with practitioners, clinics, and hospitals to assess the reduction in anxiety and vulnerability of patients treated for stress and trauma using APA guidelines.
   B. Check with school teachers and administrators to assess the extent to which students and parents are more independent in their thinking and resistant to conformity pressures after taking part in ACT, the Global Psychology Project, US and THEM, and similar programs.
   C. Include assessments of ethnocentrism in all measurements of resilience to ensure that any improvements are not a function of scapegoating and enemy imaging.

In chapter 10, "Cities of Fear, Cities of Hope: Public Mental Health in the Age of Terrorism," Stout and Weine challenge the "war on terror" metaphor. They maintain that it has stress-inducing effects and implies military solutions at the expense of social, economic, political, and psychological initiatives. The authors advocate for a number of improvements in our country's mental health delivery system aimed at reducing the potential impact of future incidents of terrorism. Their recommendations focus on the future, with an emphasis on having services in place to minimize the emotional damage of future terrorism—for example, through optimizing "community resilience." They stress the importance of collaboration among mental health experts and a variety of other groups—hospitals, physicians, government agencies, the media, and community leaders—in creating such resilience.

In chapter 8, "Psychological Effects of the Virtual Media Coverage of the Iraq War," Serlin decries the media's war coverage. She explores its impact on three Vietnam War veteran clients. She deplores the practice of using embedded journalists not only as observers, but also as participants in the events they are reporting. She provides examples of war reporting morphing into "infotainment" with the media glorifying and sanitizing the war. In the Iraq war coverage, Serlin notes the paucity of coverage of refugee camps and other sobering elements of traditional war coverage in favor of high-tech images of "the deceptive beauty of war." She cites a *London Daily Times* report documenting the Bush administration's having journalists on the payroll, and creating an enemies' list of news organizations. She ties psychological damage such as the loss of identity, derealization, and depersonalization to such media developments.

Serlin recommends additional training for psychologists to help their clients deal with the impact of this media coverage of postmodern warfare and its associated vicarious traumatization. Thus, her focus, like Stout and Weine's, is on the enhancement of emotion-focused coping in vulnerable mental health clients.

Another APA task force member also emphasized an emotion-focused coping response: the upgrading of America's primary care training (Heldring, 2005). She identified a need for famil physicians, pediatricians, nurse practitioners, general internists, obstetricians-gynecologists, community health clinicians, and public health department staff to help patients cope with the psychological impact of terrorism. Her article, "Mental Health and Primary Care in a Time of Terrorism: The Psychological Effect of Public Communication about Risk" (2005), is based on focus group surveys in 14 U.S. cities that addressed the kinds of emotional problems primary care professionals have seen in their patients since 9/11. Like some of the other authors in this book, she questioned the administration's focus on ineffectual problem-directed coping steps (such as duct tape and plastic sheeting) and recommended public service communiqués that are credible, specific, and informative, acknowledging the emotional impact of a threat. She contrasted the leadership of New York City's Mayor Giuliani to the Bush administration's handling of the terrorist threat. She advocated for primary care physicians' training not only in bioterrorism, but also panic management.

Problem-Directed Coping Recommendations

The third and fourth recommendations in the task force's report to the APA are problem-directed strategies for coping with the threat of terrorism. The third recommendation describes how the APA could promote programs to train security personnel to defuse conflicts. The fourth recommendation addresses the establishment of risk assessment approaches to evaluate the effectiveness of current antiterrorism measures. The task force report and this book are the beginnings of such risk assessment.

3. The APA should sponsor and promote programs to train security personnel to understand how to recognize and defuse potential conflict situations.

    A. Contact public service organizations that are hiring more armed security guards and offer to help them evaluate their training programs in light of current knowledge about what works.
    B. Sponsor evaluations of the performance of security personnel in conflict situations. These could be surveys of those being "guarded" and observations of critical incidents. Publicize the results.
    C. Develop new training programs in light of the evaluations mentioned above and make them available to all.

4. The APA should establish a committee to develop valid and reliable measures of the potential for terrorism in different populations. These measures could be used as outcome variables in research assessing the effectiveness of current government and media efforts to prevent terrorism. Examples of such research are assessments of the following:

    A. The color-coded alert system.
    B. The peacekeeping efforts in Iraq and Afghanistan.

C. The incarceration programs in Iraq, Cuba, and elsewhere.
D. Immigration programs and restrictions.
E. Training programs for security personnel.

Wessells's chapter 9 "The Impact of U.S. Antiterrorism Interventions on Terrorist Motivation: Preliminary Research in Afghanistan and Iraq" reports the results of studies he conducted in these countries with the help of local experts. His recommendations are all examples of problem-directed coping approaches to threat. They are aimed at reducing youth radicalization, terrorist recruitment, and, ultimately, the incidence of terrorism. For example, he recommends avoiding wars and occupations not sanctioned by the UN Security Council. He found in 2003 that the Iraqi war was inflaming future terrorist motivation in the Muslim world. In his recommendation to limit the excessive use of military force, he emphasizes the need to avoid any use of torture.

Wessells argues for more comprehensive and proactive planning for the establishment of civilian security and humanitarian support systems following possible future military actions. Specifically, he notes that humanitarian assistance must be separate from military operations and be performed by well-trained relief and reconstruction professionals in settings made relatively safe by multilateral security personnel. The association of humanitarian and military personnel in Iraq is fostering a wider sense of domination among the people and is resulting in attacks on relief workers.

Wessells suggests the establishment of a wide array of policies and practices supportive of Muslims in his last two recommendations: making U.S. economic support of Israel contingent on its adherence to human rights standards and employing culturally sensitive humanitarian initiatives in Muslim countries.

In chapter 4, "The Social Psychology of Punishing Dissent: Negative Reactions to Antiwar Views in the United States," Lott investigates the chilling impact of threats such as terrorism to independent and realistic thinking. She argues for social studies and citizenship education at various levels to identify and change this tendency. Greater understanding of the pressures to conform will help reduce groupthink at times of crisis and promote what Sternberg (2003) has called "the 'other three Rs'—reasoning, responsibility and resilience." Examples of problem directed coping recommendations that Lott makes include school exercises coupled with class discussions to teach students about the pressure for uniformity and foster their abilities to analyze the consequences of conforming or dissenting.

In chapter 3, "Jujitsu Politics: Terrorism and Responses to Terrorism," McCauley recommends U.S. policy and research programs directed toward the prevention of terrorist attacks. His suggestions are all examples of problem-directed approaches to cope with the threat of terrorism. He advocates tracking polls in the United States and in Muslim countries to assess attitudes toward the United States and its antiterrorist policies and toward terrorists and their acts. McCauley states that scientific polling practices can help the United States in the "war of ideas." He cautions against unidirectional communication—that is, shaping only Muslim opinion without any corresponding changes in U.S. attitudes. Such an approach could be seen as intellectual imperialism in the Muslim world.

McCauley recommends the development of databases with timelines linking terrorist actions and state responses to determine what works best in reducing the risk of terrorism. He advocates for more research addressing the radicalization and recruitment of individuals into terrorist groups.

Such research has been done by Wessells (in this volume) and by Crenshaw (2001), Horgan (2003), Silke (2003a, 2003b), Staub (2003a, 2003b), and Stern (2003). I will highlight the work of Borum (2003) in delineating the development of the "terrorist mind," and a related model of large group behavioral regression that can foster the development of terrorism described by Volkan (2004). (See the section in this chapter titled "The Making of a Terrorist" for the special meaning of *regression* in this context.)

Combination of Emotion-Focused and Problem-Directed Coping Recommendations

In the Foreword, Zimbardo discusses the color-coded terror alerts. He persuasively argues that the system actually reinforces the impact of terrorism by fostering unnecessary and sustained anxiety about possible attacks, while undermining realistic preparations and eroding civil liberties. So he addresses both emotion-focused (he calls it "pre-traumatic stress syndrome") and problem-directed (the desensitization of "crying wolf") coping liabilities in the current terror warning system in the United States. He suggests that the system increases the public's willingness to support military incursions, invasive homeland security measures, and intelligence-gathering approaches such as torture. He concludes that a revamping of the alert system using sound psychological principles is needed.

Hodson, Esses, and Dovidio examine the psychological effects of efforts to prevent terrorism on U.S. and Canadian immigration policies in their chapter titled, "Perceptions of Threat, National Representation, and Support for Procedures To Protect the National Group." They discuss the emotional impact of U.S. efforts to prevent terrorism on the population and the effect such steps have on immigration in the United States and in Canada. Thus, they focus on emotion-focused issues of threat perception but in relation to a social problem (immigration) and so also have a problem-directed focus. They found that some U.S. efforts to deal with terrorism, such as the overuse of terror alerts, have created a xenophobic reaction that has compromised immigration policies in the two countries since 9/11. The greater the sense of terrorist threat, the more narrowly the host group defines itself, seeing potential immigrants as more threatening. People from countries associated with terrorism are most likely to be the target of more restrictive immigration screening.

They recommend educational programs that emphasize the benefits of maintaining a flow of immigrants to the two countries to enhance their role in the world economy. They also support promoting a recategorization of the United States and Canada as "immigrant nations, not so different than the newcomers." Such an expansion of the definition of the in-group can foster changes as "they" become associated with "us." The authors contend that governments and the media should de-sensationalize the link between Arab and Muslim immigrants and the risk of terror.

In chapter 7, "Efforts To Prevent Terrorism: Impact on Immigrant Groups," Thomas also looks at immigration. Her work addresses failures of our war on terrorism immigration policies in terms of emotion-focused and problem-directed coping. She notes that the average length of detention for cleared detainees was 80 days (78 days longer than FBI directives) and that the "special registration" system for noncitizen, nonimmigrant men resulted in no terrorism charges among the 85,581 registrants as of May 2003. Such policies have alienated the communities whose cooperation law enforcement most needs in antiterrorist intelligence-gathering. The targeting of Muslim and Arabs in the United States has amplified anti-American views abroad.

Thomas gathered data from mental health professionals and advocates for immigrants, refugees, and undocumented residents in the United States and searched a variety of government and nongovernmental sources. She found a dramatic increase in psychological problems in immigrant groups since 9/11. In particular, she highlights the re-traumatizing effect of antiterrorism policies on previously traumatized asylum-seekers, refugees, and undocumented people who have fled war, genocide, and persecutory regimes, a similar finding to that of Serlin with Vietnam veterans (chapter 8 in this volume).

In chapter 5, "Untangling the Web: Threat, Ideology, and Political Behavior," Unger describes the impact of 9/11 on the level of anxiety, trauma, and anger in U.S. citizens, especially students. She also describes the effect on their attitudes about in-group and out-group thinking—including nationalism and patriotism. She writes, "Us against them was a common theme following the terrorist attacks. This rhetorical framing (see Introduction note one for a definition of rhetorical framing) evoked an essentialist and divisive definition of being an American." *Essentialism* refers to a world view that stereotypes groups of people as having a nature; immutable characteristics that are essential to being a group member.

Unger found that threats such as terrorism undermine one's tolerance for cognitive complexity. The resulting need for simple answers can weaken critical thinking. She recommends research into this area, and the development of curricula that foster cognitive complexity at all levels of education. So she addresses emotion-focused coping directed toward the problem of understanding and moderating groupthink—personally, in the media, and in public policy.

In chapter 2, "9/11 Aftershocks: An Analysis of Conditions Ripe for Hate Crimes," Christie focuses on the impact of terrorism on domestic hate crimes in the United States. He recommends a fuller range of noncoercive international policies, leading to less retaliation and resulting cycles of violence, abroad and at home. Christie cites research showing an increase in the cohesion of the target group—in this case, countries with high concentrations of Muslims (Olson, 2002). And he sees polarized "us and them" thinking fueling the upswing in domestic hate crimes toward people viewed as Muslim after 9/11. So Christie is concerned with the emotional impact of counterterrorist efforts by the United States on target populations internationally and domestically. However, his chapter is also problem-directed in that it discusses reducing the prevalence of domestic hate crimes.

Christie mentions the increase since 9/11 in antibias curricula designed to reduce violence toward Arabs and Muslims. He recommends that psychologists partner with organizations developing and disseminating antibias curricula designed to reduce the incidence of hate crimes. The last section of this chapter describes such a program designed for use by psychologists.

The Making of a Terrorist

Four-Stage Model

Borum (2003) has developed a model of the evolution of the terrorist mindset and the expansion of terrorism. In the first stage, groups of individuals conclude that ("it's not right"); that their life circumstances include deprivation, disenfranchisement, repression, stress, or rapid changes in societal mores. In stage 2 ("it's not fair"), the group's lot is compared with another group's who are better off through no efforts of their own nor faults of the first group. These comparisons breed resentment and a desire to determine the cause of this inequity. In stage 3 ("it's your fault"), the cause of the injustice is attributed to an out-group, alien culture, or corrupt regime. All the complex factors that have determined the less fortunate circumstances of the in-group are collapsed into a simplistic blaming of "them." And in the fourth stage, the perceived exploiters are dehumanized and demonized ("they are evil") so that any corrective action on the in-group's part is not only justified, but required—and, ultimately, revered.

Large Group Behavioral Regression Model

Large groups fall into predictable ways of thinking and interacting under protracted privation, stress, and threat—for example, war, oppression, terror, and repressive leadership. (In this context, *regression* refers to exhibiting less mature behavior and cognitive, attitudinal and affective reactions in these situations.) Volkan (2004) lists 20 characteristics of large groups that he describes as regressed. These characteristics include losing a sense of individuality, rallying blindly around a leader, becoming divided into "good" segments—those who obediently follow the leader—and bad—those perceived to oppose the leader, and developing a sharp "us" and "them" division between itself and the "enemy" (usually neighboring) groups. He describes 16 more characteristics that may reflect large group regression and states that such regressed groups become breeding grounds for terrorism.

Individual members of groups in intense, protracted conflicts have the tendency to split good and bad, assigning virtuous and justifiable motives to the good "us" and externalizing blame to the bad "them" (Volkan, 1988). And, ultimately, the target out-group becomes dehumanized.

Other Relevant Research

Because terrorism is one of the most extreme manifestations of prejudice and conflict that one group's members can perpetrate on another's, it is important to apply psychological theories and research findings such as those in this book to the issue of terrorism risk reduction. We know that applied programs in intergroup prejudice and conflict reduction are relevant to this issue.

There is a wealth of theory, research, and applied programs in conflict resolution (Deutsch & Coleman, 2000) and in prejudice reduction (Oskamp, 2000). Social psychologists have studied why individuals identify with one group (their reference group) and counteridentify with others (Tajfel & Turner, 1979; Turner, 1985). These studies are relevant in understanding terrorist development and recruitment and the support that terrorists receive within their communities (Wessells, 2004). Research has clarified the conditions under which intergroup prejudice (Oskamp, 2000) and conflict (Fisher & Keashly, 1991) escalate and intensify terrorist threat, as indicated by Volkan. The role of social identity, intergroup contact, competition, individual psychodynamics, power, and social cognition in prejudice and conflict and, by extension, terrorism, has recently been reviewed (Fabick, 2002). I focus here on intergroup contact, given its relevance to the processes used in the US & THEM Program described later in this chapter.

The Contact Hypothesis (Allport, 1954) is one of the most researched theories of intergroup conflict and prejudice. That research has demonstrated that a lessening of intergroup conflict and prejudice requires equal status between the conflicting groups, shared goals, personal contact (the chance to get to know out-group members as individuals), and endorsement of such contact by each group's leaders. Such conditions optimize the development of interdependence and empathy. The Contact Hypothesis has been supported by many studies (Pettigrew, 1998).

Intergroup contact under the wrong conditions, however, deleteriously affects relationships. For example, disproportionate group size, power, and status; great density of the minority population in a certain area; and opportunities for superficial (and potentially competitive) contact between the groups are variables that increase conflict. These factors can increase the sense of threat experienced by those who consider themselves the majority. Forbes (1997), a political scientist, emphasized the negative influence of contact between groups when their larger communities are not supportive of such contact, are in conflict, and are disproportionate in size. The US & THEM Program described below applies these findings in structuring intergroup interaction.

Multitrack Diplomacy

Multitrack diplomacy recognizes the peacemaking potential of nongovernmental leaders (Diamond & McDonald, 1993). The US & THEM Program is a track four diplomacy approach. There are nine tracks in the multitrack diplomacy system: government; professional conflict resolution; business; private citizen; research, training, and education; activism; religion; funding; and media or public opinion. While including negotiation between official representatives of states, the emphasis in most multitrack diplomacy is on less traditional avenues to international tension reduction. For example, in track two diplomacy, mid-level leaders from groups in protracted conflict work with conflict resolution experts to resolve their issues. Such interchanges rely heavily on psychological research and the skills of facilitators (Lederach, 1995; Rouhana & Kelman, 1994). In track three diplomacy, leaders in conflicting business communities recognize the economic and social benefits in working toward solutions between their groups.

In track four diplomacy, grassroots community leaders work to promote mutual understanding through structured intergroup contact—for example, dialogue groups. The US & THEM: Moderating Group Conflict Program described below is designed to promote such prejudice and conflict reduction through optimally structured intergroup contact. It is an example of a problem-solving approach in coping with the threat of terrorism as defined earlier in this chapter.

The US & THEM: Moderating Group Conflict Program

Need

People tend to split good and bad; that is, to externalize unacceptable aspects of themselves onto others. Similarly, within each group of people, there is some tendency to attribute disowned aspects of the group to certain target groups. Historically, this tendency has been adaptive; but as our world shrinks and nuclear risk and terrorist threats grow, we must adapt our thinking about good and bad. Changes in our technology require changes in our psychology.

Purpose

US & THEM is designed to help participants understand and moderate their prejudices and ultimately to moderate conflict between groups.

Description

The US & THEM program highlights the dynamics common to prejudice and conflict along many dimensions—for example, race, class, culture, nationality, religion, and ethnicity. Education about these common dynamics in the US & THEM workshop relies on a balance of (1) teaching basic concepts, (2) experiential learning through structured activities, and (3) post-workshop dialogue and action.

The concept of "us and them" refers to the polarization of two or more groups. Such divisiveness is fueled by an exaggerated sense of one's own group as special and good. Other groups are devalued and feared. The universal tendency to identify with our group and counteridentify with other groups has to do with issues of identity, comfort, and survival. Group boundaries give cohesiveness to groups and exclude disavowed parts of group members. They provide order in a chaotic world. Group identity confers a sense of belonging, goodness, and worth.

"Us and them" thinking is magnified by intergroup conflict of interests, such as intensified economic competition, religious conflict, or territorial dispute. And although we realize that prejudice and conflict also have important historical, economic, and political causes, we focus in the US & THEM Program on how such tensions are fueled psychologically—and how we can moderate them.

Group Process Considerations

We use methods to reduce prejudice and conflict identified by the Conflict Hypothesis. *A sense of equality* among participating group members is fostered by: balancing pre-workshop contact with group representatives; egalitarian seating arrangements in the workshop; balancing the number of participants from involved groups; striving for approximately equal status of each group's participants; and using presenters who are either not from participating groups or equally representative of them. Presenters model *respect* for all participants and respect for *healthy diversity.*

Workshop presenters facilitate participants' *common goals* by: emphasizing the reduction of intergroup misunderstanding and tension and encouraging participants to engage in a *collaborative process* through introspection of their own attitudes, education about the other group members' experiences to enhance empathy, and activities that create greater connection with participants from the other group(s). Group *interdependence* is highlighted and valued.

Presenters establish a forum for participants to get to know "them" as individuals through the exploration of common interests, experiences, and aspirations; *socialization* opportunities; and structured dialogue and exercises designed to increase participants' empathic understanding of "them." Such personal contact with out-group members promotes recategorization and cross-categorization (Urban & Miller, 1998) and also decategorization (Wilder, 1986).

Presenters seek the endorsement of participating groups' community leaders. In some communities, it is not advisable to implement the US & THEM Program until tensions decline. If resources permit, holding the program outside the region may provide the psychological space and security needed to open participation in such situations.

Postscript

On September 27, 2001, Michael Rosenberg, Director of the Center for Nonviolent Communication (www.NonviolentCommunication.com), issued a statement imploring Americans to seek security, not retribution. The following excerpt captures my hope that US & THEM and similar intergroup dialogue programs can help us find our way.

> I, and others in my organization, have worked with people from the warring factions in Rwanda, Burundi, Sierra Leone, Nigeria, South Africa, Serbia, Croatia, Israel and Palestine. Our experience has taught us that real safety and peace can be achieved, despite enormous odds, only when people are able to see the "humanity" of those who attack them. This requires something far more difficult than turning the other cheek; it requires empathizing with the fears, hurt, rage and unmet human needs that are behind the attacks.
>
> Our work is designed to help people learn to empathize with one another's needs and concerns, and begin to see that the "other side" is simply a group of humans trying to protect themselves and meet their

needs. We have seen hatred and desire for punishment transformed into hope—when people received empathy from those who had killed their families. We have seen those who committed the violence sincerely mourn—when they received empathy from those who had been violated by their actions. We have seen people on both sides lose the desire to punish each other—and then work together to ensure that everyone's needs are met. We have seen former enemies create programs together to make up for the harm they created and ensure the safety of future generations.

Sponsoring Organization

Psychologists for Social Responsibility (PsySR) is a U.S.-based, nonprofit organization that draws upon the research, knowledge, and practice of psychology to promote durable peace at community, national, and international levels. With members in 47 states and 39 other countries, PsySR is building networks to facilitate communication about building cultures of peace.

References

Allport, G. (1954). *The nature of prejudice.* Cambridge, MA: Addison-Wesley.

American Psychological Association. (2002). *Road to Resilience project and brochure.* Washington, DC: Author.

Borum, R. (2003). Understanding the terrorist mindset. *FBI Law Enforcement Bulletin,* July 7–10.

Crenshaw, M. (2001). The psychology of terrorism: An agenda for the 21st century. *Political Psychology, 21,* 405–420.

Deutsch, M., & Coleman, P. (Eds.). (2000). *The handbook of conflict resolution: Theory and practice.* San Francisco: Jossey-Bass.

Diamond, L., & McDonald, J. (1993). *Multi-track diplomacy: A systems guide and analysis.* Washington, DC: U.S. Institute for Peace.

Fabick, S. (2002). US & THEM: Reducing the risk of terrorism. In C. Stout (Ed.), *The psychology of terrorism* (Vol. 2, pp. 225–241). Westport, CT: Praeger.

Fisher, R., & Keashly, L. (1991). A contingency approach to third party intervention. In R. Fisher (Ed.), *The social psychology of intergroup and international conflict resolution.* New York: Springer-Verlag.

Forbes, H. (1997). *Ethnic conflict: Commerce, culture, and the contact hypothesis.* New Haven, CT: Yale University Press.

Gerrig, R., & Zimbardo, P. (2002). *Psychology and life* (16th Ed.). Boston: Allyn and Bacon.

Heldring, M. (2005). Mental health and primary care in a time of terrorism: The psychological effect of public communication about risk. In the Kimmel (2005) Report of the Task Force on the Psychological Effects of Efforts To Prevent Terrorism. Unpublished.

Horgan, J. (2003). The search for the terrorist personality. In A. Silke (Ed.), *Terrorists, victims and society: Psychological perspectives on terrorism and its consequences.* Chichester, England: Wiley.

Kimmel, P. (2005) The Report of the Task Force on the Psychological Effects of Efforts to Prevent Terrorism. Unpublished.

Lederach, J. (1995). *Preparing for peace: Conflict transformation across cultures.* Syracuse, NY: Syracuse University Press.

Olson, B.D. (2002). Applied social and community interventions for crisis in times of national and international conflict. *Analysis of Social Issues and Public Policy, 2,* 118–129.

Oskamp, S. (Ed.). (2000). *Reducing prejudice and discrimination.* Mahwah, NJ: Erlbaum.

Pape, R. (2003). Dying to kill us. *New York Times,* September 22.

Pettigrew, T. (1998). Intergroup contact theory. *Annual Review of Psychology, 49,* 65–85.

Pyszczynski, T., Solomon, S., & Greenberg, J. (2003). *In the wake of 9–11: The psychology of terrorism.* Washington, DC: APA Books.

Rouhana, N., & Kelman, H. (1994). Promoting joint thinking in international conflicts: An Israeli-Palestinian continuing workshop. *Journal of Social Issues, 50,* 157–178.

Silke, A. (2003a). Becoming a terrorist. In A. Silke (Ed.), *Terrorists, victims and society: Psychological perspectives on terrorism and its consequences.* Chichester, England: Wiley.

Silke, A. (2003b). The psychology of suicidal terrorism. In A. Silke (Ed.), *Terrorists, victims and society: Psychological perspectives on terrorism and its consequences.* Chichester, England: Wiley.

Staub, E. (2003a). Notes on cultures of violence, cultures of caring and peace, and the fulfillment of basic human needs. *Political Psychology, 24,* 1–21.

Staub, E. (2003b). *The psychology of good and evil: Why children, adults and groups help and harm others.* New York: Cambridge University Press.

Stern, J. (2003). *Terror in the name of god: Why religious militants kill.* New York: Harper Collins.

Sternberg, R.J. (2003, May). The other three Rs: Part three, resilience. *Monitor on Psychology,* 5.

Tajfel, H., & Turner, J. (1979). An integrative theory of intergroup conflict. In W.G. Austin & S.Worchel (Eds.), *The social psychology of intergroup relations* (pp. 33–48). Monterey, CA: Brooks/Cole.

Turner, J. (1985). Social categorization and the self-concept: A social cognitive theory of group behavior. In E. J. Lawler (Ed.), *Advances in group processes* (Vol. 2, pp. 77–122). Greenwich, CT: JAI Press.

Urban, L., & Miller, N. (1998). A theoretical analysis of crossed categorization effects: A meta-analysis. *Journal of Personality and Social Psychology*, 74, 894–908.

Volkan, V. (1988). The need to have enemies and allies: From clinical practice to international relationships. Northvale, NJ: Jason Aronson.

Volkan, V. (2004). Blind trust: Large groups and their leaders in times of crisis and terror. Charlottesville, VA: Pitchstone.

Wessells, M. (2004). The impact of U.S. anti-terrorism interventions on terrorist motivation: A preliminary study in Afghanistan and Iraq. American Psychological Association Task Force on the Psychological Effects of Efforts To Prevent Terrorism. Unpublished report.

Wilder, D. (1986). Social categorization: Implications for creation and reduction of intergroup bias. In L. Berkowitz (Ed.), *Advances in Experimental Social Psychology* (Vol. 19, pp. 291–355). Orlando, FL: Academic Press.

CHAPTER 2

9/11 Aftershocks: An Analysis of Conditions Ripe for Hate Crimes

Daniel J. Christie

This chapter offers an explanation for the surge in hate crimes that followed the attacks of 9/11. Drawing on research literature, I describe the cultural context in which the attacks of 9/11 occurred and point out that the attacks occurred at a time when nationalistic sentiments already were running high and the political culture was dominated by the political ideology called *realism.* (Chapter 1 contains an explanation of *essentialism.*) These cultural or macrolevel conditions were further fueled by the U.S. administration's divisive rhetorical framing (see Introduction, note 1) that emphasized essentialism and moral mandates. Using an ecological model (Bronfenbrenner, 1979), I demonstrate that macrolevel variables, combined with the attacks themselves and the administration's reactions to the attacks, heightened mortality salience, fear, and anger in the populace. As a result, a relatively small number of people in the United States—those who were most receptive to the climate of fear and anger and the ideology of exclusion and retribution—became perpetrators of hate crimes. In short, by using an ecological model, I illustrate how the cultural climate at the time of 9/11 interacted with a host of situational and personality variables and resulted in a spike in hate crimes (see Figure 2.1). Research and educational implications also will be presented.

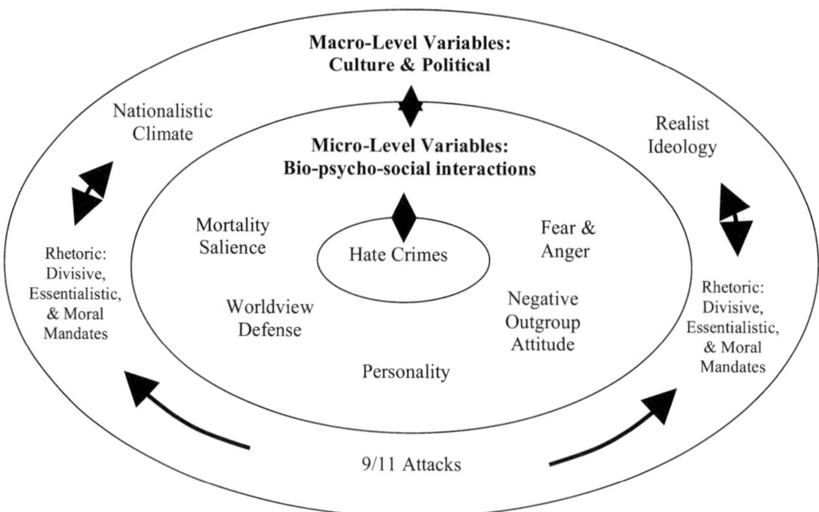

Figure 2.1 An ecological model illustrating macro- and microinfluences on hate crimes.

The Surge in Domestic Hate Crimes: Macroinfluences

The Rhetorical Framing of the Problem in Terms of Realpolitik

On September 11, 2001, a group of 19 men hijacked four transcontinental flights, two from Boston's Logan International Airport, one from Newark International Airport, and one from Washington's Dulles International Airport. One of the airliners crashed into the north tower of the World Trade Center in New York, and within 20 minutes a second airliner crashed into the south tower. About 30 minutes later, a third airliner crashed into the Pentagon. Within the next 30 minutes, the fourth airliner crashed in the Pennsylvania countryside.

The largest single terrorist attack ever experienced in the United States reverberated throughout the country. Thousands died and tens of thousands knew someone who was killed or injured in the 9/11 attacks. Within three to five days after the attacks, 44 percent of Americans reported at least one symptom of post-traumatic stress disorder (Schuster et al., 2002). One to two months after the attack, a national sampling indicated that approximately 4 percent of the population had signs of post-traumatic stress disorder (PTSD). The prevalence among New York City residents was 11 percent (Schlenger et al., 2002). No one has reported the prevalence of PTSD among those who were in positions of political power in the United States at the time.

On the evening of 9/11, President George W. Bush met with a small group of key advisors. By then, they were aware that Osama bin Laden was responsible for the attack. CIA Director Tenet noted that al Qaeda and the Taliban in Afghanistan were essentially one and the same, to which the president responded, "Tell the Taliban we're finished with them." The president continued by saying: "I want you all to understand that we are at war and we will stay at war until this is done. Nothing else matters. Everything is available for the pursuit of this war. Any barriers in your way, they're gone. Any money you need, you have it. This is our only agenda" (Clarke, 2004, p. 24).

The president and his administration quickly seized the concept of "war" and by so doing adopted political "realism" as a conceptual frame to organize their thoughts and direct their actions. From such a perspective, the 9/11 attack by al Qaeda called for swift retaliatory action by the United States. Recently, a task force of the American Psychological Association (APA) noted that the metaphor of "war" in the "war on terrorism" evokes in the public and in officials cognitions, emotions, and behaviors that promote conflict escalation and violence while inhibiting conflict management approaches (Kimmel, 2005). Within one month of 9/11, the United States was waging a war in Afghanistan, and even before that, there was a spike in hate crimes in the United States, directed at people who were thought to resemble the hijackers. Arab Americans, Muslims, and South Asians were victims of hate crimes. (The South Asians were not Muslims, but Hindu Sikhs.)

The concept of security was construed narrowly, as "peace through strength," and on Friday, September 14, President Bush announced his intention to "rid the world of evil," a view that would become thematic for the administration. Over the weekend, two hate crime deaths occurred.

The kinds of hate crimes that have occurred since 9/11 are wide ranging. The Council on American-Islamic Relations has documented and classified them. They include employment discrimination, verbal harassment, and so-called profiling, to mention a few. Individual incidents such as the following are typical:

> On March 11th [2003], hate literature was found at the local Islamic center in Honolulu, Hawaii, warning Muslims that they will be watched by "patriotic residents." Hundreds of small leaflets, headlined "ATTENTION RAG HEADS" were reportedly thrown into the fenced yard of the mosque. The leaflet read in part, "During the war on terrorism, the vigilant, patriotic residents of Hawaii will be keeping an eye on our Muslim friends." It also warned "every curry fundraiser will be checked to ensure that funds are not being funneled to support terrorist

> groups. Anyone found in violation will be strapped with explosives and shipped to Iraq. MAY GOD (NOT ALAH) BLESS AMERICA!! (Council on American-Islamic Relations Research Center, 2004, pp. 22–23)

> On April 24th, 2004, A Muslim woman and her son were harassed, threatened and attacked by another woman while shopping in Pennsylvania. The woman yelled that American troops were fighting in Iraq and Afghanistan so that women did not have to dress like her and also hit her with her cart repeatedly. Employees of the store refused to call security when she requested that they do so and did not assist her in finding a phone to call the police. (Council on American-Islamic Relations Research Center, 2005, p. 52)

It is not uncommon to see domestic backlashes when heads of state declare that a country is at war or when leaders vigorously pursue peace through the projection of force. Indeed, some of the most egregious domestic crimes against humanity can occur under such conditions (Staub, 1992). In the United States, the mass incarceration of Japanese Americans that took place during World War II is one example. Rhetorical framing that heats up nationalistic impulses can stir strong in-group identification and bonds of solidarity (Turner, Hogg, Oakes, Reicher, & Wetherell, 1987) and authoritarianism and intolerance of out-group members (Druckman, 2001; Van Evera, 1994).

A Growing Nationalistic Climate

Even before the attacks of 9/11, survey research was indicating that Americans were experiencing extremely high levels of nationalism when compared to other countries (Smith & Jarkko, 1998). In the month following the attack, nationalistic sentiments reached even higher levels (Smith, Rasinski, & Toce, 2001), with 97 percent agreeing that they would rather be Americans than citizens of any of other country (an increase of 7 percentage points) and 85 percent reporting that America was a better country than others (5-point increase). Nearly half (49 percent) agreed that the "world would be a better place if people from other countries were more like the Americans" (11-point increase), and disagreement with the idea that there are aspects of America to be ashamed of was up 22 points (from 18 percent to 40 percent). The nationalistic climate was fueled by rhetoric that emphasized essentialism, divisiveness, and moral mandates.

Essentialistic Rhetorical Framing

On the evening of September 11, President George W. Bush returned to Washington, DC, and gave a brief televised speech to the American people. The tenor of the speech was nationalistic, echoing if not enhancing the nationalistic impulses of the public while laying the groundwork for rhetoric that would underscore the goodness and resolve of the United States and cast the war against terrorism as an epic struggle between the forces of good and evil:

> These acts of mass murder were intended to frighten our nation into chaos and retreat. But they have failed. Our country is strong. A great people has been moved to defend a great nation. Terrorist attacks can shake the foundations of our biggest buildings, but they cannot touch the foundation of America. These acts shatter steel, but they cannot dent the steel of American resolve. (see Day of infamy, 2001)

The rhetoric used by the president can affect the way in which citizens understand the meaning of national unity and the degree to which they are likely to tolerate cultural differences. After 9/11, the president emphasized the fixed and immutable character of American identity (e.g., great people with resolve of steel), thereby defining national unity as an underlying essence unique and common to all Americans (Yzerbyt, Rocher, & Schadron, 1997). He also emphasized people coming together at a particular point in time to achieve shared goals (Hamilton, Sherman, & Lickel, 1998).

His use of essentialistic rhetorical framing united Americans but had some profoundly negative repercussions, not least of which was a decrease in tolerance for diversity. Evidence that bears on the relationship between rhetorical framing and tolerance was garnered by Li and Brewer (2004) in the weeks following 9/11. These investigators examined the effects of priming different construals of American unity. In one condition, American unity was construed in terms of "the core essence of what it means to be an American"; in another condition, participants were primed with a passage that focused on the "common purpose" Americans have in fighting terrorism and helping victims of the tragedy. In the core essence condition, higher levels of patriotism were associated with negative attitudes toward other nations (i.e., nationalism) and intolerance for cultural and lifestyle diversity within a nation. When priming emphasized "common purpose," high levels of patriotism were more weakly associated with nationalistic attitudes and were not incompatible with tolerance for diversity. Clearly, rhetoric matters, and, to the extent that Americans interpreted the president's rhetoric as fostering an exclusionary type of patriotism, one would expect greater intolerance for diversity.

Divisive Rhetoric

In addition to underscoring the fixed and immutable character and inherent goodness of Americans, the rhetoric of the U.S. administration sought to divide the world into allies and enemies, drawing a sharp distinction between those who were aligned with the United States and those who were not. In an address to a joint session of Congress and the American people on September 20, President Bush made a stark statement: "Every nation, in every region, now has a decision to make. Either you are with us, or you are with the terrorists. From this day forward, any nation that continues to harbor or support terrorism will be regarded by the United States as a hostile regime."

From a psychological perspective, we know quite a bit about the impact of such divisive rhetoric. Research on social cognition has identified some of the factors that are at play when sharp distinctions divide people into categories (Gerstenfeld, 2002). The formation of social categories simplifies our complex social world by accentuating differences between groups and attenuating differences within social categories (McGarty & Penny, 1988). The attenuation of out-group differences, known as the homogeneity effect, can account for the perception that out-group members all appear to be the same. Those who perpetrated hate crimes viewed members of the out-group (e.g., Middle Easterners) as all the same and included in that social category even Hindus and Sikhs, as illustrated in these examples from the Council on American-Islamic Relations (2005):

> December 1st, 2004—In Chesterfield, Virginia, a Sikh-owned gas station was destroyed by fire and anti-Muslim graffiti was found on a nearby trash container and shed. The fire is being investigated as an arson and possible hate crime. (p. 53)
>
> March 2nd, 2004—In San Diego, a man of Portuguese descent was beaten by a group of four white men who mistook him for being Middle Eastern. They yelled racial slurs at him and told him to go back to Iraq. (p. 52)

Dividing people into allies and enemies is consequential in another way; it yields more positive evaluations of the in-group, including the in-group's competency, friendliness, and strength as compared to the out-group (Messick & Mackie, 1989).

For several days following 9/11, the president's bellicose rhetorical framing continued. After two people were killed by hate crimes, President Bush spoke at the Islamic Center in Washington, DC, on Monday, September 17. He noted that these acts of violence against innocent people "violate the fundamental tenets of the Islamic faith. And it's important for my fellow Americans to understand that" (Islam is peace, 2001).

After the speech, there were no further recordings of hate crime deaths that were thought to be connected with 9/11. Amnesty International and other nongovernmental organizations applauded the president's denouncement of the incidents of hate crime, but the administration sent mixed messages as the Department of Justice (DOJ) rounded up and imprisoned, without charges, over one thousand individuals of Arab or Muslim heritage. Detainees were not given access to an attorney, and family members were not contacted. The DOJ also mandated that local police conduct interrogations of more than five thousand Arab and Muslim immigrants (National Asian American Pacific Legal Consortium, 2003).

When defining a hate crime, the Federal Bureau of Investigation (FBI) uses the definition of the American Psychological Association: "not only an attack on one's physical self but also an attack on one's very identity." Although statistical estimates vary, the FBI reported a 17-fold nationwide increase in anti-Muslim crimes in the year 2001 as compared to 2000 (Federal Bureau of Investigation, 2003). National trends were mirrored in major cities across the United States. In Los Angeles County and Chicago, officials reported 15 times the number of anti-Arab and anti-Muslim crimes in 2001 compared to the preceding year (National Asian American Pacific Legal Consortium, 2003). The year 2001 ended with a level of hate crimes against Arab Americans and Muslims that rivaled all previous years for which data had been collected (Federal Bureau of Investigation, 2003).

Moral Mandates

But spikes in nationalistic sentiments reflect attitudes, not necessarily behavior. It is not possible to know for certain whether nationalistic attitudes led directly to hate crimes, because there are many other variables. However, research on moral mandates offers some rather convincing evidence of an attitude-behavior link in hate crimes (Skitka & Mullen, 2002).

Moral mandates are strong attitudes that share three qualities with all strong attitudes: extremeness, certainty, and importance

(Petty & Krosnick, 1995). Moral mandates develop out of a person's moral convictions. Like attitudes, they have a feeling and belief component; in addition, they have built-in behavioral tendencies that are either prosocial or antisocial. For people who have a moral mandate, due process is irrelevant (Skitka & Mullen, 2002); instead, any procedure can be justified as long as the mandated end is achieved. There were moral mandates in the message delivered by President George W. Bush to the American people on the evening of 9/11, when he said: "The search is underway for those who are behind these evil acts. I've directed the full resources for our intelligence and law enforcement communities to find those responsible and bring them to justice. We will make no distinction between the terrorists who committed these acts and those who harbor them."

It remains uncertain how many people took it upon themselves to carry out this moral mandate. Some perpetrators of hate crimes may have even felt that their assaults were their patriotic duty (Perry, 2001). What we do know is that a number of people with strong negative attitudes committed hate crimes toward others who appeared to look like Osama bin Laden and they had no interest in due process.

Microlevel Processes: Of Cognition, Affect, and Personality

Pyszczynski, Solomon, and Greenberg (2003) have proposed that terror management theory (TMT) provides a compelling account of the psychological dynamics that drove the behavior of both elite decision makers and the public in the wake of 9/11. Central among their concepts is mortality salience.

Mortality Salience

From the perspective of TMT, humans are vulnerable to existential terror because of our unique ability to be aware of our own mortality. The terror that such awareness engenders can be mitigated by culture, which provides us with humanly constructed and shared beliefs that mold our transient experiences into a worldview that imbues reality with order, stability, meaning, and permanence. Therefore, "the function of culture is not to illuminate the truth but rather to obscure the horrifying possibility that death entails the permanent annihilation of the self" (Pyszczynski et al., 2003, p. 22). What makes the attacks of 9/11 particularly threatening is that they were aimed at the symbols that are seen to represent the American way of life, if not our worldview. The World Trade Center represented American economic dominance, while the Pentagon is emblematic of American global military dominance.

The literature on mortality salience is voluminous, but a selection of some pertinent findings can illustrate its application to reactions to 9/11. Typically, in experimental studies on mortality salience, participants in the experimental group are induced to make mortality momentarily salient by having them think about their own demise and death. Using this procedure, Greenberg et al. (1990) demonstrated Christian college students evaluated Jewish students more negatively when mortality was salient than in the control condition when mortality was not salient. Not only do attitudes toward the out-group become more negative when mortality is salient, but some research indicates that mortality salience affects behavior in more subtle ways. In one such study, mortality salience led to a preference for sitting next to someone of the same nationality (Ochsmann & Mathy, 1994). In another study, students in the mortality salience group deliberately gave more hot sauce to those who opposed their political beliefs than those in a control condition who did not (McGregor et al., 1998). In short, having people reflect on their own mortality is associated with derogation of the out-group, physical distancing from the out-group, and even physical aggression toward those who have a different political worldview.

Nearly all the research literature on TMT shows that when people are made aware of their own mortality, the defense of their worldview intensifies. Of course, the U.S. war on terrorism has been framed as the clash of two very different worldviews. According to Pyszczynski et al. (2003), there are a number of ways to deal with existential threats when worldviews are in contention with one another: conversion (of the other), derogation, assimilation, and accommodation are all possibilities. But when strongly held worldviews are incompatible, and the existence of one view means the destruction of the other view, the preferred strategy of defense is annihilation. The call for jihad by Osama bin Laden and his associates puts in bold relief two incompatible worldviews and the call for annihilation:

> All these crimes and sins committed by the Americans are a clear declaration of war on Allah, his messenger, and Muslims . . . jihad is an individual duty if the enemy destroys the Muslim countries. . . . Nothing is more sacred than belief except repulsing an enemy who is attacking religion and life. On that basis, and in compliance with Allah's

> order, we issue the following fatwa to all Muslims: The ruling to kill the Americans and their allies—civilians and military—is an individual duty for every Muslim who can do it in any country in which it is possible to do it, to liberate the al-Aqsa Mosque and the holy mosque [Mecca] from their grip, and in order for their armies to move out of all the lands of Islam, defeated and unable to threaten any Muslim. . . . We also call on Muslim ulema, leaders, youths, and soldiers to launch the raid on Satan's U.S. troops and the devil's supporters allying with them, and to displace those who are behind them so that they may learn a lesson. (Jihad against Jews and crusaders, 1998)

Pyszczynski et al. (2003) maintain that ultimately all wars are holy wars. Perhaps as they suggest, George W. Bush was just being honest when he said in one of his first unscripted comments about 9/11: "This crusade, this war on terrorism is going to take a while."

Under such tense conditions, a resolute leader can be most assuring to the public. As Wyatt (2005) suggests, religious fundamentalism and political conservatism have converged and together provide the public with a familiar and comfortable moral vision in the aftermath of 9/11. Not surprisingly, the sale of flags and bibles flourished after the attacks, as did the approval rating of President Bush, culminating in an unprecedented 94 percent approval rating within a month of 9/11 (Morin & Deane, 2001).

Emotions as a Moderating Variable

Although the powerful impact of mortality salience on intergroup attitudes has been well documented, it is unclear precisely what emotions are activated by reflection on one's mortality. Some investigators have suggested that mortality salience merely represents one instance of a larger class of aversive events that create anxiety by disrupting an adaptive mechanism that is involved in the formation of social networks, attachments, and coalitions (Navarrete, Kurzban, Fessler, & Kirkpatrick, 2004). Other investigators have provided evidence for the proposition that the relationship between mortality salience and outcomes such as worldview defense is not mediated by the actual experience of anxiety but the potential to experience anxiety (Greenberg et al., 2003).

In any case, the available evidence suggests that anxiety plays a central role in worldview defense, and anxiety was frequently reported in response to 9/11. But the dominant response that the U.S. administration conveyed to the public after 9/11 was anger. On the evening of 9/11, when the president was speaking with advisors about retribution, Secretary of Defense Rumsfeld pointed out that international law only allows force to prevent future attacks and not for retribution. In response, the president said: "I don't care what the international lawyers say, we are going to kick some ass" (Clarke, 2004, p. 24). When addressing the nation that same evening, President Bush noted: "The pictures of airplanes flying into buildings, fires burning, huge structures collapsing have filled us with disbelief, terrible sadness and a quiet, unyielding anger."

Survey research indicates that the emotional state of the U.S. public resonated with the president. When asked what feelings they had when they first heard about the terrorist attacks, 65 percent of people reported anger as among their very deepest feelings. This was followed by worries about how one's own life would be affected (28 percent) and worries about whether anyone was safe (27 percent). Some felt shame (22 percent), concern about foreign relations (20 percent), domestic politics (17 percent), and a sense of confusion (16 percent). Only 6 percent felt that the nation brought the terrorist attacks on itself. The general pattern among New York City residents was similar, except anger was more dominant, reported to be among their deepest feelings by 73 percent of the sample (Smith, Rasinski, & Toce, 2001).

Lerner, Gonzalez, Small, and Fischhoff (2003) have examined how emotion affects responses to terrorism. Drawing on appraisal-tendency theory, these investigators provide evidence that anger produces a different set of policy preferences than fear. According to appraisal-tendency theory, cognition drives emotions, and emotions elicit specific cognitive appraisals that help the individual cope with the event that evoked the emotion. Moreover, appraisals persist beyond the triggering event and become a perceptual lens for interpreting subsequent events. For example, in laboratory studies, one's appraisal of risk varies depending on the emotion being experienced. Anger evokes optimistic risk estimates and risk-seeking choices; in contrast, fear evokes pessimistic risk estimates and risk-averse choices (Lerner & Keltner, 2001). Lerner et al. (2003) were able to demonstrate that priming anger (e.g., "What aspect of the terrorist attacks makes you the most ANGRY?") or fear (e.g., "What aspect of the terrorist attacks makes you most AFRAID?") in response to 9/11 produced the expected pattern: optimism and risk-seeking choices for anger; pessimism and risk-averse choices for the fear condition. The same pattern was found when they examined the naturally occurring emotions that people experienced shortly after 9/11. Thus, both laboratory work and naturalistic study yield similar policy preferences. Compared with people who experienced fear, those who experienced anger increased their support of a vengeful policy and decreased their support of a conciliatory-contact policy.

Not only is an angry populace likely to make policy choices that are different from a fearful one, but people can continue to be emotionally manipulated long after the triggering event (Fischhoff, Gonzalez, Lerner, & Small, 2005). In a 2002 study, people felt there was less risk of terror than in 2001, a finding that was not surprising because very few people in the study actually experienced terror-related events or disruptions in the year following 9/11 (e.g., being hurt by terror, traveling less, trouble sleeping, etc.). However, even though a year had passed since the attacks, the investigators were able to induce either fear or anger once again by introducing selected articles from the national news media and combining them with personal reflection. And once again, the fear-induced manipulation increased people's risk appraisals while anger induction reduced risk estimates. As Fischhoff et al. point out: "Anger's unrecognized effects can exaggerate the perceived effectiveness of personal and public actions (e.g., going to war); fear can do the opposite" (p. 126). The lesson: People can be emotionally manipulated, and, if they can be made angry enough, they will accept aggressive policies, even when the policies are unlikely to succeed.

Anger also is related to fear. One way to deal with intense fear is to focus attention on anger, the emotion that instills a sense of safety and control (Shay, 1994). Moreover, in times of great threat and uncertainty, fear can also be a tool to increase the support for candidates who are resolute, magnetic, and offer the promise of restoring a sense of self worth (Becker, 1973). Cohen, Solomon, Maxfield, Pyszczynski, and Greenberg (2004) demonstrated that mortality salience increased people's preference for candidates who emphasized an overarching vision (e.g., democratization of the Middle East), confidence in subordinates, and willingness to engage in risky but calculated behavior. Mortality salience decreased their preference for candidates who emphasized relationship building, civility, and consensus.

In a related study that examined voting preferences, mortality salience increased support for President Bush and decreased support for Senator John Kerry. In September 2004, registered voters were asked which candidate they planned to vote for in the upcoming November elections. In the control condition, mortality salience was not induced and voters were more likely to vote for Kerry. In contrast, when people were reminded of death, Bush was favored over Kerry (Cohen, Ogilvie, Solomon, Greenberg, & Pyszczynski, 2005).

While 9/11 made the vulnerability of the United States salient and instilled anger in many Americans, not many Americans engaged in hate crimes. There were individual differences in the reactions that people had, differences due to the interaction of situational and personality factors. The question arises: Are there certain personality features or traits that are more receptive to the climate of anger and ideologies of exclusion?

Personality Variables and Violent Reactions

The best known effort to link personality types with prejudice attitudes was carried out by Adorno and colleagues in the aftermath of World War II (Adorno, Frenkel-Brunswick, Levinson, & Sanford, 1950). Attempting to explain the atrocities committed by the Nazis, Adorno et al. proposed that individuals with certain traits that comprise the authoritarian personality type might be unusually receptive to ideologies of exclusion. Authoritarian personality type individuals are overly deferential and anxious toward authority figures and see the world in rigid, black-and-white, terms. Moreover, people with authoritarian personalities tend to be hostile toward others who are not members of the in-group.

People who rate themselves high on measures of authoritarian personality also tend to be high on xenophobia (Campbell & McCandless, 1951), antiblack prejudice (Pettigrew, 1958), and ethnocentrism (Meloen, Hagendoorn, Raaijmakers, & Visser, 1988). These relations hold across many cultures. In India, for example, among high-caste Hindu men, high scores on authoritarian personality are associated with prejudice against Muslims (Sinha & Hassan, 1975).

While the concept of authoritarian personality continues to be widely studied, particularly in political psychology, the original explanation of the authoritarian personality as a function of ego-defensive processes in the service of a vulnerable sense of self (Adorno et al., 1950) has been largely supplanted by social learning (Altemeyer, 1988), group identification (Duckitt, 1988), and other theoretical perspectives. The original measure of authoritarianism also has been replaced by other measures, most notably the Right Wing Authoritarian scale (RWA), developed by Altemeyer (1981). The RWA scale corrected some of the problems with Adorno's measure and tapped three major beliefs: conventionalism, authoritarian aggression, and authoritarian submission. Although some evidence suggests the scale is primarily a measure of political conservatism rather than authoritarian personality (Ray, 1985), RWA has been shown to correlate positively not only with political conservatism (Altemeyer, 1988), but also with beliefs in religious fundamentalism (Altemeyer & Hunsberger, 1992) and negative attitudes toward out-group members (Laythe, Finkel, & Kirkpatrick, 2001).

There is evidence that individuals who score high on RWA are more sensitive to threat than those who score low, as demonstrated, for example, on tests that measure how quickly people recognize and respond to threatening words (Lavine, Lodge, Polichak, & Taber, 2002). In addition, threats can activate RWA tendencies. When people are presented with written scenarios that depict the future as threatening, authoritarian scores tend to increase, particularly among those who already believe the world is a dangerous and threatening place (Duckitt & Fisher, 2003). In addition, when threat is manipulated by encouraging people to think about the inevitability of their own death (i.e., increasing mortality salience), those who are high on RWA tend to rate others with dissimilar social attitudes more negatively than those who are low on RWA (Greenberg et al., 1990). A recent thrust in research on RWA and other ideologies related to conservatism is to interpret these orientations as motivated social cognitions that are activated by threats to various needs, most notably epistemic (e.g., uncertainty avoidance), existential (e.g., loss prevention), and ideological needs (e.g., preservation of group-based dominance) (Jost, Glaser, Kruglanski, & Sulloway, 2003).

Is there any evidence that the attacks of 9/11 actually activated authoritarian sentiments? Perrin (2005) drew a stratified random sample of letters to the editor and examined their content. The results indicated that both authoritarian and antiauthoritarian sentiments increased in the aftermath of 9/11. In short, research on RWA suggests that there are indeed certain personality types that are particularly receptive to ideologies of exclusion. Moreover, threats can activate an authoritarian orientation and negative out-group attitudes, and it is clear that 9/11 did just that.

Another measure of personality that engenders an exclusionary ideology is social dominance orientation (SDO), which refers to the tendency to endorse the belief that human relations ought to be hierarchically organized, with superior groups dominating inferior groups. For individuals who are high in social dominance orientation, equality between groups is neither desirable nor necessary (Sidanius & Pratto, 1999). What may be necessary is the use of force to maintain patterns of dominance (Pratto, Sidanius, Stallworth, & Malle, 1994). SDO is associated with negative affect toward members of low status groups

(Levin & Sidanius, 1999); ideologies that maintain a group's dominance; and a variety of political attitudes, including conservatism, racism, and sexism (Pratto et al., 1994).

Although SDO shares variance with RWA, there are important differences that can be seen when examining support for "terrorism" versus counterterrorism or "antiterrorism" violence (Henry, Sidanius, Levin, Pratto, & Nammour, 2005). In a study of Muslim and Christian students at American University in Beirut, support for "terrorism" increased with increased religious identification among Muslims. In contrast, support for "terrorism" decreased among Christians as religious identification increased. For these Muslim students RWA was positively related and SDO was negatively related to support for "terrorism". For the Christian students SDO was positively related to increased support for antiterrorist violence. Consistent with Sidanius and Pratto's (1999) contention that those who are high in SDO prefer current power arrangements, Henry et al. (2005) found high SDO was associated with opposition to "terrorist" violence of the weak against the strong but favored "antiterrorist" violence of the strong against the weak.

Hence, terrorism can be viewed as a tool for social change, especially for people who lack power, wish to upset the status quo, have a strong Muslim identity, and authoritarian tendencies. In contrast, SDO tends to be high among those who have power, a fundamentalist Christian identity, and who favor the status quo arrangement of power and the use of force to maintain current power arrangements.

Summary

From a psychological perspective, the attacks of 9/11 made mortality salient and elicited anger in many Americans who were already enveloped in a nationalistic climate that was further inflamed by the rhetoric of the U.S. president. Based on research on mortality salience, these conditions yield a number of predictable outcomes, including a strengthening of worldview defense, negative attitudes toward others who threaten one's worldview, and a tendency to use aggression against out-group members. When anger is the dominant emotional response, people are more likely to endorse risky policies and to desire retribution. When fear is dominant, people favor candidates who advocate actions that appear decisive in pursuit of a grand vision and the restoration of self-worth. Personality also plays a role and accounts for individual differences in receptivity to the rhetorical framing of exclusion and violence.

Some Research and Educational Implications

Research Implications

A Realistic Personal Security

The problem of domestic hate crimes is inextricably woven into the fabric of violent international relations, and, therefore, part of the solution to the problem of domestic hate crimes is a more peaceful international system. However, it may seem odd to question the use of force by the United States after the attacks of 9/11. Having identified the Taliban as among those who harbor terrorists, it might seem inevitable that the United States would go to war in Afghanistan. From the viewpoint of realist scholars, the basic motivation underlying state behavior is the struggle for power, and, therefore, state actions can be reduced to efforts that attempt "to keep power, to increase power, or to demonstrate power" (Morgenthau, 1948, pp. 21–22). More recently, Mearsheimer (2001) argued that maximizing one's power relative to other states is essential for survival in an anarchic international system.

If one believes the realist assumptions about the nature and imperatives of the international system, the violent U.S. reaction to al Qaeda leaves little room for a psychological analysis. Although al Qaeda is not a state, the organization threatened U.S. power in the international system, and, therefore, it was imperative for the United States to demonstrate its power and reclaim its hegemony. In the case of Iraq, realists argue that the United States was justified to topple the Iraq government because the promise of a democratic Iraq could begin a domino effect in the Middle East and extend the sphere of U.S. influence.

However, the perspective taken in this chapter is not the classical realist perspective. Similar to Waltz's (1979) conception of power, it is suggested that power in an anarchic international system is more usefully viewed as a means than an end. From a psychological perspective, the goal is not the acquisition of power, but, instead, a stronger sense of *realistic personal security*, and the demonstration of power may or may not serve that end. Framed against the backdrop of realistic personal security, the question is: Why did the United States choose the use of force to pursue military security rather than employing the full range of tools at its disposal, including noncoercive forms of influence, particularly when coercive actions lay the groundwork for retaliation and resultant cycles of violence?

The realist perspective provides a rough, and often misleading, fit with international interactions and relations largely because it makes numerous assumptions about what is happening at the microlevel, where the dynamics of human psychology operate. Accordingly, there is a great need for psychological research to flesh out these microprocesses and offer alternative views on the means to human security.

One entry point for developing research programs that deepen our understanding of human security is to examine some of the current research being done on attachment theory (e.g., Hart, Shaver, & Goldenberg, 2005). Based in part on Bowlby's theoretical work on attachment, Hart et al. propose a "tripartite model of security maintenance" in which three processes—attachment, self-esteem, and worldview—work together to provide the individual with a sense of security. Threats to any one of the processes produces a compensatory action in the remaining processes to shore up one's sense of security. Thus, an attack on one's worldview can be compensated for by bolstering self-esteem and a sense of attachment to others, thereby maintaining a sense of security. Although this kind of research is just beginning to have an impact on peace research, peace psychologists will find this work promising for the development of theory and practice aimed at mitigating the cognitive, affective, and behavioral sequelae that follow threats to human well-being.

Distinguishing Patriotism from Nationalism

Ever since Allport's (1954) classic study on prejudice, there has been growing recognition among psychologists of the independence of in-group amity (e.g., patriotism) and out-group enmity (e.g., nationalism). According to Allport, attachment to one's in-group does not require out-group hostility, a proposition that has been supported by laboratory and field research (Brewer, 1979; Brewer & Campbell, 1976; Hinkle & Brown, 1990), nor out-group aggression (Struch & Schwartz, 1989).

Kosterman and Feshbach (1989) underscored the ambivalence some people have toward patriotism as they walk a fine line between pride and jingoism, feeling comfortable with patriotism but uncomfortable with nationalism. Through factor analysis they were able to demonstrate that patriotism and nationalism were distinct constructs, the former associated with love of country, pride in being an American, and attachment to the nation; the latter associated with beliefs about America's moral and material superiority and the desire to have other countries fashion their governments after ours. These results suggested the independence and distinctiveness of these constructs: hence, one might be highly patriotic (love one's country) but not nationalistic (feel superior to other countries).

While the us-versus-them language used by the president may have shored up domestic support for a war on terrorism, an unintended consequence of attacking another group is an increase in the cohesion of the target group, in this case, countries with high concentrations of Muslims (Olson, 2002). Even before the war in Iraq, support for the U.S. war on terror was low in predominantly Muslim countries, ranging from 13 percent to 38 percent favor in five countries, as contrasted with relatively high support from European countries that varied from 69 percent to 81 percent in four countries (Pew Global Attitudes Project, 2005).

In addition to delineating clearly friends and enemies, President Bush failed to distinguish patriotism from nationalism so that those who opposed the war on Afghanistan or Iraq were regarded as unpatriotic; although the accusation was somewhat mitigated by peace communities such as United for Peace & Justice (www.unitedforpeace.org) that reacted by arguing that one can be patriotic and also opposed to war.

In short, there are serious problems with approaches to security that emphasize nationalism. Research that further clarifies the distinction between patriotism, nationalism, and other isms, can deepen our understanding of the origins of intolerance, and methods to change intolerant attitudes. Such research can help people reduce the ambivalence they have when their critical analysis of policies does not match those of the ruling party, an important marker of a mature democracy.

Education and Prevention

The administration's narrow approach to security contributed mightily to the growth in peace education and antibias curricula designed to reduce the violence that Arabs and Muslims in the United States experienced after 9/11. More broadly, as one might expect when the "politics of opposites" are at play in a democracy (Nincic, 1988), the "peace through strength" approach produced a counter-reaction of "peace through cooperation" (Kimmel, 1985) with social scientists, peace activists, and others who opposed the projection of deadly force arguing for a greater understanding of the roots of terrorism, a deepening of democracy, and more peace education efforts (Friedman, 2003; Galtung & Fischer, 2002; Moghaddam & Marsella, 2004).

The rise in peace education efforts following a major episode of violence is a typical pattern of the twentieth century (Harris & Morrison, 2003). Even a cursory look at the last century makes the point: growth in peace education occurred in response to the authoritarianism of the 1940s and again when U.S. military involvement in the Vietnam War escalated in the 1960s and 1970s. In the 1980s, the Cold War and the threat of nuclear war gave rise to increased peace education efforts.

Antibias education units and curricula were quickly developed in response to the surge in hate crimes. Although these initiatives were designed to address the problem of hate crimes in general, many were specifically aimed at the problems faced by Arabs and Muslims in the United States. South Asian Americans were most at risk, particularly Sikh (Hindu) Americans in part because their turbans and long beards resembled Osama bin Laden in the eyes of many. The violence included murders, physical assaults, death threats, arson, public harassment, vandalism to places of worship, and other property damage (Human Rights Watch, 2002).

Within one week after 9/11, a team of researchers and curriculum writers from the Education Development Center began disseminating a 25-page educational unit entitled "Beyond Blame: Reacting to the Terrorist Attack." The unit was designed to help middle school and high school students reduce the hostile climate toward Arab Americans. Comparisons to the Japanese internment were drawn and emphasis was placed on promoting social justice (Education Development Center, 2001).

Educators for Social Responsibility (ESR, 2003) also developed educational units to reduce the incidence of hate crimes. The units introduce the problems of prejudice, discrimination, scapegoating, and harassment to various age groups but are particularly well suited for high school and college levels. The purposes of the units are to help students understand the causes and consequences of prejudice and other attitudes that can be harmful. This antibias work was prompted by stories ESR staff had heard from teachers about incidents of bias and discrimination in their schools or communities.

Members of the Islamic Networks Group (ING) stepped up their efforts to educate and reduce bias following 9/11. Students of Muslim or Middle Eastern descent were particularly at risk, and it is noteworthy that perpetrators of harassment included fellow students, teachers, and administrators (Islamic Networks Group, 2003). Harassment occurred most often on school grounds, especially in hallways, bathrooms, and cafeterias. Girls who wore the hijab (traditional Muslim dress) and Sikh boys were often victims.

ING began its work during the period preceding the Gulf War of 1991 because hate crimes had begun at that time. One initiative was taken by Muslim leaders who worked with the media to correct inaccurate reporting. Realizing that education might be a more proactive way of dealing with the problem, ING developed training in cultural sensitivity for schools, police, social service agencies, and several other public institutions.

Psychologists have a key role to play in partnering with educational and other organizations that are interested in developing and disseminating antibias curricula and educational units designed to reduce the incidence and prevalence of hate crimes. The field of psychology is particularly well suited to offer concepts, theories, and training venues because hate crimes have affective, cognitive, and behavioral components. Psychologists are also trained to help with the evaluation and modification of existing programs.

At the national level, psychologists have a role to play in facilitating dialogue among the FBI leadership and leaders of various organizations and ethnic communities, such as Arab Americans, Muslims, and Sikhs. One challenge is to help law enforcement officials become sensitized to incidents of hate crime and to provide them with communication and conflict-resolution skills to reassure local Arab and Islamic communities of their commitment to providing a safe place for all residents.

Psychologists who are politically astute and trained in cultural sensitivity can heighten public awareness when political events place certain segments of the population at risk for hate crimes. This applied focus needs to be informed by research and evaluation that identifies reliable and valid indicators for early warning purposes.

Finally, given that future acts of terrorism in the United States and conflicts in the Middle East can be expected to generate new outbreaks of violence against members of Arab and Muslim communities, there should be a proactive effort to develop plans at the local, state, and national levels to prevent and mitigate backlash violence.

Acknowledgment

The author appreciates the assistance of Aleksandr Kvasov, who helped locate some of the articles cited herein.

References

Adorno, T. W., Frenkel-Brunswick, E., Levinson, D. J., & Sanford, R. N. (1950). *The authoritarian personality.* New York: Harper.

Allport, G. W. (1954). *The nature of prejudice.* Reading, MA: Addison-Wesley.

Altemeyer, B. (1988). *Enemies of freedom: Understanding right-wing authoritarianism.* San Francisco: Jossey-Bass.

Altemeyer, B., & Hunsberger, B. (1992). Authoritarianism, religious fundamentalism, quest, and prejudice. *International Journal for the Psychology of Religion, 2,* 113–133.

Altemeyer, R. A. (1981). *Right-wing authoritarianism.* Winnipeg, Canada: University of Manitoba Press.

Becker, E. (1973). *The denial of death.* New York: Free Press.

Brewer, M. B. (1979). Ingroup bias in the minimal intergroup situation: A cognitive motivational analysis. *Psychological Bulletin, 86,* 307–329.

Brewer, M. B., & Campbell, D. T. (1976). *Ethnocentrism and intergroup attitudes: East African evidence.* New York: Sage.

Bronfenbrenner, U. (1979). *The ecology of human development.* Cambridge, MA: Harvard University Press.

Campbell, D. T., & McCandless, B. R. (1951). Ethnocentrism, xenophobia, and personality. *Human Relations, 4,* 185–192.

Clark, R. A. (2004). *Against all enemies: Inside America's war on terror.* New York: Free Press.

Cohen, F., Ogilvie, D. M., Solomon, S., Greenberg, J., & Pyszczynski, T. (2005). American roulette: The effect of reminders of death on support for George W. Bush in the 2004 presidential election. *Analysis of Social Issues, 5,* 48–62.

Cohen, F., Solomon, S., Maxfield, M., Pyszczynski, T., & Greenberg, J. (2004). Fatal attraction: The effects of mortality salience on evaluations of charismatic, task-oriented, and relationship-oriented leaders. *Psychological Science, 15,* 846–851.

Council on American-Islamic Relations. (2004). *The status of Muslim civil rights in the United States 2004.* Washington, DC: Council on American-Islamic Relations Research Center.

Council on American-Islamic Relations. (2005). The status of Muslim civil rights in the United States 2005. Washington, DC: Council on American-Islamic Relations Research Center.

Day of infamy. (2001). *Time* (12 September), http://www.time.com/time/nation/article/0,8599,174502,00.html).

Druckman, D. (2001). Nationalism and war: A social-psychological perspective. In D. J. Christie, R. V. Wagner, & D. D. Winter (Eds.), *Peace, conflict, and violence: Peace psychology for the 21st century* (pp. 49–65). Upper Saddle River, NJ: Prentice-Hall.

Duckitt, J. (1988). Normative conformity and racial prejudice in South Africa. *Genetic, Social, and General Psychology Monographs, 114*, 413–437.

Duckitt, J., & Fisher, K. (2003). The impact of social threat on worldview and ideological attitudes. *Political Psychology, 24*, 199–222.

Education Development Center. (2001). Beyond blame: Reacting to the terrorist attack. Retrieved October 24, 2003, from https://secure.edc.org/publications/prodview.asp?1479.

Educators for Social Responsibility. (2003). Teaching students to recognize and counter discrimination. Retrieved October 24, 2003, from http://www.esrnational.org/sp/we/end.htm.

Federal Bureau of Investigation. (2003). Uniform crime reports. Retrieved October 25, 2003, from http://www.fbi.gov/ucr/ucr.htm.

Fischhoff, B., Gonzalez, R.M., Lerner, J.S., & Small, D. (2005). Evolving judgments of terror risks: Foresight, hindsight, and emotion. *Journal of Experimental Psychology: Applied, 11*, 124–139.

Friedman, T. (2003). *Longitudes and attitudes: Exploring the world after September 11*. East Rutherford, NJ: Penguin Books.

Galtung, J., & Fischer, D. (2002). To end terrorism, end state terrorism. Retrieved November 17, 2005, from http://www.wagingpeace.org/articles/2002/09/20_galtung_end-terrorism.htm.

Gerstenfeld, P. B. (2002). A time to hate: Situational antecedents of intergroup bias. *Analysis of Social Issues and Public Policies, 2*, 61–67.

Greenberg, J., Martens, A., Jonas, E., Eisenstadt, D., Pyszczynki, T., & Solomon, S. (2003). Psychological defense in anticipation of anxiety: Eliminating the potential for anxiety eliminates the effect of mortality salience on worldview defense. *Psychological Science, 14*, 516–519.

Greenberg, J., Pyszczynski, T., Solomon, S., Rosenblatt, A., Veeder, M., Kirkland, S., & Lyon, D. (1990). Evidence for terror management theory II: The effects of mortality salience on reaction to those who threaten or bolster the cultural worldview. *Journal of Personality and Social Psychology, 58*, 308–318.

Hamilton, D.L., Sherman, S.J., & Lickel, B. (1998). Perceiving social groups: The importance of the entitiativity continuum. In C. Sedikides, J. Shopler, & C. Insko (Eds.), *Intergroup cognition and intergroup behavior* (pp. 47–74). Mahwah, NJ: Erlbaum.

Harris, I., & Morrison, M.L. (2003). *Peace education*. Jefferson, NC: McFarland.

Hart, J., Shaver, P.R., & Goldenberg, J.L. (2005). Attachment, self-esteem, worldviews, and terror management: Evidence for a tripartite security system. *Journal of Personality and Social Psychology, 88*, 999–1013.

Henry, P.J., Sidanius, J., Levin, S., Pratto, F., & Nammour, D. (2005). *Social dominance orientation, authoritarianism, religious identification and support for terrorism in the Middle East*. Working Paper #186. New York: Russell Sage Foundation.

Hinkle, S., & Brown, R. (1990). Intergroup comparisons and social identity: Some links and lacunae. In D. Abrams & M. Hogg (Eds.), *Social identity theory: Constructive and critical advances* (pp. 48–70), Hemel Hempstead, England: Harvester Wheatsheaf.

Human Rights Watch. (2002). *The September 11 backlash.* Retrieved October 25, 2003, from http://hrw.org/reports/2002/usahate/usa110204.htm#P349_57452.

Islamic Networks Groups. (2003). School program to prevent hate, particularly during a crisis in the Middle East. Retrieved October 24, 2003, from http://www.ing.org/prevent_hate/default.asp.

Islam is peace: Remarks by the president at Islamic Center, Washington. (2001). American Rhetoric Online Speech Bank, The Rhetoric of 9-11, http://www.americanrhetoric.com/speeches/gwbush911islamispeace.htm.

Jihad against Jews and crusaders. (1998). World Islamic Front Statement (23 February) http://www.fas.org/irp/world/para/docs/980223-fatwa.htm.

Jost, J.T., Glaser, J., Kruglanski, A.W., & Sulloway, F.J. (2003). Political conservatism as motivated social cognition. *Psychological Bulletin, 129,* 339–375.

Kimmel, P. (1985). Learning about peace: Choices and the U.S. Institute of Peace as seen from two different perspectives. *American Psychologist, 40,* 525–541.

Kimmel, P. (2005) Report of the Task Force on the Psychological Effects of efforts to Prevent Terrorism. Unpublished.

Kosterman, R., & Feshbach, S. (1989). Toward a measure of patriotic and nationalistic attitudes. *Political Psychology, 10,* 257–274.

Lavine, H., Lodge, M., Polichak, J., & Taber, C. (2002). Explicating the black box through experimentation: Studies of authoritarianism and threat. *Political Analysis, 10,* 342–360.

Laythe, B., Finkel, D., & Kirkpatrick, L.A. (2001). Predicting prejudice from religious fundamentalism and right-wing authoritarianism: A multiple-regression approach. *Journal for the Scientific Study of Religion, 40,* 1–10.

Lerner, J.S., Gonzalez, R.M., Small, D.A., & Fischhoff, B. (2003). Effects of fear and anger on perceived risks of terrorism: A national field experiment. *Psychological Science, 14,* 144–150.

Lerner, J.S., & Keltner, D. (2001). Fear, anger, and risk. *Journal of Personality and Social Psychology, 81,* 146–159.

Levin, S., & Sidanius, J. (1999). Social dominance and social identity in the United States and Israel: Ingroup favoritism or outgroup derogation? *Political Psychology, 20,* 99–126.

Li, Q., & Brewer, M. (2004). What does it mean to be an American? Patriotism, nationalism, and American identity after 9/11. *Political Psychology, 25,* 727–739.

McGarty, C., & Penny, R.E.C. (1988). Categorization, accentuation, and social judgment. *British Journal of Social Psychology, 27,* 147–157.

McGregor, H., Lieberman, J., Greenberg, J., Solomon, S., Arndt, J., & Simon, L. (1998). Terror management and aggression: Evidence that mortality salience promotes aggression toward worldview-threatening individuals. *Journal of Personality and Social Psychology, 74*, 590–605.

Mearsheimer, John J. (2001). *The tragedy of great power politics.* New York: Norton.

Meloen, J.D., Hagendoorn, L., Raaijmakers, Q., & Visser, L. (1988). Authoritarianism and the revival of political racism. *Political Psychology, 9*, 419–429.

Messick, D., & Mackie, D. (1989). Intergroup relations. *Annual Review of Psychology, 40*, 45–81.

Moghaddam, F.M., & Marsella, A.J. (Eds.). (2004). Understanding terrorism: Psychosocial roots, consequences, and interventions. Washington, DC: American Psychological Association.

Morgenthau, Hans J. (1948). *Politics among nations* (1st ed.). New York: Knopf.

Morin, R., & Deane, C. (2001, October 8). Public support is overwhelming; poll finds 94% favor Bush's ordering strikes on Afghanistan. *Washington Post*, A5.

National Asian American Pacific Legal Consortium. (2003). Backlash: When America turned on its own. Retrieved October 24, 2003, from http://www.napalc.org/literature/annual_report/9-11_report.htm.

Navarrete, C.D., Kurzban, R., and Fessler, D.M.T., & Kirkpatrick, L.A. (2004). Anxiety and intergroup bias: Terror management or coalitional psychology? *Group Processes & Intergroup Relations, 7*, 370–397.

Nincic, M. (1988). The United States, the Soviet Union and the politics of opposites. *World Politics, 40*, 452–475.

Ochsmann, R., & Mathy, M. (1994). *Depreciating of and distancing from foreigners: Effects of mortality salience.* Unpublished manuscript, Universitat Mainz, Mainz, Germany.

Olson, B.D. (2002). Applied social and community interventions for crisis in times of national and international conflict. *Analysis of Social Issues and Public Policy, 2*, 118–129.

Perrin, A.J. (2005). National threat and political culture: Authoritarianism, antiauthoritarianism, and the September 11 attacks. *Political Psychology, 26*, 167–194.

Perry, B. (2001). *In the name of hate: Understanding hate crimes.* New York: Routledge.

Pettigrew, T.F. (1958). Personality and sociocultural factors in intergroup attitudes: A cross-national comparison. *Journal of Conflict Resolution, 2*, 29–42.

Petty, R.E., & Krosnick, J.A. (Eds.). (1995). *Attitude strength: Antecedents and consequences.* Hillsdale, NJ: Erlbaum.

Pew Global Attitudes Project. (2005). Support for terror wanes among Muslim publics: 17-nation Pew global attitudes survey. Retrieved on November 17, 2005, from www.pewglobal.org.

Pratto, F., Sidanius, J., Stallworth, L.M., & Malle, B.F. (1994). Social dominance orientation: A personality variable predicting social and political attitudes. *Journal of Personality and Social Psychology, 67*, 741–763.

Pyszczynski, T., Solomon, J., & Greenberg, J. (2003). *In the wake of 9/11: The psychology of terror.* Washington, DC: American Psychological Association.

Ray, J.J. (1985). Defective validity in the Altemeyer authoritarianism scale. *Journal of Social Psychology, 125*, 271–272.

Schlenger, W., Caddell, J., Ebert, L., Jordan, B.K., Rourke, K., Wilson, D., Thalji, L., Dennis, J. M., Fairbank, J., & Kulka, R. (2002). Psychological reactions to terrorist attacks: Findings from the National Study of Americans' Reactions to September 11. *Journal of the American Medical Association, 288*(5), 581–588.

Schuster, M.A., Stein, B.D., Jaycox, L.H., Collins, R.L., Marshall, G.N., Elliot, M.N., Shou, A.J., Kanouse, D.E., Morrison, J.L., & Berry, S.H. (2002). A national survey of stress reactions after the September 11, 2001, terrorist attacks. *New England Journal of Medicine, 345*(20), 1507–1512.

Shay, J. (1994). *Achilles in Vietnam: Combat trauma and the undoing of character.* New York: Atheneum.

Sidanius, J., & Pratto, F. (1999). *Social dominance: An inter-group theory of social hierarchy and oppression.* New York: Cambridge University Press.

Sinha, R.R., & Hassan, M.K. (1975). Some personality correlates of social prejudice. *Journal of Social and Economic Studies, 3*, 225–231.

Skitka, L.J., & Mullen, E. (2002). The dark side of moral conviction. *Analysis of Social Issues and Public Policy, 2*, 35–41.

Smith, T.W. & Jarkko, L. (1998). National pride: A cross-national analysis. *GSS cross-national report no. 19.* Chicago: National Organization for Research at the University of Chicago.

Smith, T.W., Rasinski, K.A., & Toce, M. (2001). *America rebounds: A national study of public response to the September 11th terrorist attacks.* Chicago: National Organization for Research at the University of Chicago.

Staub, E. (1992). *The roots of evil: The origins of genocide and other group violence.* New York: Cambridge University Press.

Struch, N., & Schwartz, S.H. (1989). Intergroup aggression: Its predictors and distinctness from in-group bias. *Journal of Personality and Social Psychology, 56*, 364–373.

Turner, J.C., Hogg, M., Oakes, P., Reicher, S., & Wetherell, M. (1987). *Rediscovering the social group: A self-categorization theory.* Oxford, England: Blackwell.

Van Evera, S. (1994). Hypotheses on nationalism and war. *International Security, 18*, 5–39.

Waltz, Kenneth N. (1979). *Theory of international politics.* New York: McGraw-Hill.

Wyatt, R. (2005). God willing? Political fundamentalism in the White House, the war on terror, and the echoing press. *Mass Communication & Society, 8*, 177–178.

Yzerbyt, V. Y., Rocher, S., & Schadron, G. (1997). Stereotypes as explanations: A subjective essentialistic view of group perception. In R. Spears, P. Oakes, N. Ellemers, & S. A. Haslan (Eds.), *The psychology of stereotyping and group life* (pp. 20–50). Oxford, England: Blackwell.

CHAPTER 3

JUJITSU POLITICS: TERRORISM AND RESPONSES TO TERRORISM

Clark McCauley

Most essays about terrorism begin with some kind of definition. Definitions are controversial, but commonly join two elements: a target element and a motivational element. The usual target specification is that terrorism is violence or threat of violence against civilians; the usual motivational specification is that the goal of terrorism is to induce fear, to intimidate and to coerce—in short to create terror to achieve a political or social goal.[1]

Definitions of terrorism referring to fear and coercion go back at least as far as the League of Nations Convention of 1937: "All criminal acts directed against a State and intended or calculated to create a state of terror in the minds of particular persons or a group of persons or the general public." The United Nations Office on Drugs and Crime also cites the language of a 1999 UN resolution: "criminal acts intended or calculated to provoke a state of terror in the general public, a group of persons or particular persons for political purposes."[2]

Similarly, the U.S. Federal Bureau of Investigation definition is "the unlawful use of force and violence against persons or property to intimidate or coerce a government, the civilian population, or any segment thereof, in furtherance of political or social objectives."[3]

Despite the popularity of such definitions, there is significant risk associated with specifying terrorist goals as part of the definition of terrorism. In general, understanding the origins of behavior is not helped by putting hypothesized origins into the definition of the behavior of interest. In particular, specifying goals of fear and coercion can distract from less obvious but perhaps more important terrorist goals, among which is the crucial need to mobilize those whose interests the terrorists claim to advance. This is a political goal, and my chapter argues that terrorism is best understood as a form of political competition. This perspective is consistent with the U.S. State Department's definition of terrorism: "premeditated, politically motivated violence perpetrated against noncombatant targets by subnational groups or clandestine agents."[4]

My starting point can be summarized in a syllogism:

War is politics by other means.
Terrorism is the warfare of the weak.
Therefore, terrorism is politics.

The first section of this chapter draws out some of the implications of this syllogism, and the second section examines several aspects of the U.S. response to terrorism in light of these implications. The third section offers conclusions and recommendations for evaluating U.S. antiterrorist policies, and for research needed to understand terrorism better.

Terrorism as Politics

Understanding terrorism as politics leads immediately to four implications. I advance each in summary form, with brief discussion and application to understanding al Qaeda, the attacks of 9/11, and the repercussions of these attacks.

1. The psychology at the bottom of terrorism is the same psychology at the bottom of less extreme forms of political action:[5] group identification—that is, the capacity to care about what happens to a cause and the group associated with that cause.[6]

Discussion

Individuals are recruited to terrorism by perceptions of threat, injury, and humiliation experienced by a group they care about, which may include direct experience of threat, injury, and humiliation to self and loved ones. The popular invocation of psychopathology or personal frustration to explain how individuals are recruited to terrorism is mistaken. Psychologically normal and personally accomplished people are recruited to terrorism by a combination of ideological appeal and intense small-group dynamics that is similar to recruitment and training in conventional armies and other groups.[7] Terrorism is a form of intergroup conflict, not an expression of individual problems and frustrations.[8]

Among scholars, at least, the pathology argument is fading. Psychiatrists[9] and social scientists[10] today usually agree that the great majority of terrorists are not suffering any form of psychopathology, at least not anything represented in the *Diagnostic and Statistical Manual of the American Psychiatric Association.*[11]

Application to al Qaeda

The 9/11 attackers were not crazy, and the leaders were men of above-average socioeconomic status from the Arab diaspora in Europe.[12] Their grievances included perceptions that the U.S. supports totalitarian governments in Arab countries, that U.S. troops stationed in Saudi Arabia are a desecration of the holy land of Mecca and Medina, that the U.S. blockade killed a million Iraqis, and that the U.S. supports Israel to kill and displace Palestinians.[13] More generally, they see the culture of the West penetrating and dominating Muslim culture since the fall of the Ottoman Empire.

These grievances were not, however, the proximate motivation of the 9/11 attackers; not, at least, if the content of what has come to be called "Atta's Manual" is any indication. This manual contained instructions for preparing the 9/11 attacks, and these were more an extended prayer than a litany of hate. The manual specifically enjoined striking for Allah and specifically warned against striking out of personal feelings of vengeance. For many terrorists and perhaps most terrorists, it is not hatred of the enemy but love of the in-group that powers sacrifice for the cause.[14]

This love does not have to be religious. Several of the 9/11 attackers were not highly religious; Ziad Jarrah for instance, while living in the United States before 9/11, drove a red sports car, drank beer, and brought his girlfriend to visit from Germany. Similarly, a survey of Islamic protestors in Europe found no relation between religiosity and interest in martyrdom or willingness to use weapons of mass destruction.[15] The Tamil Tigers, who represent a national rather than religious cause, have produced at least 75 suicide bombers.[16]

Even when terrorism appears to be about religious differences, these differences are often only imperfect markers for competition between two ethnic groups—that is, between two groups that see themselves defined by descent. This is the case for the conflict between Palestinians and Jews: the issue is not Islam versus Judaism but two ethnic groups claiming the same land. The fact that most Palestinians are Muslim and most Israeli Jews practice Judaism does not make the conflict a religious conflict—that is, it does not mean that the conflict is about religion. Similarly for the conflict between Catholics and Protestants in Northern Ireland: there are irreligious individuals among the militants of both sides. The issue is two descent groups claiming the same land.

2. Politics is competition, and terrorist groups are in constant competition with governments, more moderate opposition groups, and, often, other terrorist groups, for the pyramid of sympathizers on whom terrorists depend for silence, support, and recruits.

Discussion

Terrorists are the apex of a pyramid of sympathizers and supporters.[17] The base of the pyramid includes all who sympathize with the goals of the terrorists, even if they disagree with the means. In Northern Ireland, for instance, the base of the pyramid for the Irish Republican Army included everyone who agrees "Brits out." Higher layers in the pyramid are associated with more radical political views, more support for violence, and more risk-taking and personal sacrifice in support of the terrorists. The terrorists at the apex depend on the lower levels of the pyramid for cover, information, material resources, and, especially, recruits. Long-term success in reducing terrorism requires cutting terrorists off from their base. The Armenian Secret Army for the Liberation of Armenia, for instance, declined quickly after it lost the support of the Armenian diaspora.[18]

The pyramid model suggests that terrorist groups can be considered a kind of social movement—the "people power" that links individual sentiments and collective action.[19] The first scholar to bring a social movement theory perspective to the study of terrorism was sociologist della Porta,[20] who focused on the Red Brigade terrorists in Italy and the dynamics by which protestors' interaction with Italian police led to an escalation to terrorism. Psychologists too have begun to theorize about the dynamics of social movements,[21] but psychological approaches have not yet been integrated with microlevel developments in social movement theory.[22]

More recently, social movement theory has been used to understand violence by Islamic political groups against their own governments. Examples of this kind of work include *The Management of Islamic Activism: Salafis, the Muslim Brotherhood and State Power in Jordan*,[23]

Why Muslims Rebel: Repression and Resistance in the Islamic World,[24] *Islamic Activism: A Social Movement Theory Approach*,[25] and *Islamic Modernism, Nationalism and Fundamentalism: Episode and Discourse*.[26] Each of these monographs examines how violent politics and terrorism arise out of the interaction of state policies with groups and organizations that contend against the state.

Further, each describes conflict among groups contending with the state. This conflict can sometimes become violent. Sendero Luminoso, a Maoist terrorist group in Peru, killed leftists who disagreed with Sendero's interpretation of Marxism.[27] Two black African groups, The African National Congress and the Inkatha Freedom Party, were in violent conflict in South Africa, even as the ANC was using terrorist tactics against the white apartheid government.[28] Other examples of terrorist-against-terrorist rivalries, some involving violence, include the Provisional Irish Republican Army versus the Official Irish Republican Army, Fatah versus Hamas, Irgun Zwei Leumi versus Irgun, Armenian Secret Army for the Liberation of Armenia versus Justice Commandos for the Armenian Genocide, and Baader versus Meinhof in the Red Army Faction.[29]

Application to al Qaeda

Al Qaeda is today thought to be more like a franchise than an army. Its leaders, including bin Laden and al Zawahiri, have been driven out of their home countries (Saudi Arabia and Egypt) after losing political contests with Arab governments that successfully repressed them. Their failures at home led to a crucial turn in strategy when al Qaeda moved from attacks on the "near enemy"—Arab governments—to attacks on the "far enemy"—U.S. and other Western targets.[30] Their goal is to divide Muslims from non-Muslims, to remove Western power and Western culture from Muslim countries, and to mobilize a billion Muslims against the West in a jihad that will return Muslim culture to power and respect.[31] Given their previous failure to mobilize support in their home countries, their strategy requires Western assistance.

3. Terrorists count on the response of the state to mobilize those who sympathize with the goals of the terrorists. State response, to the extent that it hurts or outrages those less committed than the terrorists, does for the terrorists what they cannot do for themselves. This is jujitsu politics: using the enemy's strength to mobilize against the enemy.

Discussion

This aspect of terrorist strategy has been recognized in one way or another by many students of terrorism[32] but has not been the focus of a sustained theoretical analysis and is only beginning to appear in the discourse of security experts, policymakers, and journalists.

Although the hallmark of terrorist violence is violence against civilians, the distinction between civilian and soldier, between combatants and noncombatants, has been eroding since the French Revolution introduced the citizen army.[33]

In *Death by Government,* Rummel offers estimates of government killing of civilians during the twentieth century. He begins with the distinction between battle deaths and civilian deaths: 34 million combatants killed in interstate and civil wars; 169 million civilians killed by government. Enemy civilians killed during war amount to 39 million; civilians killed by their own government total 130 million. Nonstate killing of civilians, including terrorism, guerilla war, and insurgency, total perhaps 500,000.

Given the imbalance of state killing and nonstate killing in recent history, there is some warrant for the terrorists' expectation that state violence will miscarry to strike other than the terrorists. The result is likely to be useful to the terrorists.

Group dynamics research provides a theoretical and empirical basis for the analysis of jujitsu politics. Group dynamics research originated in Festinger's work on informal social influence, was extended in Festinger's theory of social comparison, and has been amplified and revised to take into account evidence indicating that different sources of cohesion have different effects on behavior.[34] Important for understanding terrorism is the ample evidence that competition or threat from an out-group has powerful effects on in-group psychology, including increased cohesion and the "authoritarian triad" of idealization of in-group norms, increased pressure on in-group deviates, and increased support for in-group leaders.[35] In short, out-group threat produces in-group mobilization in small face-to-face groups and, I argue, similarly produces in-group mobilization in large ethnic and national groups.[36]

A quick review of the American experience after 9/11 illustrates the impact of out-group threat on in-group dynamics. After 9/11, American cohesion—patriotism—was very high, with flags and flag decals displayed in profusion. American values and the American way of life were reiterated and reinforced in response to the terrorist challenge. Increased pressure on deviates was obvious in the hostility toward anyone who might question U.S. bombing attacks on Afghanistan, try to understand the attackers, or even suggest, as Bill Maher did, that driving an airplane into a tower was not an act of cowardice.[37] Finally, there was increased support for group leaders, especially the president.

Gallup polling[38] in the week before the 9/11 attacks showed 56 percent of Americans approving "the way George W. Bush is handling his job as president." The week after the 9/11 attacks, approval had risen to 86 percent. Approval for "the way George W. Bush is handling the economy" went from 54 percent before the attacks to 72 percent after the attacks. The latter result is perhaps the more surprising, because it indicates the generality of the rising tide of support for the president. In the absence of any new terrorist attacks on the U.S. homeland and the war dragging on in Iraq, U.S. polls in 2005 show much weaker support for President Bush.

Application to al Qaeda

In "Psychological Issues in Understanding Terrorism and the Response to Terrorism,"[39] I suggest that al Qaeda had jujitsu politics in mind in planning the 9/11 attacks. Bin Laden's right-hand man, Dr. Ayman al Zawahiri wrote in "Knights under the Banner of the Prophet" that if the shrapnel of war were to hit U.S. bodies, the United States would have to come out from behind its Arab and Jewish surrogates to attack Muslims directly.[40] The result would be jihad: a general mobilization of Muslims against the West. The United States did indeed respond to 9/11 by attacking the Taliban in Afghanistan, an attack that al Qaeda anticipated by assassinating Sheik Massoud, the leader of the only remaining Afghan resistance to the Taliban, a few days before 9/11.

Al Qaeda was disappointed in the relatively small collateral damage inflicted by U.S. forces in Afghanistan: perhaps 2,000 to 3,000 civilian deaths. But their hopes for more casualties and more Muslim outrage remain high as Western forces stay in Afghanistan to pacify the country. These hopes are expressed in bombings and suicide bombings against soft targets such as schools and hospitals in Afghanistan and Pakistan; at a minimum, these attacks will decrease the penetration of Western culture and sharpen the boundary between Muslims and Westerners. From al Qaeda's point of view, a further goal is to elicit the U.S. response that will radicalize more Afghans behind al Qaeda leadership.

The U.S. invasion of Iraq is an additional opportunity for al Qaeda, as Muslim militants from all over the world converge on Iraq to join in attacking U.S. forces.[41] Training in combat against Americans in Iraq can replace the training camps al Qaeda lost in Afghanistan. Expertise with improvised explosive devices can be exported to Afghanistan and, perhaps, to Europe. Al Qaeda began as the organizational base for bringing Muslims to fight the Russians in Afghanistan. In 2005 Abu Musab al Zarqawi's "al Qaeda in Mesopotamia" is the organizational base for bringing Muslims to fight the Americans in Iraq.

In Iraq, as in Afghanistan, shootings and bombings punish those who work for the Americans—not only those recruited to American-supported police and military forces but those who work for the Americans as translators, drivers, or hotel keepers. Attacks on Americans and those who work for Americans are helping to separate Western forces from Iraqis. When U.S. forces respond to these attacks, breaking down doors must substitute for language skills and the result is increasing opposition from Iraqis.[42] Jujitsu politics is the strategy behind attacks against Westerners from Morocco to Indonesia, the Philippines, and Malaysia—wherever Westerners and Western culture are penetrating the Muslim world.

Attacks on civilians in Madrid (March 11, 2004) and London (July 7, 2005) are similarly motivated. These attacks are retribution for Spanish and British participation with the United States in the war in Iraq, but have as well the possibility of eliciting Spanish and British reactions against Muslims that will radicalize Muslims who are, from the Islamist point of view, getting on too comfortably with Western culture and politics.

4. Understanding terrorist behavior requires understanding the relationship between terrorist acts and state responses. These form a dynamic of violence and counterviolence that must be seen as a whole, as a pattern, to make progress against the terrorists.

Terrorists may not always have an explicit or abstract understanding of jujitsu politics. Even when they do not, they can profit by its power. For the state targeted by terrorist attacks, effective response to terrorism requires attention to jujitsu politics regardless of whether the terrorists understand it. Of course the domestic political value of foreign attack is no mystery; state elites are not surprised by the kind of patriotic rallying to the government that the United States experienced after 9/11. The parallel effect of state response in rallying support for the terrorists is perhaps not so obvious, especially for policymakers who, as in the United States, are accustomed to focusing on domestic issues. Nevertheless, jujitsu politics may be, in the long run, the most powerful weapon the terrorists have; any state that ignores this power is delivering a major advantage to the terrorists.

The most important implication of jujitsu politics is that terrorist attacks and state responses form a dynamic system. Understanding terrorism means understanding the interactions between terrorist attacks and state responses. Evaluating success against terrorism means understanding the trends over time in the nature of these interactions. The first requirement of such understanding is to have a record of state actions that can be put on the same time line as the record of terrorist actions.

There are half a dozen major databases that track terrorist attacks, especially for international terrorists, and scholars can hold a terrorist group's actions against their writings and pronouncements.[43] But attention to the terrorists has not been matched by attention to state responses to terrorism. There is, to my knowledge, nothing like a complete account of state responses for any terrorist group. A database tracking state responses would indeed be complex, including military, police, legislative, judicial, insurance, investment, and public relations initiatives. Records of these initiatives are the essential first step toward evaluating what does and does not work against terrorism.

An interesting example of the kind of data needed is the work of Maoz on Israeli responses to Palestinian terrorist bombers.[44] This research suggests that states, too, are capable of using jujitsu politics: when pressures for peace are seen as inconvenient, Israelis use targeted assassinations of Palestinian leaders to draw Palestinian reprisals that relieve the pressure. It is difficult to press peace negotiations in the aftermath of a suicide bombing.

In sum, jujitsu politics means that the response to terrorism can be more dangerous than the terrorists. Rather than brief application of this generalization to al Qaeda, as in previous sections, I will consider in some detail in the next section the U.S responses to terrorism after 9/11.

Jujitsu Politics and the War on Terrorism

Criminal Justice versus War

Since 9/11, two kinds of discourse are commonly used to frame the U.S. response to terrorism: criminal justice and war. Both of these can still be heard in the rhetorical framing (see Introduction note 1) of U.S. political leaders, but the dominant rhetorical framing since 9/11 has been in terms of the "war on terrorism." The rhetorical framing in terms of war dominates despite the fact that the first attack on the World Trade Center in 1993 was followed by a successful criminal justice response: perpetrators were tracked down, extradited, charged, tried, and imprisoned. Of course, it can be objected that the criminal justice response did not succeed in preventing the 9/11 terrorist attacks. The obvious rejoinder is that criminal justice is not usually given up because it does not eliminate crime; indeed no one today suggests that the war on terrorism will eliminate terrorism.

Much depends on which frame is dominant.[45] When the response to terrorism is criminal justice, terrorists are seen as relatively few and atypical of their ethnic or national group, terrorism is understood as a problem to be controlled rather than eliminated, civil rights are seen as part of an effective response, and terrorism is seen as one of many problems with claims on state resources. When the response to terrorism is war, the enemy are seen as many and representative of their ethnic or national group, terrorism is understood as a battle that can be "won," civil rights are seen as an impediment to effective response, and other problems are invisible or subordinated for the duration of the war. War is moral judgment against a group; justice is moral judgment against an individual. War thus paves the way for violence against an enemy defined by group membership, violence that can include internment, torture, and death. At home, war claims without argument resources that might in better times go to investments in economic development, education, or health care.

In general, a criminal justice response short-circuits the psychology of jujitsu; a war on terrorism reinforces this psychology.

Hostility toward Arabs, Muslims, and Those Thought To Be Arab or Muslim

It should amaze us that the actions of 19 Arab Muslims on 9/11 could lead many Americans to fear of and hostility toward all Arabs and Muslims in the United States. "In the aftermath of the September 11, 2001, terrorist attacks, Arabs and Muslims in the United States, and those perceived to be Arab or Muslim, such as Sikhs (Hindus) and South Asians, became victims of a severe wave of backlash violence. The hate crimes included murder, beatings, arson, attacks on mosques, shootings, vehicular assaults, and verbal threats. This violence was directed at people solely because they shared or were perceived as sharing the national background or religion of the hijackers and al Qaeda members deemed responsible for attacking the World Trade Center and the Pentagon."[46] Would an attack by 19 French ecoterrorists produce similar fear and hostility toward French-origin people in the United States?

Attribution theory has not had much to say about when groups are seen as responsible for the acts of individuals; instead, most attribution research is about situational versus dispositional attributions for individual behavior.[47] The relatively few studies of group-level attributions tend to focus on perceptions of group homogeneity or extremity.[48] Perhaps the individualist culture of Western scholars gets in the way of asking about group guilt. In contrast, scholars interested in the contact hypothesis maintain that positive relations between individual members of groups in conflict can generalize to more positive attributions about the groups from which these individuals come.[49] It seems likely that the rhetorical framing in terms of war facilitates broad negative attributions for the actions of a few. Unfortunately, hostility toward Arabs and Muslims in the United States tends to undermine their support for cooperation with U.S. security agencies.

Reduced Civil Rights for Arabs, Muslims, and Those Thought To Be Arab or Muslim

The U.S. government imprisoned hundreds of Arab and Muslim men after 9/11; the prisoners were not publicly charged or tried, were held without counsel, and many were deported months and years later for visa violations.[50] Male immigrants from 25 predominantly Muslim countries were summoned for visa checks, and many were arrested in the federal buildings to which they had been summoned.[51] The October 6, 2005, threat of a terrorist attack on New York City subways brought renewed calls for the so-called profiling of Arab Americans.[52] The result of these policies of discrimination, internment, and deportation is that planeloads of young men are returning to places like Pakistan with the news that the United States is no place for a Muslim. In the United States, a "not-welcome" sign has undermined Muslim cooperation with antiterrorist investigations.[53]

A special case of reduced civil rights is the internment at Guantanamo Bay, Cuba, of hundreds of individuals captured in Afghanistan. These and other internees in Iraq and Afghanistan have been subjected to stresses that many would consider torture.[54] The U.S. claim that these prisoners should not enjoy the protections of prisoner-of-war status is widely rejected in other countries and is seen by many Muslims as another kind of bias against Muslims.[55] Many Americans are coming to see the treatment of these prisoners, and those at Abu Ghraib in Iraq and Bagram Air Force Base in Afghanistan, as violations of American values and traditions.[56]

Visa Policies

Since 9/11, it has become difficult to the point of impossible for men from Arab and Muslim countries to get visas for entry to the United States. The result is fewer students coming to study in the United States and fewer professors, journalists, government personnel, and nongovernmental organizations visiting the United States for professional reasons.[57] These policies may increase security in the short term, but in the longer term U.S. visa policy helps build the wall al Qaeda wants between Muslims and Americans.

International Relations

The United States has undertaken a new foreign policy posture that assumes the right to intervene in any country that might harbor or support terrorists. The result is that more people around the world begin to join with al Qaeda in resentment and fear of U.S. power.[58]

The war on terrorism has been pressed with the insistence that every country must choose to be with the United States or against the United States.[59] This pressure leaves little room for Muslim leaders and parties who are fundamentalist in religion but not violent in politics.[60] It is these conservatives (not the much sought after "moderates") who are the natural competitors of al Qaeda for the sympathies of the Muslim "street."

One unhappy result of the pressure to join in the war on terrorism has been additional support among Muslims for the mullahs commanding Iran. More moderate and modern leadership was winning democratic support in Iran until U.S. troops arrived next door in Iraq and the United States threatened Iran about its nuclear programs. The rally of support for the president in the United States after 9/11 offers some indication of the dynamic of U.S. threats against Iran. Just as external threat moved Americans to support their president after 9/11, external threat moves Iranians to support their current leaders.

Support for authoritarian and repressive regimes that join in the war on terrorism has meant increased U.S. support for repressive governments around the world. Examples include U.S. support for "antiterrorist" violence in Chechnya, Xingjiang, and Tibet; this violence looks more like genocide to those experiencing it. New alliances with authoritarian regimes are also associated with a string of post-9/11 U.S. military bases in the predominantly Muslim states (Kyrgyzstan, Uzbekistan, and Tajikistan) that emerged from the southern border about a crusade against Muslims, even as they worry Russians who feel encircled by U.S. power.[61]

Already noted is the value to al Qaeda of U.S. troops in Afghanistan and Iraq. Foreign troops trying to police an unfamiliar country in an unfamiliar language are a prescription for misunderstanding, mistakes, and misdirected violence. Incidents in which U.S. troops kill the wrong Iraqis multiply as U.S. troops respond to their own increasing casualties. If al Qaeda was disappointed with the level of collateral damage as the United States fought the Taliban, it must have renewed hope in seeing the current difficulties of U.S. pacification programs in Afghanistan and Iraq.

There is one positive development that should be noted in the international picture. The United States is removing its troops from Saudi Arabia, thanks to building replacement bases in Qatar. This removes what was once bin Laden's principal grievance and a recruiting tool for al Qaeda in Saudi Arabia. It is interesting to note that the United States has not made much public use of this withdrawal as evidence of respect for a Muslim ally. Perhaps acknowledging retreat is seen as more costly than the potential value of acknowledging respect for Saudi preferences.

Conclusions

Since 9/11, the U.S. war on terrorism has probably exceeded al Qaeda's best hopes for the power of jujitsu politics. A wall is rising between Muslims and the West: Arabs and Muslims in the United States are discriminated against, Arabs and Muslims cannot get visas to visit the United States, and Westerners have been deterred from living in or visiting Muslim countries or restricted to defensive enclaves in these countries. U.S. foreign policy has given people of many countries—not only Arabs and Muslims—reason to fear and resent U.S. power. Some sense of the significance of these trends is available in polls showing that in Indonesia, the largest Muslim country, 61 percent held a positive view of the United States in mid-2002, but only 15 percent had a positive view in June 2003.[62] More recent polling finds somewhat more positive views, but still generally unfavorable views of the United States (e.g., 38 percent in Indonesia favorable toward the United States in 2005).[63]

Al Qaeda seeks a "culture war" between Muslims and the West. Jujitsu politics is making progress everywhere that bombs and suicide bombers can elicit bias against, separation from, and attacks on Muslims who are not yet terrorists. If the response to terrorism mobilizes terrorists faster than the United States can kill them, al Qaeda cannot lose.

Policy Recommendations

The perspective of jujitsu politics leads to recommendations for U.S. response to terrorism.

1. The United States should support regular tracking polls among those likely to sympathize with the cause terrorists claim to represent. Polling in predominantly Muslim countries is not easy, but the Pew Global Attitudes Project has shown the way.

Polls in Muslim countries should assess attitudes toward the terrorist group and moral judgment of terrorist acts. Similarly these polls should assess attitudes toward the United States and moral judgment of U.S. antiterrorist policies. As focus groups and polls are used to pretest policy initiatives in the United States, so focus groups and polls in Muslim countries could be used to pretest new antiterrorist initiatives before the United States implements them. As partisan research in the United States looks for wedge issues that can advance a particular candidate, so polling in Muslim countries could look for issues that can advance U.S. interests against the terrorists. It may be, for instance, that most Muslims have nationalist sentiments that oppose bin Laden's goal of a pan-Islamic caliphate. Zogby polls in six Muslim countries in 2005 found that only six percent of respondents sympathized with this goal.[64]

2. U.S. policymakers should evaluate antiterrorist policies in relation to poll results. It is not enough to assess success in terms of terrorists killed and captured, assets frozen, and attacks prevented. Nor is it enough to assess U.S. public approval of these policies. Long-term success against terrorism requires cutting the terrorists off from their pyramid of supporters and sympathizers.

This is politics, and U.S. expertise in political campaigns can be brought to bear. Political campaigns in the United States depend on two-way communication, with constant interplay between what politicians say and do and what politicians learn about the evolving beliefs and preferences of citizens. The same kind of communication can connect U.S. policies with the beliefs and preferences of Muslims. The result will be reduced support for Islamic terrorists from Muslims worldwide.

Opinion research can thus be the foundation for the war of ideas that is currently led by Karen Hughes, who was nominated by President George W. Bush on June 29, 2005, to serve as Under Secretary of State for Public Diplomacy and Public Affairs. She was confirmed by the United States Senate on July 29, 2005, and sworn in on September 9, 2005. Her agenda for U.S. public diplomacy will succeed to the extent that she learns as much about Muslim politics as she has learned about U.S. politics.

3. One U.S. antiterrorist policy deserves particular attention, because it seems to promise victory over terrorism without communication or, more precisely, with unidirectional communication. This policy can be interpreted as suggesting that the United States can change Islam in ways that will make it unnecessary for the United States to change at all.

The war of ideas against terrorism currently targets Islamic schools, radio and television stations, mosques, and monuments.[65] These initiatives stem from a revision of the National Security Strategy for Combating Terrorism, a revision approved by President Bush in 2004. The new strategy, Muslim World Outreach, reflects a judgment that fighting terrorism requires taking a hand in what happens in Islamic countries and even within Islam itself. Islam, one might say, is too important to be left to the Islamists. As part of this strategy, the U.S. Agency for International Development is spending over $10 billion a year in Muslim countries. The State Department and the Central Intelligence Agency are cooperating in the Muslim World Outreach Program. This program has a potential downside. Osama bin Laden claims that the West is mounting a crusade against Islam. If he can show the United States taking its crusade inside the structure of Islam—show the United States trying to tinker with the meaning and essence of Islam—his appeal to a billion Muslims could be multiplied far beyond what Abu Ghraib and the war in Iraq accomplished. Western Christians might imagine, for instance, their reaction to learning that billions of Arab petrodollars are funding efforts to change the message of the Bible in directions favorable to Muslims.

Research Recommendations

The perspective of jujitsu politics also leads to suggestions for research.

1. Research is needed to develop databases that record both terrorist actions and state actions on the same time line.

Current research focuses on terrorist attacks on the state power they oppose, with some attention to terrorist texts and public statements, terrorist organization, and terrorist leadership. Terrorist attacks are usually recorded in terms of date, place, weapons, and casualties. Actions relevant to the political appeal of a terrorist group are much broader, however, and include educational activities, social welfare activities, fundraising, security for supporters, discipline for deviates, and competition with other groups claiming the same cause. Records of the whole spectrum of terrorist activities are required to understand the political position of the terrorists.

Even more underdeveloped are the records of state responses to a terrorist group. As indicated earlier, the data required will include initiatives of many different kinds—not just military and police initiatives but intelligence, legislative, judicial, diplomatic, and mass media initiatives. For each initiative, the record should include the date of announcement of the new program, date of implementation, dates of any major modifications, and, if relevant, the date on which the initiative is withdrawn or terminated. Some estimate of the cost of an initiative would also be useful.

Only study of both kinds of data—terrorist actions and state responses—can determine what works better and worse against terrorism.

2. Even the best research on terrorist actions and state responses is already too late. Because prevention is better than cure, research should aim to understand how a group moves from protest to violent protest to terrorism.

Scholars interested in terrorism have focused on the study of existing terrorist groups, especially the relatively few international terrorist groups that attack Western interests and citizens. This amounts to selecting on the dependent variable of interest such that the origins of terrorism are obscured. More research is needed that takes a social movement approach, such as was pioneered by della Porta with the Italian Red Brigades and, more recently, employed by scholars of Islamic political violence such as Hafez, Moaddel, and Wictorowicz.[66]

Only comparison of groups and movements that did and did not make the transition to terrorism can find predictors of this transition.

Acknowledgment

This research was supported by the United States Department of Homeland Security through the National Consortium for the

Study of Terrorism and Responses to Terrorism, grant number N00140510629. However, any opinions, findings, and conclusions or recommendations in this document are those of the author and do not necessarily reflect views of the U.S. Department of Homeland Security.

Notes

1. Ruben Ardilla, "The Psychology of the Terrorist: Behavioral Perspectives," in *The Psychology of Terrorism*, ed. Christopher Stout (Westport, CT: Praeger, 2002); Steven S. Olweean, "Psychological Concepts of the "Other": Embracing the Compass of the Self," in *The Psychology of Terrorism*, ed. C. Stout (Westport, CT: Praeger, 2002); William H. Reid, "Controlling Political Terrorism: Practicality, Not Psychology," in *The Psychology of Terrorism*, ed. C. Stout (Westport, CT.: Praeger, 2002).

2. United Nations Office on Drugs and Crime, *United Nations Resolution* (2005), http://www.unodc.org/unodc/en/terrorism.html.

3. U.S. Government Printing Office via GPO Access, *Code of Federal Regulations, 20cfro.15* (2005), http://frwebgate.access.gpo.gov/cgi-bin/get-cfr.cgi.

4. U.S. State Department Office of Counter Terrorism, *Foreign Terrorist Organizations Fact Sheet, October 11* (2005), http://www.state.gov/s/ct/rls/fs/37191.htm.

5. Donald R. Kinder, "Opinion and Action in the Realm of Politics," in *The Handbook of Social Psychology*, eds. Daniel T. Gilbert, Susan T. Fiske, and Gardner Lindzey (New York: McGraw-Hill, 1998).

6. Clark McCauley, "The Psychology of Group Identification and the Power of Ethnic Nationalism," in *Ethnopolitical Warfare: Causes, Consequences, and Possible Solutions*, eds. Daniel Chirot and Martin E.P. Seligman (Washington, DC: APA Books, 2001); Clark McCauley, "What Do Terrorists Want?" *Psychological Science Agenda* 14, no. 6 (2001.); Donald M. Taylor and Winifred R. Louis, "Terrorism and the Quest for Identity," in *Understanding Terrorism: Psychosocial Roots, Consequences, and Interventions*, eds. F.M. Moghaddam and A.J. Marsella (Washington, DC: American Psychological Association, 2004).

7. Clark McCauley, "Terrorism Research and Public Policy: An Overview," *Journal of Terrorism and Political Violence* 3 (1991); Clark R. McCauley and Mary E. Segal, "Social Psychology of Terrorist Groups," in *Review of Personality and Social Psychology*, ed. C. Hendrick (Beverly Hills, CA: Sage, 1987).

8. J. Donovan, *U.S.: Analysts See Weak Link between Poverty and Terrorism*, Radio Free Europe/Radio Library (2002), http://www.rferl.org/nca/features/2002/11/27112002205339.asp.

9. Ibid.

10. Scott Atran, "Genesis of Suicide Terrorism," *Science*, 7 March 2003.

11. Jonathan Drummond, "From the Northwest Imperative to Global Jihad: Social Psychological Aspects of the Construction of the Enemy, Political Violence, and Terror," in *The Psychology of Terrorism*, ed. C. Stout (Westport, CT: Praeger, 2002); T.G. Goetzel, "Terrorist Beliefs and Terrorist Lives," in *The Psychology of Terrorism*, ed. C. Stout (Westport, CT: Praeger, 2002); Ervin Staub, "Preventing Terrorism: Raising 'Inclusively' Caring Children in the Complex World of the Twentieth Century," in *The Psychology of Terrorism*, ed. C. Stout (Westport, CT: Praeger, 2002).

12. Clark McCauley, "Psychological Issues in Understanding Terrorism and the Response to Terrorism," in *The Psychology of Terrorism*, ed. Christopher Stout (Westport, CT: Praeger, 2002).

13. Osama bin Laden et al., *Jihad against Jews and Crusaders: World Islamic Front Statement* (1998), http://www.fas.org/irp/world/para/docs/980223-fatwa.htm.

14. McCauley, "Psychological Issues in Understanding Terrorism."

15. Ayla Schbley and Clark McCauley, "Political, Religious, and Psychological Characteristics of Muslim Protest Marchers in Eight European Cities: Jerusalem 2002," *Terrorism and Political Violence*, in press.

16. Mia Bloom, *Dying To Kill: The Allure of Suicide Terror* (New York: Columbia University Press, 2005); Robert A. Pape, *Dying To Win: The Strategic Logic of Suicide Terrorism* (New York: Random House, 2005).

17. McCauley, "Psychological Issues in Understanding Terrorism"; McCauley, "Terrorism Research and Public Policy."

18. Julie Huang et al., "Toward Understanding Desistence from Terrorism: The Case of the Armenian Secret Army for the Liberation of Armenia" in preparation.

19. Charles Tilly, *From Mobilization to Revolution* (Reading, MA: Addison-Wesley, 1978).

20. Donnatella della Porta, *Social Movements, Political Violence, and the State; A Comparative Analysis of Italy and Germany* (Cambridge, England: Cambridge University Press, 1995).

21. Dominic Abrams and Georgina Randsley de Moura, "The Psychology of Collective Political Protest," in *The Social Psychology of Politics*, eds. Victor C. Ottati et al. (New York: Kluwer Academic/Plenum, 2002); Tom R. Tyler and Heather J. Smith, "Social Justice and Social Movements," in *The Handbook of Social Psychology*, eds. D.T. Gilbert, S. Fiske, and G. Lindzey (New York: McGraw-Hill, 1998).

22. Douglas McAdam, Sidney Tarrow, and Charles Tilly, *Dynamics of Contention* (New York: Cambridge University Press, 2001).

23. Quentan Wiktorowicz, *The Management of Islamic Activism: Salafis, the Muslin Brotherhood and State Power in Jordan* (Albany: State University of New York Press, 2001).

24. Mohammed H. Hafez, *Why Muslims Rebel: Repression and Resistance in the Islamic World* (Boulder, CO: Lynne Rienner, 2003).

25. Quintan Wiktorowicz, ed. *Islamic Activism: A Social Movement Theory Approach* (Bloomington: Indiana University Press, 2004).

26. Mansoor Moaddel, *Islamic Modernism, Nationalism, and Fundamentalism* (Chicago: University of Chicago Press, 2005).

27. Goetzel.

28. C. Higson-Smith, "A Community Psychology Perspective on Terrorism: Lessons from South Africa," in *The Psychology of Terrorism*, ed. C. Stout (Westport, CT: Praeger, 2002).

29. McCauley and Segal.

30. Farhad A. Gerges, *The Far Enemy: Why Jihad Went Global* (New York: Cambridge University Press, 2005).

31. R. B. Hamud, ed., *Osama Bin Laden: America's Enemy in His Own Words* (San Diego, CA: Nadeem, 2005).

32. Atran; Martha Crenshaw, "The Causes of Terrorism," in *Violence: A Reader*, ed. C. Besteman (New York: New York University Press, 2002); Martha Crenshaw, "The Effectiveness of Terrorism in the Algerian War," in *Terrorism in Context*, ed. M. Crenshaw (University Park: Pennsylvania State University Press, 1995); Higson-Smith; Winifred R. Louis and Donald M. Taylor, "Understanding the September 11 Terrorist Attack on America: The Role of Intergroup Theories of Normative Influence," *Analyses of Social Issues and Public Policy* (2002); Ian S. Lustick, "Terrorism in the Arab Israeli Conflict: Targets and Audiences," in *Terrorism in Context*, ed. M. Crenshaw (University Park: Pennsylvania State University Press, 1995); Carlos Marighella, *Minimanual of the Urban Guerrilla*, trans. J. Butt and R. Sheed (Havana: Tricontinental, 1970; reprinted in C. Marighella, *For the Liberation of Brazil* (Harmondsworth, England: Penguin Books, 1971), pp. 61–97.

33. Clark McCauley, "Terrorism and the State: The Logic of Killing Civilians," in *The Making of a Terrorist: Recruitment, Training and Root Causes*, ed. J. Forest (Westport, CT: Praeger, in press).

34. Kurt Back, "Influence through Social Communication," *Journal of Abnormal and Social Psychology* 42 (1951); Leon Festinger, "Informal Social Communication," *Psychological Review* 57 (1950); Leon Festinger, "A Theory of Social Comparison Processes," *Human Relations* 7 (1954); Clark McCauley, "Group Dynamics in Janis's Theory of Groupthink: Backward and Forward," *Organizational Behavior and Human Decision Processes* 73 (1998).

35. John Duckitt and Kirstin Fisher, "The Impact of Social Threat on Worldview and Ideological Attitudes," *Political Psychology* 24, no. 1 (2003); Robert A. LeVine and Donald T. Campbell, *Ethnocentrism* (New York: Wiley, 1972); Muzafer Sherif et al., *The Robbers' Cave Experiment* (Norman: University of Oklahoma Press, 1961).

36. McCauley, "The Psychology of Group Identification"; Clark McCauley, "The Psychology of Terrorism," in *After September 11: Perspectives from the Social Sciences* (2001); Clark McCauley, "War Versus Justice in Response to Terrorist Attack: Competing Frames and Their Implications," in

Psychology of Terrorism, eds. Bruce Bongar and Larry E. Beutler (New York: Oxford University Press, in press).

37. News Hour, *Limits of Dissent*, PBS News (2001), http://www.pbs.org/newshour/bb/media/july-dec01/dissent_10-16.html.

38. Poll Gallup, *Presidential Ratings - Job Approval* (2005), http://poll.gallup.com/content/default.aspx?ci=1723.

39. Clark McCauley, "Psychological issues in understanding terrorism and the response to terrorism." In *The Psychology of Terrorism*. Vol III, *Theoretical Understandings and Perspectives*, ed. C. Stout. pp. 3-30. (Westport, CN: Praeger).

40. Ayman al Zawahiri, *Knights under the Banner of the Prophet* (2001), http://www.fas.org/irp/world/para/ayman_bk.htm.

41. Dexter Filkins, "Foreign Fighters Captured in Iraq Come from 27, Mostly Arab, Lands," *New York Times*, October 21, 2005.

42. Dexter Filkins, "The Fall of the Warrior King," *New York Times Magazine*, October 23, 2005.

43. Hamud.

44. Zeev Maoz, "The Unlimited Use of the Limited Use of Force: Israel and Low Intensity Warfare, 1949-2004." Paper presented at the 45th Annual International Studies Association Convention, Montreal, Canada, 2004.

45. McCauley, "War Versus Justice."

46. Human Rights Watch, *"We Are Not the Enemy": Hate Crimes against Arabs, Muslims, and Those Perceived To Be Arab or Muslim after September 11* (2002), http://www.hrw.org/reports/2002/usahate/index.htm#TopOfPage.

47. Miles Hewstone, "The Ultimate Attribution Error? A Review of the Literature on Intergroup Causal Attribution," *European Journal of Social Psychology* 20 (1990).

48. Henry Rothgerber, "External Intergoup Threat as an Antecedent to Perceptions of in-Group and out-Group Homogeneity," *Journal of Personality and Social Psychology* 73 (1997).

49. Thomas F. Pettigrew, "Intergroup Contact Theory," *Annual Review of Psychology* 49 (1998).

50. John N. Paden and Peter W. Singer, "America Slams the Door (on Its Foot): Washington's Destructive New Visa Policies," *Foreign Affairs* (2003).

51. Joseph Feuerherd, "Critics Say Immigration Tactics Threaten Security," *National Catholic Reporter*, March 28, 2003.

52. Edward Epstein, *Calls for Racial, Ethnic Profiling Renewed after Transit Attacks. Critics Say It Unfairly Singles out Minorities* (August 10, 2005), http:sfgate.com/cgi-bin/article.cgi?f=/c/a/2005/08/10/MNG16E5JTC1.DTL.

53. Feuerherd.

54. Mark Danner, *Torture and Truth: America, Abughraib, and the War on Terror* (New York: New York Review of Books, 2004).

55. Hamud.

56. Frontline, *The Torture Question*, PBS (2005), http://www.pbs.org/wgbh/pages/frontline/torture/.

57. Paden and Singer.

58. A. Kohut, *Anti-Americanism: Causes and Characteristics*, Pew Research Center (2003), http://people-press.org/commentary/display.php3?AnalysisID=77.

59. CNN, *You Are Either with Us or against Us* (2001), http://archives.cnn.com/2001/US/11/06/gen.attack.on.terror/.

60. Emmanuel Karagiannis and Clark McCauley, "Hizb Ut-Tahrir Al-Islami: Evaluating the Threat Posed by a Radical Islamic Group that Remains Nonviolent," *Terrorism and Political Violence* (in press).

61. "U.S. Military Bases and Empire," *Monthly Review*, March 1, 2002.

62. Kohut; David E. Sanger and Jane Perlez, "Bush Woos Skeptics in Visit to Bali," *International Herald Tribune*, October 23, 2003.

63. Pew Global Attitudes Project, *U.S. Image up Slightly, but Still Negative*, Pew Research Center (2005), http://pewglobal.org/reports/display.php?ReportID=247.

64. Elizabeth Bumbiller, "21st-Century Warnings of a Threat Rooted in the 7th," *New York Times*, December 12, 2005.

65. David E. Kaplan, *Hearts, Minds, and Dollars: In an Unseen Front in the War on Terrorism, America Is Spending Millions . . . To Change the Very Face of Islam* U.S. News & World Report (April 25, 2005), http://www.usnews.com/usnews/news/articles/050425/25roots.htm.

66. della Porta; Hafez; Mohammed H. Hafez and Quentan Wiktorowicz, "Violence and Contention in the Egyptian Islamic Movement," in *Islamic Activism: A Social Movement Theory Approach*, ed. Q. Wiktorowicz (Bloomington: Indiana University Press, 2004); Moaddel; Wiktorowicz, *Islamic Activism.*

CHAPTER 4

The Social Psychology of Punishing Dissent: Negative Reactions to Antiwar Views in the United States

Bernice Lott

The definition of social psychology as the study of social influence[1] encourages examination of conformity to group norms and majority opinions and the consequences of deviating from them. This chapter presents examples of reactions to political dissent gathered from the U.S. press to illustrate social psychological processes relevant to majority pressures for uniformity, in this case for *prescriptive patriotism*, a phrase from Platt and O'Leary.[2] These examples are media-reported reactions to antiwar views by supporters of the Iraq war. My focus is on responses by individuals, by *private actors*, not responses by government, such as the PATRIOT Act, Department of Defense databases, or surveillance.[3]

The chapter includes a call for education about the problems inherent in conformity pressures and an explanation of how such pressures threaten independent decision-making and can undermine the democratic process. Research on independent thinking has lagged behind the study of conformity but is a vital complement to it. We need to identify variables related to the acquisition, reinforcement, and maintenance of independence. An empirical focus on independence will provide data that are as essential to an understanding of the social psychology of attitudes, beliefs, and behavior as are data on conformity.

Context

After the events of 9/11, a heightened sense of threat in the United States was followed by a lower tolerance for dissenting views on governmental measures to deal with terrorism. An often-repeated message was that "You are either with us or against us." Criticism of the preemptive war against Iraq evoked especially strong negative reactions to dissenters. While efforts to unify public opinion may be expected in the face of external threat, uniformity pressures can undermine democracy by restraining minority views. Democracy, however, requires that views critical of the status quo and of government policies can be expressed without fear of retribution. The verbal attacks on those criticizing the Iraq war thus merit critical examination, because such criticism is essential to protect democracy and guarantees of the First Amendment.

Following the U.S. invasion of Iraq, messages that "'love of country' means 'no questions asked'" were widely circulated.[4] One commentator noted that "tolerance for dissent in America has been visibly frayed"[5] and another that in " today's chilly climate . . . the forecast for dissent is cloudy with a chance of consequences."[6] Media reports of responses to voices opposed to the war illustrate such consequences.

Dissent and Stigmatization

Richard, Bond, and Stokes-Zoota[7] examined 322 meta-analyses of social psychological phenomena studied during the last 100 years. The hypothesis that people who deviate from a group are rejected by it, tested by 23 meta-analyses, was supported by a strong average effect size (r) of .60. Of the 474 hypotheses tested in these meta-analyses, only 24 were supported by average effect sizes of .50 or higher. Avoiding rejection is a powerful motive for conformity, and rejection can take many forms—being ignored, excluded, belittled, derided, threatened with harm.

Letters to U.S. newspaper editors voicing objections to statements critical of the Iraq war frequently accused dissenters of threatening group unity. Dissent was said to be OK, but only at the right time and right place.[8] Thus, two politically moderate guests on a PBS news show agreed that, while a war is on, opponents should keep quiet.[9] A CBS movie miniseries about Hitler's rise to power was called disruptive to national solidarity after the producer, in an interview, compared the fearfulness rampant in post–World War I Germany with the prevalent fear in this country. He expressed the belief that fear had helped the U.S. public accept a pre-emptive war.[10] And when Ted Koppel of *Nightline* proposed reciting the names of all the U.S. troops killed in Iraq on his program, he was accused of planning to undermine the war effort. The Sinclair Broadcast Group, judging the program to be "an anti-war statement," did not permit its TV stations to air the broadcast.[11]

Yanay,[12] in writing about the hate letters received by members of a dissident Israeli left-Zionist party, describes how exclusion is used as a method of punishment. The letter writers told the dissidents: "You don't belong to the Jewish people . . . to our community" (p. 55). The threat of social ostracism is clear. In two experimental studies, Williams, Cheung, and Choi[13] manipulated ostracism by having some players of an Internet game ignored by the others. The result was that the targets of the rejection were more likely to conform later to the incorrect judgments of a new group.

Political dissenters become stigmatized. They acquire the "social identity" of troublemakers or outsiders whose views are disrespected and disallowed. Crocker, Major, and Steele[14] discuss social stigma as resulting from the rejection of persons who "deviate from cultural norms" (p. 510). The stigmatized person is devalued, and the more powerful stigmatizers put forward their position as superior and their worldview as correct.

Critics of the war and occupation of Iraq are accused of identifying with the enemy, and their patriotism is questioned. For example, a Fox official called CNN correspondent Christine Amanpour a "spokeswoman for al Qaeda" after she spoke publicly of the influence of intimidation on some of CNN's prewar news reports.[15] A letter to the editor in one newspaper accused Gary Trudeau of "providing comfort to the enemy" in his *Doonesbury* cartoons and undermining the spirit of U.S. troops.[16] A New York City newspaper listed 13 actors and musicians with antiwar views as "Saddam Lovers."[17] And when Congresswoman Pelosi questioned the president's leadership, Tom DeLay accused her of "putting American lives at risk."[18] After the release of Michael Moore's film *Fahrenheit 9/11*, one irate letter-to-the-editor writer asked whether Moore was "working for America, or . . . working for the enemy,"[19] and a columnist claimed that Moore's views were no different from those of Hezbollah.[20]

A Florida pastor, publicly critical of the war in Iraq, was rejected for membership in her local garden club, despite the fact that she had previously been a featured speaker at the club and was the author of two garden books.[21] In addition to outright rejection, a frequent negative response to dissenting views is derision. Hollywood celebrities who spoke against the war during the 2003 Academy Award ceremonies were described as being airheads with hot air opinions;[22] the antiwar statements of Tim Robbins were dismissed as "foolish rantings";[6] and Barbra Streisand was said to have a "big mouth."[23] The Dixie Chicks (whose lead singer said that she was ashamed President Bush was from her state of Texas) were called traitors, Dixie sluts, and Saddam's angels.[24, 25]

While celebrity dissenters are easy targets for derision, the opinions of others have also been ridiculed. Senator McCain reportedly told President Carter to "shut up" after the latter questioned the preemptive war; and Representative DeLay told Senator Daschle to do the same, calling him "the senator from France."[17] The poet laureate of Rhode Island was called "an uneducated man" by a letter-to-the-editor writer[26] after his public criticism of the president.

Conformity and Groupthink

Conformity is tempting because it avoids rejection. It also helps us feel correct, diminish conflict, and take our place among those we admire and see as similar to or more powerful than ourselves.[27] Conformity reduces the stresses involved in arguing and the effort of having to formulate and support a contrary position.[28] Dissenting is a strain on one's resources of energy and ideas and a source of anxiety about potential negative consequences.

Negative reactions to dissent can lead to a social psychological phenomenon called *groupthink* that inhibits criticism and attention to new ideas by discrediting contrary information and encouraging the conviction that the majority is smarter than and morally superior to those who disagree with it.[29] In the negative responses to dissenting views about the Iraq war are subtle references to sources of power: the majority, not the minority, has the resources to provide desired or aversive outcomes; has superior knowledge; and includes the country's most respectable people and its most legitimate leaders. Unger[30] has proposed that a "hidden ideology" characterizes those who do not question their own values and beliefs, and who "demonize" those who do not accept their worldview as "the only true one" (p. 48).

Threatening Responses to Dissent

Some negative reactions to antiwar voices contain threats of job loss or potential violence. For example, a parent in Rhode Island, whose high school child had gone to hear Howard Zinn's critical remarks about the Iraq war, called for firing the teacher who had invited Zinn.[31] A Vermont teacher whose students produced a poster critical of the president as part of an assignment on Iraq was removed from the course, and other administrative action against him was reportedly being pursued.[32] A Florida teacher with 11 years of service was suspended after he participated in a peace march.[4] Comedian Bill Maher's remark about the 9/11 suicide attackers not being cowards cost him his job. First, Sears and FedEx pulled out as his sponsors; then his show was cancelled.[8] The producer of the miniseries on Hitler mentioned earlier was fired.[10]

An antiwar minister in California was greeted by a sign that read "Why don't you leave America now!"[8] A Catholic priest[33] with outspoken antiwar views was awakened early one morning by 75 National Guard soldiers outside his house and church in a "tiny, remote" desert town in New Mexico "shouting . . . 'Kill, Kill, Kill!'" After actor Tim Robbins spoke of a "climate of fear" before the National Press Club, radio commentator Rush Limbaugh said, "Good. You should be afraid."[8] The antiwar comments of a college commencement speaker provoked boos and shouts of "send him to France"; his microphone was unplugged twice, and some people climbed the platform in an attempt to remove him from behind the speaker's stand.[34] At a performance in Las Vegas, Linda Ronstadt dedicated an encore song, *Desperado,* to Michael Moore for his film *Fahrenheit 9/11.* About a quarter of those in attendance left, and others "spilled drinks, tore down posters and demanded their money back."[35] Ronstadt was ejected from the hotel and told that she would not be welcomed back.[36] And rock band Nine Inch Nails, which was invited to perform during the MTV Movie Awards, canceled its performance after being told that its plan to perform a song that was critical of the war against a backdrop image of President Bush, was an unacceptable "partisan political statement."[37]

Effects on Observers and Dissenters

What is particularly striking about these examples of negative responses to dissenting views on the Iraq war reported in the U.S. press is that they were not efforts to influence the thoughts, feelings, and actions of the dissenters. The punishing words and consequences could be expected to have a potential effect primarily on observers—on those who read or heard about them via the media. The implied message was: this is what *you* can expect if you stray from the normative or prescribed views of the majority.

Experiments by Janes and Olson[38] found conformity by those who merely observed derision that was directed at others. They tested the assumption that ridicule punishes group members who do not adhere to social norms by having some students observe others being ridiculed. These students were later significantly more conforming on a task and reported being more afraid of failing than other participants. Those who observed others being ridiculed were not themselves potential targets; yet they presumably became sensitized to their own vulnerability to negative treatment, an awareness that Janes and Olson suggest "can limit and constrain subsequent behavior" (p. 484).

Even when there is no overt rejection or threat of rejection, those who have minority opinions may feel pressures to conform. This hypothesis was tested by Bassili.[39] He predicted that persons with minority opinions on such social policy issues as affirmative action or simple likes and dislikes about foods and celebrities would exhibit hesitancy in expressing their views. The hesitancy was seen as reflecting conflict between a desire to conform and having opinions that do not match the assumed dominant position on an issue. Response latencies assessed in five computer telephone surveys indicated that minority views were consistently expressed more slowly on a variety of social policy and personal matters. These results supported a "minority slowness effect." Bassili concluded that this effect is "pervasive and robust." Its consequences for social life may be serious and far-reaching, since, as Bassili noted, "hesitancy is often a precursor of inaction" (p. 274).

Such findings suggest that those who castigate and deride persons with minority views hope to cause dissenters or potential dissenters to self-doubt and keep quiet. Fear of negative consequences has social influence effects as a result of the direct consequences to dissenters that follow their behavior and from the knowledge that observers have of these negative sanctions. While approval and social harmony are the expected consequences for conforming to majority views or social norms, rejection and denigration are the expected consequences for not conforming. Observers learn that dissenters should not be attended or listened to. Thus, while a democratic society may provide the right to free speech, the impact of dissenting views can be minimized when listeners do not give them "a respectful hearing" (p. 212).[40] It is the constraining of overt behavior or verbal expression that is the objective of punishing dissent and that has such serious consequences for a democratic society.

A defining feature of democracy is that it provides opportunities for the free expression of differences through the ballot box and through all forms of public discourse. Criticism of different positions is also protected, but we need to understand that minority views are particularly vulnerable to conformity pressures, especially when subjected to a wide range of negative sanctions from derision to threats.

Social Norms

The negative responses to antiwar views reported in the U.S. media serve as a case study of factors that maintain uniformity in beliefs and behavior and achieve conformity to norms. Cialdini and Trost[41] define social norms as "rules and standards that . . . guide and/or constrain social behavior without the force of laws . . . and any sanctions for deviating from them come from social networks, not the legal system" (p. 152). It is precisely this phenomenon of social sanctions that is illustrated by the range of negative reactions to dissent that have been briefly presented here. These serve to punish dissenters through rejection, name-calling, derision, and threats and to inform would-be dissenters of the consequences of deviating from the majority view.

Our knowledge of the conditions that increase the probability of conformity to majority views does not help us identify the conditions that are sufficient or necessary for independent behavior. What may be operating in dissent or independence is the existence of competing reference groups[42] that support different behaviors. Showing independence from the norms of one group may show allegiance with those of another. We need to formulate a research agenda that will uncover antecedents of independence, identify consequences, and test hypotheses about the relationships between such behavior and both personal and situational variables. Democracy rests on the free expression of different views so that decisions can be made by weighing the strengths and weaknesses of alternative positions. It is therefore vital that pressures to conform to a majority view are not so overwhelming that minority positions quickly give way. We need to understand how continued maintenance of an independent minority position can be achieved.

Under certain conditions, for example, there are positive payoffs for persons who dissent. In the case of the Dixie Chicks, their popularity may have increased. At one concert, scenes of marches for civil rights and abortion rights were projected on video screens and scenes of people destroying Dixie Chicks records. "There were cheers when Ms. Maines sang, 'I don't think I'm afraid anymore.'"[43] The group has reported sold-out concerts and increased record sales.[44] We need to identify the variables related to positive consequences for dissenters.

Recommendations

With respect to policy, we must persuade educators that social studies and citizenship classes at various levels would profit greatly from information and discussion about the consequences of conforming and independent behavior in the realm of values and politics. School exercises and class discussions should be developed to explore pressures for uniformity, definitions of deviance, reactions to nonconformity, and the role of the media. We need to help students identify techniques—seen in their extreme form when used by cults, for example[45]—that are part of the everyday arsenal of uniformity-inducing strategies. When being "part of the group," "not making waves," "not making trouble," and "blending in" are personal goals that receive reinforcement from schools and media, we need to help students analyze the consequences of pursuing them.

Discussions of issues related to conformity and independence are vital for constructive citizenship and active community participation. The benefits of dissent in contributing new information and ideas that stimulate discussion and argument need to be recognized. Greenberg[9] has argued that antiwar movements have produced valuable social and political works of art, philosophy, and criticism and have also given rise to lasting and influential organizations. We should recognize this and inform our students, for example, that Thomas Jefferson was among the targets of the Alien and Sedition Acts of 1798 that made it illegal to say harshly critical things about the U.S. government.[8]

A major strategy for those in public policy positions is to foster ways to increase our knowledge of, and attention to, variables related to the expression of opinions and values. Sternberg[46] has proposed that our schools should teach "the 'other three Rs'—reasoning, responsibility and resilience" (p. 55). I would add to this the teaching of "independence"—not an R, but a behavior related to all three of his additions to the school curriculum and vital to the maintenance of a vibrant democratic society.

Readers can work locally for this objective by attempting to educate and persuade members of school boards and school personnel about the value of teaching for independence. Psychologists and other social scientists can put empirical questions about independence high on their research agenda lists, thus recognizing its significance for theory, practice, and a vital democratic society.

Acknowledgment

Some portions of this chapter were presented at a colloquium at the Department of Psychology, University of California, Santa

Cruz, on March 5, 2004, and at a symposium at the annual convention of the American Psychological Association in Honolulu, Hawaii, on July 28, 2004.

References

1. Allport, G.W. (1968). The historical background of modern social psychology. In G.A. Lindzey & E. Aronson (Eds.), *The handbook of social psychology* (Vol. 1, pp. 1–46). Reading, MA: Addison-Wesley.

2. Platt, J. & O'Leary, C. (2003). Patriot Acts. *Social Justice*, 30, pp. 5-21.

3. Scordata, M.R. & P.A. Monopoli (2003). Free speech rationales after September 11: The First Amendment in post-World Trade Center America. *Stanford Law Policy Review*, 13, pp. 185-203.

4. Haynes, C. (2002, October 13). In climate of fear, people are punished for speaking out. *Freedom Forum*. Retrieved Oct. 28, 2002 from http://www.freedomforum.org/templates/document.asp?documentID = 17104.

5. Grieve, T. (2003, March 14). Equal time for protest signs. *Salon.com, Inc.* Retrieved Mar. 30, 2003 from http://archive.salon.com/news/feature/2003/03/14/flag/.

6. Paynter, S. (2003, January 15). A sister of conscience confronts a lack of tolerance for dissent in the post-9/11 world. *Seattle Post-Intelligencer*, E1.

7. Richard, F.D., Bond, C.F. Jr., & Stokes-Zoota, J.J. (2003). One hundred years of social psychology quantitatively described. *Review of General Psychology*, 7, 331–363.

8. Duryea, B. (2003, April 20). The death of dissent. *St. Petersburg Times* (Florida), 1D.

9. Greenberg, D. (2003, March 26). Advise and dissent. *Slate Magazine*. Retrieved Mar. 30, 2003 from http://slate.msn.com/id/208073.

10. DeMoraes, L. (2003, April 11). Producer is a casualty in CBS's "Hitler" miniseries. *Washington Post*, C7.

11. Stanley, A. (2004, May 2). *Nightline* show a moving tribute. *Providence Journal*, A17.

12. Yanay, N. (2002). Understanding collective hatred. *Analyses of Social Issues and Public Policy*, 2, 53–60.

13. Williams, K.D., Cheung, C.K.T., & Choi, W. (2000). Cyberostracism: Effects of being ignored over the Internet. *Journal of Personality and Social Psychology*, 79, 748–762.

14. Crocker, J., Major, B., & Steele, C.M. (1998). Social stigma. In D.T. Gilbert, S.T. Fiske, & G. Lindzey (Eds.), *The handbook of social psychology* (Vol. 2, pp. 504–553). New York: McGraw-Hill.

15. Krugman, P. (2003, October 10). Lessons in civility. *New York Times*. Retrieved Oct. 11, 2003 from http://www.nytimes.com/2003/10/10/opinion/10KRUG.html.

16. Kizior, R. (2004, June 14). Doonesbury's Trudeau aiding the enemy. *Providence Journal*, A13.

17. Polman, D. (2003, March 23). A clash over who is a patriot. *Philadelphia Inquirer.* Retrieved Mar. 30, 2003 from http://www.philly.com/mld/philly/5457504.htm.

18. Pelosi questions Bush's competence. (2004, May 20). *CNN.* Retrieved June 1, 2004 from http://cnn.com/2004/ALLPOLITICS/05/20/pelosi.bush/index.html.

19. Uscio, F. (2004, July 16). American undermined by enemies within. *Providence Journal,* B5.

20. May, C.D. (2004, July 12). Michael Moore, Hezbollah heartthrob. *Providence Journal,* A9.

21. Schaper, D. (2003, May 2). A heretic amid the hibiscus. *New York Times.* Retrieved May 3, 2003 from http://www.nytimes.com/2003/05/02/opinion/.

22. Hot air from celebrities. (2003, March 31). *Providence Journal,* A10.

23. Scott, W. (2003, April 6). Personality parade. *Parade Magazine,* 2.

24. Horowitz, D. (2002, March 27). Yes, Virginia, there is a " decent left." *Salon.com.* Retrieved Oct. 30, 2003 from http://archive.salon.com/news/col/horo/2002/03/27/walzer/.

25. People. (2003, April 26). *Providence Journal,* D1.

26. Riggs, D. (2003, April 20). Poet in the hot seat. *Providence Sunday Journal,* E1.

27. Nail, P.R., MacDonald, G., & Levy, D.A. (2000). Proposal of a four-dimensional model of social response. *Psychological Bulletin, 126,* 454–470.

28. Quinn, A., & Schlenker, B.R. (2002). Can accountability produce independence? Goals as determinants of the impact of accountability on conformity. *Personality & Social Psychology Bulletin, 4,* 472–483.

29. Nowak, A., Vallacher, R.R., & Miller, M.E. (2003). Social influence and group dynamics. In T. Millon & M.J. Lerner (Eds.), *Handbook of psychology: Personality and social psychology* (Vol. 5, pp. 383–417). Hoboken, NJ: Wiley.

30. Unger, R.K. (2202). Them and us: Hidden ideologies—differences in degree or kind? *Analyses of Social Issues and Public Policies, 2,* 43–52.

31. Students aren't sponges. (2004, March 18). *South County Independent,* A 7.

32. Rothschild, M. (2003a, May 10). Cop makes midnight raid of teacher's classroom. *The Progressive.* Retrieved Dec. 15, 2003 from http://www.progressive.org.

33. Dear, J. (2003, November 29). The soldiers at my front door. *Common Dreams.* Retrieved Dec. 15, 2003 from http://www.CommonDreams.org.

34. Rothschild, M. (2003b, May 21). Pulitzer Prize-winner heckled during his commencement address. *The Progressive.* Retrieved Dec. 15, 2003 from http://www.progressive.org.

35. Casino ejects Ronstadt over "Fahrenheit" praise. *CNN.* Retrieved July 22, 2004 from http://www.cnn.com/2004/Showbiz/music/07/19/ronstadt.reut/index.html.

36. Desperadoes. (2004, July 21). *New York Times.* Retrieved July 22, 2004 from http://www.nytimes.com/2004/07/21/opinion/21wed4.html.

37. People. (2005, May 29). *Providence Journal,* A2.

38. Janes, L.M., & Olson, J.M. (2000). Jeer pressures: The behavioral effects of observing ridicule of others. *Personality & Social Psychology Bulletin, 26,* 474–485.

39. Bassili, J.N. (2003). The minority slowness effect: Subtle inhibitions in the expression of views not shared by others. *Journal of Personality and Social Psychology, 84,* 261–276.

40. Sunstein, C.R. (2003). *Why societies need dissent.* Cambridge, MA: Harvard University Press.

41. Cialdini, R.B., & Trost, M.R. (1998). Social influence: Social norms, conformity, and compliance. In D.T. Gilbert, S.T. Fiske, & G. Lindzey (Eds.), *The handbook of social psychology* (Vol. 2, pp. 151–192). New York: McGraw-Hill.

42. Blanton, H., & Christie, C. (2003). Deviance regulation: A theory of action and identity. *Review of General Psychology, 7,* 115–149.

43. Pareles, J. (2003, June 23). Down-home and defiant again. Retrieved June 24, 2003 from http: /www.nytimes.com/2003/06.23/arts/music/23CHIC.html.

44. Hawkes, E. (2003, Summer). Shock and jaw. *Ms., 13*(2), 31–39.

45. Dittman, M. (2003, November). Lessons from Jonestown. *Monitor on Psychology, 34*(10), 36–38.

46. Sternberg, R.J. (2003, May). The other three Rs: Part three, resilience. *Monitor on Psychology, 34*(5), 5.

CHAPTER 5

UNTANGLING THE WEB: THREAT, IDEOLOGY, AND POLITICAL BEHAVIOR

Rhoda Unger

After September 11, 2001, Americans lost their sense of invulnerability. An observation that appeared frequently in the media announced that "nothing would ever be the same." The purpose of this chapter is to explore what this statement means from the perspective of social psychology. Many studies were begun shortly after September 11 on the response to terrorism. Researchers have continued to extend this work to explore the psychological impact of domestic programs and foreign policies developed to fight the "war on terror."

These studies indicate that effects extend well beyond the personal trauma suffered by those near the sites of the terrorist attacks. This chapter focuses on how perceptions of group threat, mediated by patriotism and nationalism, produce harmful consequences for both individuals and society. It discusses the relationship between threat and a number of attitudinal constructs that function as system-justifying ideologies. These include right-wing authoritarianism, social dominance orientation, positivism, belief in a just world, and political conservatism. These ideologies motivate individual perceptions, cognitions, and actions, which, in turn, influence social and political reality.

The chapter also discusses empirical evidence that explores the role that group threat has played in recent changes in U.S. polices at home and abroad with a particular focus on research using experimental methodology. Finally, the chapter examines the psychological and social implications of continued perceptions of ongoing threat and offers some suggestions about what psychologists can do to minimize its harmful consequences.

The Impact of Terrorism

There is no doubt that the terrorist events of September 11 had a major impact on the nation's psychological well-being. The first published studies appeared shortly after the attacks and focused on individuals who were most directly affected by them. It soon became evident, however, that the impact of these events was not limited to the communities directly affected. Data from a nationwide sample collected within three weeks of September 11 showed that 17 percent of the U.S. population outside of New York City reported symptoms of post-traumatic stress.[1] In another study, only small differences in stress between students in New York City and those at a Midwestern university were found.[2] And, although some proximity effects have been reported, they have declined over time. Nevertheless, the events of September 11 continued to take a psychological toll on the nation more than a year later.[3]

Doing Research on a Moving Target

The passage of time is not, in itself, a meaningful psychological variable. Potentially traumatizing events have continued to occur in the years since September 11, 2001. These include further threats of biological and chemical terrorism, such as the contamination of the U.S. mail with anthrax; the initiation of procedures to improve homeland security, such as: the use of color-coded security alerts; increased surveillance at airports and other forms of public transportation; the closing of city streets; screenings at public venues; and the implementation of international policies designed to deal with terrorists abroad, including the invasion of Afghanistan and, somewhat later, the invasion of Iraq.

All of these events were intensively covered by the media. Media coverage of these events has been incessant and nationwide and may have contributed to a kind of vicarious traumatization of individuals who were not directly involved in them. Several studies have documented a relationship between media exposure (number of hours of television watched) and symptoms of psychological stress.[4, 5]

However, media effects extended beyond the expected signs of mental distress. Degree of dependency on the media after the attacks has been found to be related significantly to the degree of threat that individuals perceived. [6] Contrary to expectations, socioeconomic status, level of social capital, and degree of connectedness to others showed no relationship to either media dependency or perceptions of threat.

Horrific and repetitive images shown on television have helped justify a cascade of voluntary and involuntary changes in the lives of all Americans. These included a period of increased fear of and a decline in air travel that had a profound effect on the U.S. economy—introducing another source of fear and insecurity. Public rhetorical framing (see Indroduction note 1) that made moral distinctions between "us and them" and the meaning of being American also heightened suspicion of others—especially those from the Middle East and South Asia. It is difficult, therefore, to distinguish the psychological impact of terrorism from the psychological effects of the fight against terrorism.

The Value and Limits of a Social Psychological Analysis

It has become clear that, in addition to personal stress, some, if not all, of these developments have had major effects in a variety of social psychological domains. Changes in beliefs, values, and attitudes and behavioral change have been empirically verified. These changes stem from a sense of collective fear and vulnerability in the American public that was triggered by the events of September 11 and has not yet dissipated. In the rest of this chapter I discuss some of the psychological consequences of heightened fearfulness. This is not a simple analysis, because psychological effects are modified by individual differences, collective identity and membership in various social networks, and the sociohistorical context of society as a whole.

This analysis is also limited by the research that has been conducted. Because no one could predict the catastrophic events of September 11, there are few studies with before-and-after comparisons. Such comparisons are limited to studies that were in process at the time. This means that the measures used are sometimes idiosyncratic and do not provide all of the data we would like to have had. But other forms of comparison are useful, and I review the findings of studies that have been conducted at various times since September 11 (usually tied to some other newsworthy and potentially fear-provoking event) as well as studies that compare attitudes and behaviors of Americans to other national groups. The results of experimental studies that examine potential causal relations between threat and fear and attitudes, cognitions, and behaviors are particularly useful.

Before and after September 11

What evidence supports the view that American's beliefs and values changed after September 11? One of the few studies to address this issue directly was conducted six months before and approximately six weeks after the terrorist attacks.[7] The study examined individuals' beliefs about their personal world, their American national group, and their perceptions about what the American national group believes about itself. As the researchers hypothesized, post-9/11 respondents reported stronger group-level perceptions of vulnerability, injustice, distrust, and superiority and a weaker group-level perception of helplessness.

These perceptions have different meaning when applied to one's group rather than one's self. In this study, post-9/11 respondents saw Americans as potential victims of pervasive and imminent threats; believed that the victimization was unjust; perceived that other groups harbored malevolent intentions toward America; and believed that our political system and way of life was morally superior, chosen, entitled, or destined for superiority over others. Helplessness, in contrast, referred to perceptions about the United States' ability to alter circumstances and fulfill its goals. The researchers suggested that perceptions of national helplessness may have been reduced because the war against terrorism in Afghanistan had already begun when the respondents were recontacted.

This study found much less change in personal beliefs. Instead, the group became more salient than the individual. Of course, the respondents had already been exposed to a number of speeches by President Bush and other public figures about the moral superiority of the United States, terrorists' hatred of our values and political system, and appeals to patriotism and nationalism that accompanied the national effort to fight terrorism at home and abroad.

The problem of disentangling the cumulative impact of terrorism, antiterrorism, and political rhetoric about terrorism can be minimized if we look at studies that were conducted just after 9/11. These studies provide convergent evidence of the powerful impact of collective threat in enhancing collective consciousness. Identification with one's group helped shape punitive attitudes about how to deal with terrorism and perceived terrorists. For example, one study of university students in New Mexico found that only threats to one's group as a whole predicted advocacy of harsh retaliatory measures against terrorists and negative attitudes toward Muslim fundamentalists.[8] Individuals who perceived the threat more personally felt more helpless and hopeless and did not endorse harsh retaliatory measures. In another study of university students in Connecticut, patriotic responses were positively correlated with suspicion of foreigners and a desire for military retaliation.[9]

Similarly, in a third study conducted at a university in New Jersey (within sight of the World Trade Center) and a university in Massachusetts (more than 200 miles away), individuals at both institutions who supported a patriotic militant response to September 11 were also significantly more likely to blame Muslim fundamentalism.[10] Individuals who scored high on patriotic militancy and low on international efforts of conflict resolution were also less likely to blame President Bush for the events of September 11. These relationships were remarkably similar for the two universities.

What do all of these studies have in common? They demonstrate a relationship between perceived threat and fear for one's group and hostile responses to other groups and nations. The events of September 11 were closely followed by enhanced perceptions of oneness with other Americans[11] and a decline in perception of similarity to other people.[12]

In sum, these studies suggest a causal relationship between the events of September 11 and a variety of negative psychological changes in beliefs and attitudes of Americans nationwide. The psychological variables measured appear to reflect views about one's group identity vis-à-vis other groups. As compared to their responses before September 11, Americans showed increased distrust of others and a greater distancing from other groups accompanied by increased willingness to express aggression and hostility against those who are perceived as inimical to the United States.

In-Group Identity, Nationalism, and Patriotism

This pattern of enhanced in-group identification and disparagement of out-groups is characteristic of nationalism and some forms of patriotism.[13, 14] There are many different definitions of both concepts that explore the positive and negative aspects of national attachment. On the positive side, group identification at the national level creates bonds of solidarity, aligns individual interests with group welfare, and provides the motivation for being a good group member or citizen. On the negative side, high levels of nationalism have been associated with authoritarianism, intolerance, and militarism.[13]

Although patriotism is often seen as benign "love for one's country," researchers have made a distinction between *constructive patriotism* and *blind patriotism*.[14] Constructive patriotism is characterized by support for questioning and criticism of current group practices that are intended to result in positive group change. Blind patriotism is characterized by unquestioning positive evaluation, unfaltering allegiance, and intolerance of criticism. The differences between these two forms of patriotism reflect the manner in which individuals relate to their country rather than their support for particular programs or policies.

In the first study designed to differentiate between these concepts, blind patriotism was found to be associated with nationalism, perceptions of foreign threat, perceived importance of symbolic behavior, and selective exposure to information that glorified rather than criticized the United States in contrast to more unbiased sources of information.[14] Constructive patriotism was found to be positively associated with multiple indicators of political involvement, including diverse forms of information seeking. It may be seen as a kind of critical loyalty, although the researchers did not use this label.

The consequences of nationalism and patriotism appear to depend on what definitions of statehood are evoked. A group may be seen, for example, as unified by the shared attributes and common heritage of its members—defining the group by its "common goals." On the other hand, a group may be defined more essentially by its fixed and immutable character—a "core essence" definition.[13] The latter definition implies potentially inaccurate comparisons with other fixed groups. National identification and high regard for one's in-group have been linked with out-group rejection mainly in contexts that evoke intergroup comparison.[15]

"Us against them" was a common theme following the terrorist attacks. This rhetorical framing evoked an essentialist (see chapter 1 for an explanation of essentialism) and divisive definition of being an American. One can ask the question, therefore, whether this rhetorical response to terrorism, in itself, produced some of the hostility toward others noted in many of the studies cited earlier.

This question was tested by a study conducted by Qi and Brewer just after 9/11. These researchers asked students and community members questions about patriotism, nationalism, and tolerance of multicultural and life-style diversity.[13] The questionnaires were preceded by two different instructions that used alternative definitions of American identity. In the "core essence" conditions, participants read the following statement:

> The tragic events of September 11 have united Americans as never before in our generation. We have come to understand what we have in common as Americans. As a nation, our focus is on the core essence of what it means to be an American.

In the common goal condition, this paragraph was replaced with the following:

> The tragic events of September 11 have united Americans as never before in our generation. We now have a common purpose to fight terrorism in all of its forms and to work together to help those who were victims of this tragedy. (p. 732)

The former, more essentialist definition of patriotism, was found to be associated with derogatory attitudes toward other nations, intolerance of deviation from a common national standard, and increased perceived distance from blacks, Asians, and Muslims. Core essence instructions also increased the relationship between patriotism and nationalism. Common goal instructions were less closely associated with nationalism. Instead, they increased the probability that those individuals who received them would be more tolerant of both foreign and domestic diversity.

Although these researchers did not discuss the relationship of essentialist and common goal definitions of patriotism to blind and constructive patriotism, these conceptualizations appear to be quite similar. Rhetorical framing in terms that idealize Americanism is more likely to heighten the nationalistic aspects of blind patriotism. The study demonstrates empirically the important role of language in altering sociopolitical identity and, thus, responses to national threat.

Ideology and Perceptions of and Responses to Terrorism

Nationalism and both kinds of patriotism are forms of ideology that link the person and the state. But there are other forms of ideology that also influence connections between how one sees one's country and how one reacts to it. John Jost has labeled these forms of ideology "system-justifying ideologies." Such ideologies allow people to justify and rationalize the way things are, so that existing social, economic, and political arrangements tend to be perceived as fair and legitimate.[16] These ideologies are important in social contexts in which the individual is threatened and feels little sense of personal control.

A number of system-justifying ideologies have been identified by psychologists and have been used to study responses to terrorism and national efforts to combat terrorism. These include belief in a just world, social dominance orientation, right-wing authoritarianism, political conservatism, and positivism. The instruments used to measure these constructs have some similar attitudinal components. These include abdication of responsibility to an outside authority, belief that one's own values and/or those of one's group are superior, and devaluation of those who are perceived as outsiders.

In a theoretical paper published just after September 11, 2001, I predicted such ideological frameworks would interact with nationalism and patriotism to influence attitudes about how the United States should deal with terrorism.

> Patriotism and nationalism are double-edged swords. At the same time as they unite us in a common purpose, they make it easy to see others as the enemy—as unlike ourselves. It is possible that the "war against terrorism" will increase "normative" levels of authoritarianism, social dominance, and positivist ideation. It might "just" make people who think in these ways more influential than they have been in recent years. Or, it may give such individuals "permission to act against those they perceive to be different from themselves. None of these are positive developments.[17] [See the subsection titled "Positivist Attitudes about Reality" later in this chapter for an explanation of the term *positivist.*]

At the time I made these predictions, there was little empirical research by psychologists to support them. However, September 11 had a major impact on the nation's psyche and was followed by major domestic and foreign policy initiatives designed to fight terrorism at home and abroad. It is not surprising that many articles on the psychological implications of both 9/11 and the war on terrorism have appeared in professional journals in the past four years.

To maximize clarity, I'll discuss separately evidence for the relationship between each ideology and attitudes about policies designed to fight terrorism at home and abroad. I'll then discuss studies that indicate the interrelationship between them and some of the nuanced differences in the attitudes that each ideology predicts.

Belief in a Just World

There is direct evidence for a connection between one system-justifying ideology—belief in a just world—and responses to terrorism. The study examined the relationship between university students' scores on the just-world scale (obtained several months before September 11) and their desire for revenge against the perpetrators of the attacks against the United States.[18] The researchers found that the more strongly students endorsed just-world beliefs prior to the attacks, the more distressed they felt about the attacks and the more they desired revenge.

Right-Wing Authoritarianism

Because right-wing authoritarianism has been repeatedly connected to ethnocentric nationalism and perception of threats from groups other than one's own,[19, 20] it is not surprising that many studies after September 11 used this measure. These studies have consistently linked high levels of right-wing authoritarianism to a harsh response to terrorism, including support for increased domestic surveillance and the use of military force abroad.[21, 22, 23] Earlier studies found that students with high authoritarian scores before the first Gulf War endorsed more aggressive actions (including the use of nuclear weapons) in response to hypothetical Iraqi actions.[24] After the war, they expressed relatively more gloating and less regret than students who scored lower in right-wing authoritarianism.

Similarly, high right-wing authoritarianism measured at the end of 2001 predicted support for the restriction of civil liberties one year later.[23] These attitudes were strengthened by perceived threat to one's group. Earlier studies have also found that people who scored high in authoritarianism became more punitive under perceived stress, whereas the opposite was true for less authoritarian individuals.[25]

Social Dominance Orientation

Concerns about American predominance characterize individuals with high levels of social dominance and those who are high in right-wing authoritarianism.[26] Social dominance orientation is an ideological construct that focuses on the extent to which an individual perceives his or her group as superior to others and desires to maintain that superiority.[27] U.S. students who perceived the United States as superior to other countries supported greater violence toward the Middle East.[28]

Social dominance and right-wing authoritarianism overlap to some extent, but also predict differing aspects of attitudes about the war against terrorism. For example, while both measures predicted support for the U.S. attack on Iraq, authoritarianism did so through stronger beliefs that Iraq threatened America. Social dominance did so through reduced concerns about the human costs of the war.[20]

McFarland's study also found that high levels of both ideologies were associated with high levels of blind patriotism. High levels of these two system-justifying ideologies may reinforce each other to produce particularly destructive effects. For example, a recent simulation study involving international relations found that individuals high in both right-wing authoritarianism and social dominance were particularly likely to seize leadership and initiate intergroup conflict.[29]

Positivist Attitudes about Reality

Nearly twenty years ago I developed a scale designed to look at people's perceptions about reality.[30] This scale is more global than those just discussed, but it overlaps somewhat with beliefs in a just world[31] and right-wing authoritarianism.[32] People with high positivist attitudes tend to believe in the power of external rather than subjective reality and the legitimacy of some authority external to themselves (*positivist* is the opposite of *constructivist*). They believe that their own group's values and those of their source of authority are universally true, favor their society's status quo, and prefer individualistic rather than collective explanations for many social issues. For example, those who score high in positivism are more likely to agree with the following statements:[30]

It is maladaptive to refuse to conform to the demands of others.

People who achieve success usually deserve it.

The more technology we develop the better our science will be.

At the present time, people are recognized for their achievements regardless of their race, sex, or social class.

The United States has the most egalitarian society in the world.

Society must protect itself from those who do not accept its rules.

Most social problems are solved by a few very qualified individuals.

Positivist beliefs predict support of U.S. militarism and aggression. As compared to less positivist individuals, positivists have been found to believe that nuclear weapons can effectively deter war, that space weapons can defend against a nuclear attack, and that government policies would ensure survival in the event of a nuclear attack.[33] During the Gulf War, positivists were found significantly more likely to support the invasion of Iraq and to allocate more blame to Saddam Hussein and less to the first President Bush for starting the war.[34]

After 9/11, positivism was found to be directly related to militant patriotism. Students who scored high in positivism were significantly more likely than less-positivist students to endorse the following statements:[10]

> Now that a war is about to start, we must support our government.
>
> The fact that many nations are supporting the U.S. means that this is a just war.
>
> The attack against the World Trade Center and the Pentagon occurred because Osama bin Laden hates U.S. democracy.
>
> The U.S. response to the events of September 11 must be tough and decisive in order to make sure that such things never happen again.
>
> The citizens of the U.S. must be willing to give up some freedoms in order to prevent terrorists from acting freely.

In contrast, positivist students were less likely to endorse international efforts toward peaceful resolution of conflict.

Those who scored high in their support of militant governmental policies both at home and abroad were also significantly more likely to blame Muslim fundamentalism and significantly less likely to blame George W. Bush for the events of September 11, 2001. The relationship between positivism and attitudes about whom to blame for the attacks and how to deal with them was stronger six months after September 11 than it was one month after the attack. This unexpected finding suggests that once the initial shock of the attacks had worn off, individual differences in worldview became a more important influence on patriotic militancy.

Political Conservatism and Its Correlates

Since political conservatism is a system-justifying ideology, it is not surprising that several studies have found significant positive correlations between various ideological scales, political identification, and attitudes about how to combat terrorism.[10, 23] Perhaps more interesting, however, are data collected from meta-analyses that show positive relationships between political conservatism and many motivational and cognitive measures such as mortality salience; dogmatism/intolerance of ambiguity; lack of openness to experience; poor tolerance for uncertainty; and need for order, structure, and closure.[35] These analyses also found a strong connection between political conservatism and fear of threat and loss.

We do not know the causal direction of these relationships. It is possible that conservative ideology is particularly attractive to individuals who are more fearful than less conservative people. It is also possible that conservative ideology makes it more likely that individuals will feel threatened by outside forces. Both possibilities are problematic because of the connection between the perception of threat and political beliefs that foster inequality and resistance to social change.

These meta-analyses also found a link between political conservatism and religious conservatism. The researchers defined religious conservatism in terms of membership in an authoritarian rather than a relatively nonhierarchical church. Other researchers have found similar links between political conservatism and self-rated levels of religious observance and/or identification as a Christian—a self-definition that puts one's fate in the hands of a personal savior and is often accompanied by belief that biblical texts are literally true.[10, 21, 36]

Religious conservatism has been linked to a number of system-justifying ideologies already discussed (e.g., right-wing authoritarianism, social dominance, and positivism).[17] It has also been linked with support of U.S. militarism, including support for the attack on Afghanistan.[10, 21] A recent analysis of students at nine colleges and universities nationwide indicated that a high level of religious observance was a major predictor of support for militarism abroad and curtailment of civil liberties at home and lack of support for international efforts toward peaceful conflict resolution.[37] Religion and religiosity were highly correlated and may help explain the differences in voting patterns between "red" and "blue" states that occurred several months after these data were collected.

Disentangling the Variables

Our understanding of the implications of these studies' results is handicapped by the fact that many are unsystematic explanations of the psychological implications of ongoing events. One could characterize them as attempts to capture a moving target. A number of domestic and foreign policies were put into place rapidly after September 11. Psychologists have been racing to catch up and have often used familiar measures and theories. Thus, although there is a considerable amount of consistency among the findings, there have been few attempts to synthesize them. How are various ideologies related and how do they mediate differing attitudinal and behavioral responses to multiple threats to personal and group security?

A few studies have begun to unravel some of the complex relationships among individual characteristics, emotions provoked by the threat of terrorism, and attitudes about how to deal with terrorism. Linda Skitka and her associates sampled a nationwide panel one and four months after September 11.[38] They examined the effects of individuals' anger and fear on their level of political tolerance just after the attacks and again four months later. Political tolerance was measured by both degree of support for the curtailment of the civil liberties of Arab Americans, Muslims, or first-generation immigrants and by the extent to which respondents agreed with the Bush administration's restrictions of civil liberties to fight terrorism.

This study found that anger and fear both decreased political tolerance, but they did so via different psychological pathways.

> In sum, immediate post-attack anger was more strongly associated than fear with subsequent higher levels of moral outrage and outgroup derogation, reactions that in turn were associated with lower levels of political tolerance. Immediate post-attack fear had more of a mixed effect on subsequent political tolerance. Specifically, fear (more than anger) led to higher levels of perceived threat and to increased in-group enhancement, reactions that were associated with weakened support for civil liberties.[38] (p. 753)

Some of the initial emotional responses to September 11 seem to be linked to the different forms of patriotism discussed earlier. Anger, for example, led to moral outrage and out-group derogation—attitudes that appear to be closely associated with blind patriotism. Fear had more complex effects. Post-attack fear was associated with both in-group enhancement (an aspect of blind patriotism) and with value affirmation (which appears to include elements of both blind and constructive patriotism). Value affirmation was measured by how much respondents felt the need to restore the moral balance by helping someone, whether they reported donating blood or increasing church attendance, and the extent to which they displayed the American flag after the attacks. Fear either increased or decreased political tolerance depending on which aspect of patriotism was activated.

Through the filter of in-group enhancement, fear reduced political tolerance (because it increased perceptions of threat). When, however, fear led to value-affirming thoughts and behaviors, it indirectly increased political tolerance. Behaviors such as donating blood and displaying the American flag increased individuals' sense of psychological closure, which, in turn, increased their political tolerance. These complex relationships reinforce the need for psychologists to consider the role of individual differences in the way individuals perceive and construct their realities when trying to understand the formation of political attitudes under frightening circumstances.

The Psychological Impact of Threat and Fear

The events of September 11 and their aftermath threatened all Americans. Americans lost their sense of invulnerability. Many believed that "everything had changed" or "nothing would ever be the same." Fear and anger appear to be almost instinctive responses to such overwhelming threat.[39]

The threat from September 11 and the U.S. government's responses to this threat continue to fuel American fear and anger. In turn, fear and anger seem to fuel attitudes that favor the restriction of civil liberties at home and military action abroad. Of course, not everyone has such attitudes. Recent social psychological research suggests that attitudes about current domestic and foreign policies are influenced, in part, by a complex interaction between threat and the dispositional characteristics and ideological beliefs already present in the individual.

These studies indicate that it is not necessary to look for new or more system-justifying ideologies in the United States (and, as yet, no one has done so) to account for changes in attitudes about foreign and domestic policies designed to deal with terrorism. Instead, it is important to determine how threat makes some ideologies more relevant and potent.

Researchers are beginning to do this. A study in New Zealand asked undergraduates to read a scenario about their country's future in which it had experienced years of severe economic decline and social disintegration with high rates of crime, violence, and social conflict.[40] Other undergraduates read scenarios that foretold a rosy future or one that was essentially unchanged. Path analyses showed that social threat induced changes in worldview that made the world seem a much more dangerous place. In turn, belief that the world is dangerous greatly increased the subsequent level of authoritarian responses.

This study also found a weak effect of threat on social dominance, but this effect was entirely mediated through authoritarianism. Right-wing authoritarianism appears to be the system-justifying ideology that is most responsive to threat. For example, although high authoritarianism, high social dominance, and political conservatism all predict support for restriction of civil liberties, only authoritarianism interacted with the threat from terrorism. Threat reinforced the positive effect of authoritarianism on support for the use of domestic surveillance.[23]

Threat also interacted with high authoritarianism to limit the kind of information individuals seek. In a laboratory experiment, students were exposed to a reminder of death and then asked to select and read one of three articles on capital punishment.[41] In the absence of threat, both high and low authoritarians were responsive to norms of even-handedness and were more likely to choose an article that presented both sides of the issue. In the presence of threat, high but not low authoritarians were significantly more likely to choose an editorial that agreed with their views (most likely one that supported capital punishment) and less likely to choose a balanced article. Selective exposure to attitude-congruent information inhibited attitude change.

Terror Management, Worldview, and Cognitive Processes

Studies of terror management reveal much about the psychological impact of fear on views about the self and attitudes about the world. Some of this research clarifies the powerful psychological impact that 9/11 and its consequences have had on Americans.

According to terror management theory, humans deal with their knowledge that death is inevitable by maintaining a strong belief in a cultural worldview. Such worldviews present a security-providing image of reality to those who share the group's culture.[42] People are highly motivated to maintain and defend their worldviews because they play a major role in controlling anxiety. They provide an explanation of reality that is ordered and stable. They also provide a basis for the establishment of self-worth by setting standards for the behavior of group members. Most, if not all, system-justifying ideologies are this kind of worldview.

Terror management studies have shown that when mortality is made salient to individuals (who are asked to think about their own deaths or are exposed to images of death and destruction), they are more likely to make active efforts to maintain their worldview and to bolster their self-esteem than individuals who are not exposed to these kinds of anxiety-provoking manipulations.[43, 44]

Making mortality salient exaggerated the tendency to rely on simple cognitive strategies to categorize others. For example, individuals exposed to thoughts of death as compared to thoughts of pain were more likely to discount information inconsistent with their previous point of view and to miscategorize others based on an overuse of representative information.[43] Two examples of such processes in the context of the war against terrorism may be instructive. Some high-ranking U.S. government officials were reluctant to give up their view that Iraq possessed weapons of mass destruction despite the lack of evidence to support this position. And, shortly after the September 11 attacks, a number of hate crimes were committed against South Asians such as Hindu Sikhs because some of these targets were (or were thought to be) Muslims.

Evocations of mortality have a greater impact on individuals who have a high need for structure than on those with less need for cognitive certainty. When exposed to mortality salience manipulations, individuals who have a high need for structure were more likely to dislike a target individual who behaved in an inconsistent or complex manner, more likely to seek disparaging information about victims of a senseless tragedy, and more likely to prefer stories that bolstered the belief that immediate negative outcomes can ultimately lead to benevolent outcomes.[43] These latter two findings support the view that concerns about death can reinforce a just world ideology. This relationship is similar to the one found between threat and authoritarianism discussed earlier.

The Rhetoric of Fear

After September 11, the people of the United States were exposed to a great deal of rhetorical framing by politicians designed to reinforce patriotism and nationalism. Much of this rhetoric cast the events in apocalyptic terms, such as portraying the U.S. response to terrorism as a "crusade against evil." Political rhetoric also portrayed the value of tough and morally righteous leadership for an effective response to the national crisis.

Changes in political language after September 11 have been documented. For example, an examination of the rhetorical content of President Bush's public speeches before and after the terrorist attacks found that their charismatic content increased.[45] This content uses a person's special knowledge, moral authority, and image to motivate trust and belief. This study found, furthermore, that the media's portrayal of Bush after the attacks reflected a similar increase in charismatic content.

Several scholars of communication have offered some intriguingly detailed analyses of differences in rhetoric before and after September 11. One such analysis was based on a photo that appeared to capture the face of a demon in a large plume of smoke from one of the twin towers of the World Trade Center. After this so-called smoke demon photograph was published, it was widely disseminated via the Internet with foreboding comments about the approach of the Christian apocalypse.[46]

The author of this article linked the use of the demonic to fundamentalist religious concerns with exorcism and conversion. He noted that use of the language of exorcism to describe purging of the nation's enemies was a common theme in President Bush's speeches after September 11.

This combination of charismatic leadership and apocalyptic language may help explain why studies have found that President Bush's policies of war in Afghanistan and Iraq were particularly popular in the conservative Christian community.[37] Strict religious beliefs have also been linked with right-wing authoritarianism and other system-justifying ideologies, political conservatism, and a variety of cognitive mechanisms related to openness to information.[35]

Other rhetorical devices have also been discussed. One communications expert has suggested that media coverage after September 11 presented a melodramatic plot line that encouraged American nationalism. In this script America was portrayed as a morally righteous victim ensnared in a position that required it to transform victimization into heroic retributive action.[47]

Similarly, British scholars argue that television coverage helped create a climate in which a pro-Iraq War position became more relevant and plausible in the United Kingdom. It did so by highlighting narratives that linked the war on terrorism to forms of military action, making both war and military spending more acceptable.[48] Brewster Smith makes a similar argument about the United States in his discussion of the metaphor of the "war on terrorism." He argues that the metaphor has facilitated the mobilization of effort, but has also made aggressive actions abroad more acceptable to the public, endangered civil liberties, and helped to stifle debate as unpatriotic.[49]

Media responses that privilege aggressive responses in times of national threat are not a new phenomenon. For example, in an archival study that looked at authoritarian themes in American comic books over a 25-year period, Bill Peterson found that comic books produced during years of relatively high social and economic threat (1978–1982 and 1991–1992) contained more aggressive imagery, more conventional themes, less introspection, and fewer spoken lines by women characters relative to comic books produced during years of relatively low threat (1983–1990).[50]

These studies do not tell us whether the media reflects reality or creates it. Some answers to this question may be found in a recent series of experiments designed to find out whether linguistic differences in reporting influence people's interpretation of violent acts as patriotism or terrorism.[51] The first study in this series was a content analysis of a national sample of newspaper articles describing violence in Iraq. This revealed that words implying destruction and devious intent were typically used to describe violent actions associated with Iraq and opponents of the United States, whereas more benign words were used to describe the actions of the United States and its allies. For example, the words *explosion*, *blast*, *threat*, and *plot* were used significantly more often in reference to Iraq and nonallies than in references to the United States and its allies. In contrast, the words *forces* and *campaign* were used significantly more often in reference to the United States than Iraq.

The researchers hypothesized that these differences in word usage established schemas that guide perception of violence as either terrorism or patriotism. To test this hypothesis they constructed two articles describing the bombing of a building—one (the "us" version) included words that had been found more frequently in news accounts of U.S. and allied actions and one (the "them" version) that used words more often found in accounts of Iraq and nonallies. College students and community members read one of the two versions and were subsequently tested on their attitudes about the event. As expected, individuals who read the "us" version of the article agreed more strongly (than those who read the "them" version) that the bombing was necessary for national defense. In contrast, those who read the "them" account agreed more strongly that the bombing was an act of terrorism.

Further studies found that even subtle differences in the wording of the articles influenced participants' memory about the presence of words connoting either patriotism or terrorism. Participants were more likely to recall falsely words associated with terrorism than patriotism when they read the "them" article. The opposite pattern emerged when they read the "us" version of the article. The researchers suggested that the differential use of language activates schema that influence people's perceptions, attitudes, and memory. These effects emerged even when the event being described was never explicitly described as terrorism.

The Politics of Fear

These studies indicate the power of words to change perceptions of reality. Other studies demonstrate more active political consequences. Earlier I discussed evidence that the charismatic components of political rhetoric have increased since September 11. Recent studies indicate, moreover, that charismatic language has an impact on perceptions of appropriate political leadership under conditions of mortal threat. Researchers using terror management theory tested this hypothesis by exposing individuals to a subtle reminder of death and then asking them to read campaign statements by charismatic, task-oriented, and relationship-oriented gubernatorial candidates.[52] As predicted, mortality salience increased support for a charismatic political candidate and decreased support for a relationship-oriented candidate.

Fear of death appears to have had a major impact on the 2004 U.S. presidential election. Researchers found that reminding people of their own mortality increased support for President Bush and his antiterrorism policies and decreased support for Senator Kerry.[53] Subliminal exposure to images from September 11 was just as effective in enhancing support for President Bush as manipulations that made personal mortality salient. It is noteworthy that President Bush repeatedly linked 9/11 and the Iraq War during his presidential campaign, despite the fact that there was no evidence to support a connection between Saddam Hussein and the terrorist attack on the United States.

Experimental research indicates that fear and threat directly influenced the results of the 2004 U.S. presidential election.[47] Following a mortality salience or control induction, registered voters were asked in late September which candidate they intended to vote for in the November election. In accordance with predictions, John Kerry received substantially more votes than George Bush in the control condition, but Bush was favored over Kerry following a reminder of death.[54]

The magnitude of difference between the two conditions is striking. In the control condition, Kerry was favored over Bush by a four-to-one margin. But Bush had a two-to-one margin following the mortality salience induction.

Fear of death was repeatedly reinforced by images of terrorism. One image that may have had a particularly powerful impact was a videotape of Osama bin Laden that was released just before the election. In the days after the release of the bin Laden tape, government agencies issued several terror warnings to state and local officials.

Although we have no direct data on the effect of government-issued terror warnings, they are, of course, a potent reminder of death. One study provides powerful, albeit indirect, empirical support for a relationship between terror warnings and increased support for President Bush. The study used a time-series analysis of warnings reported in the *Washington Post* between February 2001 and May 2004 and Gallup poll data on Americans' opinions of President Bush.[55] It found a consistent, positive relationship between terror warnings and presidential approval. Government issued warnings also increased support for President Bush's handling of the economy. Unfortunately, the duration of these effects could not be ascertained.

Lessons from History

One of the unresolved questions among researchers interested in the social psychological factors associated with the U.S. response to terrorism is whether increases in nationalism, patriotism, and the level of various system-justifying ideologies were inevitable. Some archival data suggest that the answer to this question is yes. For example, there is evidence that U.S. citizens elected presidents who radiated strength and energy by wide margins during years of high threat.[56] Authoritarianism appears to play a role in such electoral decisions. In both the 1996 and 2000 U.S. presidential elections, students who supported more conservative Republican candidates were found to be higher in authoritarianism than those who supported more liberal Democratic candidates.[57]

The impact of threat extends beyond political behaviors. During periods of threat, Americans have been found to be more likely to attend churches that strictly adhered to doctrine as compared to attending less orthodox churches.[58] Researches have developed a number of other archival indicators of authoritarianism, such as Ku Klux Klan activity. They, too, have found that authoritarian behaviors were greater during years of relatively high economic and social threat compared to years of relatively low threat.[59]

Lessons from Context and Culture

Cross-Cultural Similarities

Another unresolved question is whether the United States is more likely to become nationalistic and authoritarian in response to threat than are other nations. The answer to this question is equivocal. Of course, an attack on members of one's group is more threatening than attacks on other groups. A week after September 11, researchers in Europe found that focusing participants' attention on an identity that included Americans as a group similar to themselves led Europeans to express more fear and stronger fear-related behaviors than when the victims of terrorism were categorized as individuals who were not like themselves.[60]

Several studies elsewhere have found associations between system-justifying ideologies and political attitudes and behaviors similar to those found in the United States. In Australia, for example, high levels of right-wing authoritarianism, identification with one's own in-group, and conservative political views predicted support for the war in Afghanistan.[61] Similarly, a study of British students indicated that both right-wing authoritarianism and belief in a just world influenced their perceptions about the causes of September 11.[62]

An Italian study found significant relationships between high need for closure (associated with authoritarianism and other system-justifying ideologies in studies discussed earlier in this chapter) and heightened nationalism, preference for autocratic leadership, and a centralized form of political power.[63] Those who were high in need for closure also valued religiosity more than individuals who scored lower on the measure and were less supportive of pluralism and multiculturalism. They were also more likely to have voted for a right-wing party than individuals with less need for closure.

Cross-Cultural Differences

Although the evidence for cross-cultural similarities between ideology, nationalism, and punitive behavior toward apparently dangerous out-groups seems clear, there is less international consensus about the sources of terrorist threats and the measures needed to deal with them. The most obvious differences are between perceptions of causality in the United States and those in the Arab world.

After September 11 the U.S. media framed terrorism in apocalyptic terms as a "clash of civilizations." This view saw the attacks as due to

Islamic hatred of American values and the belief that those who hold such values are the "enemies of God." But researchers who examined attitudes about September 11 among Lebanese undergraduates a few months after the attack found much more evidence of an "anti-dominance perspective."[64]

These students saw the attacks as a response to perceived American and Israeli oppression of Arabs in general and of Palestinians in particular. Those who saw the attack as a legitimate response to American dominance were also more willing to justify it. In contrast, perceptions of the attack as a "clash of civilizations" were unrelated to support for Islamic terrorist organizations. Contrary to expectations, authoritarianism had little impact on Lebanese students' fear of violence, although it influenced American students' concern about the possible loss of international dominance by the United States.[26]

National groups also differed in their attitudes about U.S. military and domestic policies designed to deal with terrorism. Shortly after the Iraq War broke out, we administered a questionnaire very similar to the one used about responses to terrorism and the war in Afghanistan (discussed earlier) to a cross-national and international selection of university students. The U.S. respondents included students from nine universities, and the international respondents included students from universities in the United Kingdom, Australia, Israel, Portugal, and Turkey.[65]

We used a very similar questionnaire to the one originally designed to look at attitudes and perceptions after the events of September 11 for several reasons. First, we wanted to determine whether responses of students nationwide would be similar to students at the two universities originally studied (as a further replication, respondents were obtained from these universities again). Second, we wanted to find out whether support of patriotic militancy at home and abroad had declined over time. And, third, we wished to know how similar the attitudes of U.S. students were to students in other countries. The countries were chosen because they varied greatly in terms of their political connection with the crisis in Iraq; for example, the United Kingdom and Australia were part of the "coalition of the willing," Portugal was a neutral observer, and Israel and Turkey are near the region of conflict. Although these latter two countries were not directly involved in the war and are both U.S. allies, their different religious identities led us to expect opposite positions on the conflict.

There were few differences in attitudes among U.S. students based on the university that they attended.[37] We also found that attitudes had changed relatively little in the time period between September 11 and the invasion of Iraq. We examined the percentage of agreement with various items shortly after 9/11 and again shortly after the invasion of Iraq. We were particularly interested in those items that loaded strongly on patriotic militancy in both questionnaires.

For item 2, "Once a war has started, people must support their government," 61 percent of U.S. students agreed with the item after September 11 (the war in Afghanistan had already started). This figure decreased to 52 percent during the Iraq War. For item 9, "The U.S. response to potential threats must be tough and decisive in order to make sure that terrorist acts never happen again," 78 percent of U.S. students agreed after 9/11 as compared to 68 percent during the Iraq War. And, for item 10, "Citizens must be willing to give up some freedoms in order to prevent terrorists from acting freely," 60 percent of the U.S. students agreed after 9/11 as compared to 46 percent during the Iraq War. The relatively high percentage of university students who are willing to trade freedom for security is particularly distressing because it indicates support for government policies that erode civil liberties in an educated population that one would expect to oppose such restrictions.

Although it is true that there has been some decline in agreement since September 11, 2001, the high percentages of agreement with these items (with correspondently low levels of disagreement and few neutral responses) are quite disturbing. Students in the United States agreed more with these items than university students in several other countries studied

The most similar levels of agreement can be found among students in the United Kingdom, which also belonged to the "coalition of the willing." Two thirds of the students in both the United States and the United Kingdom agreed with the statement that tough and decisive action is necessary to combat terrorism. It is also disturbing that nearly half of the students in the United States and the United Kingdom were willing to trade some freedoms for security. The only other country with a comparable level of agreement was Turkey, which has had a series of military dictatorships in the past 20 years. In contrast, only about a quarter of students in Israel were willing to trade security for freedoms, despite the fact that this nation has been exposed to terrorist attacks for many years.

The item "The war against Iraq is due to U.S. support of Israel" was not included in the scale because it did not correlate with any of the other items. The item, however, provides some indication of national attitudes about U.S. support of Israel. There is very little agreement with this item except among Turkish students. Their response is similar to that found among students in Lebanon just after September 11.[64] As one would expect, over 80 percent of Israeli students disagreed with it.

U.S. students' perceptions about responsibility for the invasion of Iraq were not always factually accurate. For example, although they assigned the most responsibility to Saddam Hussein (36 percent) and George W. Bush (30 percent), they also assigned a considerable share of the blame to Osama bin Laden (27 percent) even though there was no evidence at the time to support the involvement of al Qaeda.

Similarly, when responsibility for the crisis was allotted among structural variables, U.S. power was attributed the most responsibility (42 percent) followed by Muslim fundamentalism (23 percent), although, again, there was no evidence of any Islamist involvement at the beginning of the conflict. These attributions did not vary much by university.

Perceptions about appropriate foreign and domestic policies were also associated with perceptions of who or what to blame for the situation. American students who supported U.S. militancy were more likely to assign significantly more blame to Saddam Hussein ($r = .52$) and Osama bin Laden ($r = .31$) and significantly less to George W. Bush ($r = -.61$). Those who supported a patriotic militant response to the Iraq conflict also considered Muslim fundamentalism significantly more responsible for the crisis ($r = .37$) and saw U.S. power as less responsible ($r = -.52$). Similar relationships were found for students in other countries.

Lessons for Psychology

There is ample empirical evidence of a connection between perceived threat to one's group and hostile responses to those perceived to be responsible for that threat. Threat increases nationalism and harmful and benevolent aspects of patriotism. Both psychological and physical coercion may be exerted on members of the in-group who do not conform to demands for national unity.

More troubling is evidence of increases in support of militancy abroad and draconian policies to ensure security at home. These attitudinal changes appear to be mediated by a number of system-justifying ideologies, including right-wing authoritarianism, social dominance orientation, positivism, belief in a just world, and conservatism. There is ample evidence that these ideologies become more salient and potent following mortal threat. Experimental studies have demonstrated that fear of death influences perceptions of political reality and political behavior and may have influenced the results of the 2004 U.S. presidential election.

The role of the media is critically important in communicating to the public information about threats and how to think about them. Rhetorical framing by politicians, reflected by media accounts, appears to have played a role in generating an "us against them" mentality and an apocalyptic view of the United States' place and role in the world. The media contributed to a perceived belief in the need for authoritarian leadership as well as the endorsement of militant foreign policies by a majority of the population.

It is also important to recognize that the perceptions of reality are readily distorted by ideological bias. For example, despite repeated attempts to convince the public about the lack of a connection between Iraq and the terrorist events of September 11, many believe in a link between them. These misperceptions influenced the acceptance of militant U.S. policies abroad and domestic security policies that erode civil liberties.

Suggestions for Change

The factors involved in the erosion of the democratic process since September 11 form a complex web. The ideological underpinnings of attitudes and perceptions about reality are particularly difficult to influence because they are implicit or unconscious. Indeed, system-justifying ideologies often lead individuals to act in ways that appear to be opposed to their own self-interest.[16]

System-justifying ideologies are associated with a number of dysfunctional cognitive strategies, including dogmatism or intolerance of ambiguity; lack of openness to experience; poor tolerance for uncertainty; and the need for order, structure, and closure.[35] Functional cognitive strategies interfere with the use of system-justifying ideologies. For example, constructionist thinking (defined as the opposite of positivism) has been repeatedly associated with higher grade point averages in university students.[10, 30] In the most recent study of this connection, grade point average, years of university education, and enrollment in an academically selective university were all associated with less support of patriotic militancy and increased support of international efforts toward peaceful resolution of international conflict.[37]

It is important, therefore, that psychologists investigate the components of critical thinking and develop curricula that foster such thinking at all levels of education. It is also important that we continue to explore the link between threat and the potency of system-affirming ideologies. Although we have little control over political rhetoric, we can promote public dialogue in the media that disrupts the dangerous connections between unrealistic fears for one's nation, support for authoritarian and charismatic leadership, and policies that endanger the United States abroad and at home.

Although there is much to learn from psychology about the processes involved, the solutions, like the problems, are not only psychological. Psychologists must join with scholars in other disciplines and with experts in public policy and the media in these efforts. Work on these problems involves blurring the distinctions between "pure" and "applied" work. The research cited in this chapter indicates that we have made a good start.

References

1. Silver, R.C., Hofman, E.A., McIntosh, D.N., Poulin, M., & Gil-Rivas, V. (2002). Nationwide longitudinal study of psychological responses to September 11. Journal of the American Medical Association, 288, 1235–1244.

2. Callahan, K.L., Hilsenroth, M.J., Yonai, T., & Waehler, C.A. (2005). Longitudinal stress responses to the 9/11 terrorist attacks in a New York metropolitan college sample. *Stress, Trauma, & Crisis: An International Journal, 8*, 45–60.

3. Blanchard, E.B., Rowell, D.L., Kuhn, E., Rogers, R., & Wittrock, D. (2005). Posttraumatic stress and depressive symptoms in a college population one year after the September 11 attacks: The effect of proximity. *Behaviour Research and Therapy, 43*, 143–150.

4. Blanchard, E.G., Kuhn, E., Rowell, D.L., Hickling, E.J., Wittrock, D., Rogers, R.L., Johnson, M.R., & Steckler, D.C. (2004). Studies of the vicarious traumatization of college students by the September 11 attacks: Effects of proximity, exposure and connectedness. *Behaviour Research and Therapy, 42*, 191–205.

5. Ahern, J., Galea, S., Resnick, H., & Vlahov, D. (2004). Television images and probable posttraumatic stress. *Journal of Nervous and Mental Disease, 192*, 217–226.

6. Lowrey, W. (2004). Media dependency during a large-scale social disruption: The case of September 11. *Mass Communication & Society, 7*, 339–357.

7. Eidelson, R.J., & Plummer, M.D. (2005). Self and nation: A comparison of Americans' beliefs before and after 9/11. *Peace and Conflict, 11,* 153–175.

8. Renfro, L., & Stephan, W.G. (2003, August). Psychological reactions to the threat posed by the terrorist attacks of 9/11. Paper presented at 111th annual meeting of the American Psychological Association, Toronto, Ontario, Canada.

9. Anthony, K., Roselli, F., & Caparyan, L. (2003). Truly evil or simply angry: Individualism, collectivism, and attributions for the events of September 11th. *Individual Differences Research, 1,* 147–157.

10. Unger, R.K., & Locher, P. (In press). Them and us: The influence of hidden ideologies on reactions to September 11, 2001. *Peace and Conflict.*

11. Silver, M.D., & Silver, L.A. (2003). American national identification among college students before, during, and after September 2001. *Psicologia Politica, 27,* 59–77.

12. Agyrides, M., & Downey, J.L. (2004). September 11: Immediate and long term effects on measures of aggression, prejudice, and person perception. *North American Journal of Psychology, 6,* 175–188.

13. Li, Q., & Brewer, M.B. (2004). What does it mean to be an American? Patriotism, nationalism, and American identity after 9/11, *Political Psychology, 25,* 727–739.

14. Schatz, R.T., Staub, E., & Lavine, H. (1999). On the varieties of national attachment: Blind versus constructive patriotism. *Political Psychology, 20,* 151–174.

15. Mummendy, A., Klink, A., & Brown, R. (2001). Nationalism and patriotism: National identification and out-group rejection. *British Journal of Social Psychology, 40,* 159–172.

16. Jost, J.T., & Hunyady, O. (In press). Antecedents and consequences of system-justifying ideologies. *Current Directions in Psychological Science.*

17. Unger, R.K. (2002). Them and us: Hidden ideologies—differences in degree or kind? *Analyses of Social Issues and Public Policy, 2,* 43–52.

18. Kaiser, C.R., Brooke, V., & Major, B. (2004). A prospective investigation of the relationship between just-world beliefs and the desire for revenge after September 11, 2001. *Psychological Science, 15,* 503–506.

19. Altemeyer, B. (1981). *Right-wing authoritarianism.* Winnipeg, Canada: University of Manitoba Press.

20. Altemeyer, B. (1988). *Enemies of freedom: Understanding right-wing authoritarianism.* San Francisco: Jossey-Bass.

21. Henderson-King, D., Henderson-King, E., Bolea, B., Koches, K., & Kauffman, A. (2004). Seeking understanding or sending bombs: Beliefs as predictors of responses to terrorism. *Peace and Conflict, 10,* 67–84.

22. McFarland, S.G. (2005). On the eve of war: Authoritarianism, social dominance, and American students' attitudes toward attacking Iraq. *Personality & Social Psychology Bulletin, 31,* 360–367.

23. Cohrs, J.C., Kielmann, S., Maes, J., & Moschner, B. (2005). Effects of right-wing authoritarianism and threat from terrorism on restriction of civil liberties. *Analyses of Social Issues and Public Policy, 5*, pp. 263–276.

24. Doty, R.M., Winter, D.G., & Peterson, B.E. (1997). Authoritarianism and American students' attitudes about the Gulf War, 1990–1996. *Personality & Social Psychology Bulletin, 23*, 1133–1143.

25. Feldman, S., & Stenner, K. (1997). Perceived threat and authoritarianism. *Political Psychology, 18*, 741–770.

26. Pratto, F., Lemieux, A.F., Glasford, D.E., & Henry, P.J. (2003). American and Lebanese college students' responses to the events of September 11, 2001. *Psicologia Politica, 27*, 13–35.

27. Sidanius, J., & Pratto, F. (2001). *Social dominance: An intergroup theory of social hierarchy and oppression.* New York: Cambridge University Press.

28. Henry, P.J., Sidanius, J., Levin, S., & Pratto, F. (2005). Social dominance orientation, authoritarianism, and support for intergroup violence between the Middle East and America. *Political Psychology, 26*, 569–583.

29. Altemeyer, B. (2003). What happens when authoritarians inherit the earth? A simulation. *Analyses of Social Issues and Public Policy, 3*, pp 15–23.

30. Unger, R.K., Draper, R.D., & Pendergrass, M.L. (1986). Personal epistemology and personal experience. *Journal of Social Issues, 42*, 67–79.

31. Draper, R.D. (1990, August). Discriminant and divergent validity of the Attitudes about Reality Scale. Paper presented at the meeting of the American Psychological Association, Boston.

32. Evans, W.J. (2000). Construct validity of the Attitudes about Reality Scale. *Psychological Reports, 86*, 738–744.

33. Columbus, P.J. (1993). Attitudes about reality and college students' opinions about nuclear war. *Psychological Reports, 73*, 249–250.

34. Unger, R.K., & LeMay, M. (1991). Who's to blame? The relationship between political attributions and assumptions about reality. *Contemporary Social Psychology, 15*, 144–149.

35. Jost, J.T., Glaser, J., Kruglanski, A.W., & Sulloway, F.J. (2003). Political conservatism as motivated social cognition. *Psychological Bulletin, 129*, 339–375.

36. Harrison, W.D., & Atherton, C.R. (1990). Cognitive maturity and the "one foundation" controversy in social work education. *Journal of Social Work Education, 26*, 87–95.

37. Unger, R.K. (2005). The limits of demographic categories and the politics of the 2004 presidential election. *Analyses of Social Issues and Public Policy, 5*, pp. 153–163.

38. Skitka, L.J., Bauman, C.W., & Mullen, E. (2004). Political tolerance and coming to psychological closure following the September 11, 2001, terrorist attacks: An integrative approach. *Personality & Social Psychology Bulletin, 30*, 743–756.

39. Freyd, J.J. (2002). In the wake of terrorist attack, anger may mask fear. *Analyses of Social Issues and Public Policy, 2,* 5–8.

40. Duckitt, J., & Fisher, K. (2003). The impact of social threat on worldview and ideological attitudes. *Political Psychology, 24,* 179–222.

41. Lavine, H., Lodge, M., & Freitas, K. (2005). Threat, authoritarianism, and selective exposure to information. *Political Psychology, 26,* 219–244.

42. Landau, M.J., Johns, M., Greenberg, J., Pyszczynski, T., Martens, A., Goldenberg, J.L., & Solomon, S. (2004). A function of form: Terror management and structuring the social world. *Journal of Social and Personality Psychology, 87,* 189–210.

43. Greenberg, J., Solomon, S., & Pyszczynski, T. (1997). Terror management theory of self esteem and cultural worldviews: Empirical assessments and conceptual refinements. In M. Zanna (Ed.), *Advances in experimental social psychology* (Vol. 29, pp. 61–139). San Diego, CA: Academic Press.

44. Pyszczynski, T., Solomon, S., & Greenberg, J. (2003). *In the wake of 9/11: The psychology of terror.* Washington, DC: American Psychological Association.

45. Bligh, M.C., Kohles, J.C., & Meindl, J.R. (2004). Charisma under crisis: Presidential leadership, rhetoric, and media response before and after the September 11th terrorist attacks. *Leadership Quarterly, 15,* 211–239.

46. Gunn, J. (2004). The rhetoric of exorcism: George W. Bush and the return of political demonology. *Western Journal of Communication, 68,* 1–23.

47. Anker, E. (2005). Villains, victims, and heroes: Melodrama, media, and September 11. *Journal of Communication, 55,* 22–37.

48. Lewis, J. (2004). Television, public opinion and the war in Iraq: The case of Britain. *International Journal of Public Opinion Research, 16,* 295–310.

49. Smith, M.B. (2002). The metaphor (and fact) of war. *Peace and Conflict, 8,* 249–258.

50. Peterson, B.E., & Gerstein, E.D. (2005). Fighting and flying: Archival analysis of threat, authoritarianism, and the North American comic book. *Political Psychology, 26,* pp. 887–904.

51. Dunn, E.W., Moore, M., & Nosek, B.A. (2005). The war of the words: How linguistic differences in reporting shape perceptions of terrorism. *Analyses of Social Issues and Public Policy, 5,* 67–86.

52. Cohen, F., Solomon, S., Maxfield, M., Pyszczynski, T., & Greenberg, J. (2004). Fatal attraction: The effects of mortality salience on evaluations of charismatic, task-oriented, and relationship-oriented leaders. *Psychological Science, 15,* 846–851.

53. Landau, M.J., Solomon, S., Greenberg, J., Cohen, F., Pyszczynski, T., Arndt, J., Miller, C.H., Ogilvie, D.M., & Cook, A. (2004). Deliver us from evil: The effects of mortality salience and reminders of 9/11 on support for President George W. Bush. *Personality & Social Psychology Bulletin, 30,* 1136–1150.

54. Cohen, F., Ogilvie, D. M., Solomon, S., Greenberg, J., & Pyszczynski, T. (2005). American roulette: The effect of reminders of death on support for George W. Bush in the 2004 presidential election. *Analyses of Social Issues and Public Policy, 5*, pp. 177–187.

55. Willer, R. (2004). The effects of government-issued terror warnings on presidential approval ratings. *Current Research in Social Psychology, 10*, 56. McCann, S.J.H. (1997). Threatening times, "strong" presidential popular vote winners, and the victory margin, 1824–1964. *Journal of Personality and Social Psychology, 73*, 160–170.

57. Kemmelmeier, M. (2004). Authoritarianism and candidate support in the U.S. presidential elections of 1996 and 2000. *Journal of Social Psychology, 144*, 218–221.

58. McCann, S.J.H. (1999). Threatening times and fluctuations in American church memberships. *Personality & Social Psychology Bulletin, 25*, 325–336.

59. Doty, R. M., Peterson, B. E., & Winter, D. G. (1991). Threat and authoritarianism in the United States, 1978–1987. *Journal of Personality and Social Psychology, 61*, 629–649.

60. Dumont, M., Yzerbyt, V., Wigboldus, D., & Gordijn, E. H. (2003). Social categorization and fear reactions to the September 11th terrorist attacks. *Personality & Social Psychology Bulletin, 29*, 1509–1529.

61. Louis, W. R., & Terry, D. J. (2003, August). Australian anti-Americanism and support for the "war on terrorism." Poster presented at 111th annual meeting of the American Psychological Association, Toronto, Ontario, Canada.

62. Reser, J. P., & Muncer, S. (2004). Sense-making in the wake of September 11th: A network analysis of lay understandings. *British Journal of Psychology, 95*, 283–296.

63. Chirumbolo, A., Areni, A., & Sensales, G. (2004). Need for cognitive closure and politics: Voting, political attitudes and attributional style. *International Journal of Psychology, 39*, 245–253.

64. Sidanius, J., Henry, P. J., Pratto, F., & Levin, S. (2004). Arab attributions for the attack on America: The case of Lebanese sub-elites. *Journal of Cross-Cultural Psychology, 35*, 403–416.

65. Unger, R. K., & Gareis, K. (Article in process). The eye of the beholder: Cultural differences in attitudes about how to deal with terrorism.

CHAPTER 6

Perceptions of Threat, National Representation, and Support for Procedures To Protect the National Group

Gordon Hodson, Victoria M. Esses, and John F. Dovidio

In the wake of the September 11, 2001, terrorist attacks, North Americans have experienced a heightened sense of vulnerability to attacks from other groups and a strengthening of national identity. Indeed, threat alerts and politicians' rhetorical framing (see Introduction note 1) have supported and enhanced such effects. In this chapter, we discuss how these effects may lead to increased support for restrictive and aggressive policies and procedures to protect the national group and may result from such policies and procedures.

Threat Perceptions in Intergroup Contexts

Threat has a profound effect on how people respond to others. Considerable evidence suggests that perceptions of threat can systematically influence behavior toward those believed to be a source of threat. For example, tangible threats to personal and group well-being and conditions of antagonistic interdependence produce negative attitudes and behaviors toward members of other groups.[1–4] From this perspective, intergroup competition over resources, real or not, contributes substantially to intergroup tension and hostility. Indeed, much tension that currently exists on the world stage comes from this type of conflict. For instance, disputes between the United States and Canada on issues such as soft-wood lumber trade[5] and the sale of beef[6] undoubtedly reflect competitive concerns between nation states of a primarily economic, resource-based nature.

In addition, threats that seem to challenge one's cherished values and principles are likely to evoke intense defensive reactions.[7–10] From this perspective, out-groups may not only threaten access to tangible resources such as housing, food, water, and power, but also symbolic aspects of a group's or a nation's identity. Much of the conflict and tension between Quebec and the rest of Canada reflects this type of threat perception, with the key issues at stake being culture, language, and identity. Recent terrorist attacks have given rise in the West to the notion of a "clash of civilizations," in which the West and Islam engage in war largely over ideological and cultural concerns.[11] Similar expressions of symbolic value threat have been expressed toward groups and individuals some believe violate cultural values (such as homosexuals),[8, 12] resulting in negative attitudes toward and restrictions on these groups. Researchers are beginning to examine the joint influence of realistic and symbolic value threats.[13] For example, Stephan, Renfo, Esses, Stephan, and Martin[14] recently found that immigrant groups seen to pose *both* realistic (i.e., tangible) and symbolic value threat were evaluated especially unfavorably.

Threat and Orientations toward the In-Group and Out-Groups

Although this research on intergroup threat seems to parallel work on how interpersonal threat promotes aggression to the source of the threat,[15–16] the effects of intergroup threat are broader. That is, intergroup threat has consequences not only for how people react to the perceived source of the threat, but also for how they think and feel about members of their own group, and how they behave toward members of other groups generally. Thus, attempts to promote security, such as the government providing regular information about the level of alert for terrorism and the media's coverage of potential terrorist activities, can exacerbate the psychological impact of threat while promoting public safety.

Threat increases in-group cohesiveness and makes common identity highly salient. Under conditions of threat to one's group, people see themselves as closer to members of their own group and value them more highly.[17–18] National crisis and threat often lead to an increased focus on national identity and renewed attachment to the nation.[19–22] In addition, under threat, people empathize more strongly with other members of their group, even those who under other circumstances would be seen as quite different and not prototypical. As a consequence, threat induces positive orientations, such as greater helpfulness and more favorable attitudes, toward a range of others identified as members of the in-group. For example, after the September 11, 2001, terrorist attacks, there was a dramatic increase in volunteerism in the United States.[23] This increase in volunteerism, which persisted for several weeks, was not focused solely on threat-related activities (e.g., helping the families of victims of the attacks), but also on assisting other members of the national in-group who are otherwise often stigmatized (e.g., helping people with AIDS). In addition, when primed by external terrorist threats to citizens of the United States generally, whites displayed greater empathy to the plight of blacks and lower levels of prejudice.[24]

At the same time as they enhance connections within one's group, conditions of threat also increase the salience of the psychological boundaries between people perceived as members of other groups. Although the distinction between one's own group and the threatening group is primary, the distinction between the in-group and any other group becomes sharpened. The ideals of the in-group are celebrated in ways that achieve "positive distinctiveness" relative to the portrayal of other groups' values.[25–27] One result of the narrowing of psychological boundaries defining the national in-group[28] is a generally decreased acceptance of "foreigners."[9, 19, 29] Thus, perceptions of threat and a narrow representation of the national in-group are likely to result in support for policies to keep foreigners out, an increased desire to monitor citizens already in the country, and an increased willingness to attack those who are seen as the source of threat.

These effects are not necessarily unidirectional. Once restrictive policies and procedures are in place to protect the national in-group, the sense of threat and a narrow definition of the in-group are likely to be reinforced. For example, the immigration policies of a nation are likely to influence the collective vision of national identity and perceptions of who is (and who is not) considered a member of the national in-group.[29] Following the September 11 terrorist attacks, public support for decreasing immigration increased in both the United States and Canada.[30–31] Restrictive immigration policies suggest to the public that foreigners are a source of threat and that the in-group is in need of protection from this threat. Similarly, willingness to have civil liberties curtailed and support for military action against other nations may be justified by heightening the sense of threat that exists.

Thus, just as perceptions of threat may lead to support for restrictive, aggressive policies and procedures, such policies and procedures may heighten one's sense of threat and increase the strength of in-group–out-group boundaries.

Such a feedback loop is a key component of the Unified Instrumental Model of Group Conflict.[13] According to this model, threats from competition (resource/power and value/cultural) are likely to result in attempts to reduce competition (e.g., decreasing out-group competitiveness; increasing in-group competitiveness), the influence of which feeds back, exacerbates, and entrenches ideologies and situational stressors that fostered perceptions of group competition in the first place. For instance, immigration can be seen as a situational stressor that may challenge the status quo and create instability, particularly when immigrants come from regions known to experience conflict and terrorist activities. To members of the host society, immigrants then become a salient out-group that is highly distinct from the in-group, and a variety of cognitive, affective, and motivational mental processes can exacerbate the perception of intergroup conflict. According to the model, a likely outcome is the attempt to remove threat posed by the immigrant group. In the present example, this may include limiting the opportunities for immigration at the border, or, upon arriving in the host society, limiting immigrants' employment or educational opportunities. In creating intergroup disparities, attempts to remove out-group threat can exacerbate situational stressors that lead to the perception of conflict, and the process can become cyclical.

Although an out-group is not necessary to increase the sense of national identity, as evidenced by increased nationalism after Hurricane Katrina struck the New Orleans area,[32] out-groups are often perceived as sources of group threat that can increase national identification. As a result, the representation of the in-group becomes increasingly narrow in its scope and definition in the presence of out-groups perceived as threatening to in-group identity. As foreigners, immigrants particularly represent a potential source of threat, both in terms of realistic threat—as they gain employment, buy housing, and access healthcare—and also in terms of cultural and value threat—as they "import" aspects of their culture to the host society that may be perceived as at odds with existing values. Immigrants may have a difficult time identifying with the host society, and this undoubtedly exacerbates the problem. For instance, recent survey evidence suggests that compared to host Canadians, immigrants are 30 percent less likely to identify themselves as Canadian, and are 30 percent less likely to engage in political activity such as voting; disturbingly, this immigrant racial divide is growing in strength rather than diminishing over time, such that the children of immigrants are integrating less well than their parents.[33] If these trends continue, immigrants will increasingly be rejected as part of the host society's national identity. Of concern to public policy, perceptions of threat are likely to reduce acceptance of immigrant cultures, paradoxically at the time when nations such as the United States and Canada are most in need of immigrants to sustain economic growth and global competitiveness.[34]

Perceptions of threat are likely to have important implications for public policy, not only toward immigration, but also toward local interventions such as increased surveillance of citizens at home and increased endorsement of military interventions against out-groups and nation states suspected of promoting or conducting terrorism.

Threat and Public Policy

From the perspective of Terror Management Theory, reminders of personal mortality can invoke a host of defensive reactions to buffer existential anxiety, including an enhanced preference for one's own culture and in-group. In support of this theory, heightened salience of terrorism has been shown to exert dramatic consequences on public policy decisions. For instance, Americans primed with reminders of their own mortality[35] or reminders of personal mortality coupled with terrorism, even at an unconscious level,[36] were significantly more likely to plan to vote for the "tough on terror" incumbent George W. Bush than for John Kerry. This research shows that dramatization can increase the salience of terrorist violence and personal mortality, which can clearly exert substantial influence on political outcomes and the formation of public policy. These political policy outcomes need not even be directly linked to the issue of terrorism. Willer's[37] time-series analyses of *Washington Post* reports and surveys of Gallup poll data over a three-year period suggest a direct positive association between terror warnings and presidential approval. In addition, the delivery of terror alerts was similarly linked to approval for the president's handling of the economy, a largely non–terrorism-relevant issue.

As these studies suggest, perceptions of threat impact and guide public policy. Figure 6.1 presents a model of likely outcomes in the aftermath of terrorist activity such as the September 11 attacks in the United States. Institutional responses, such as the issuing of terror

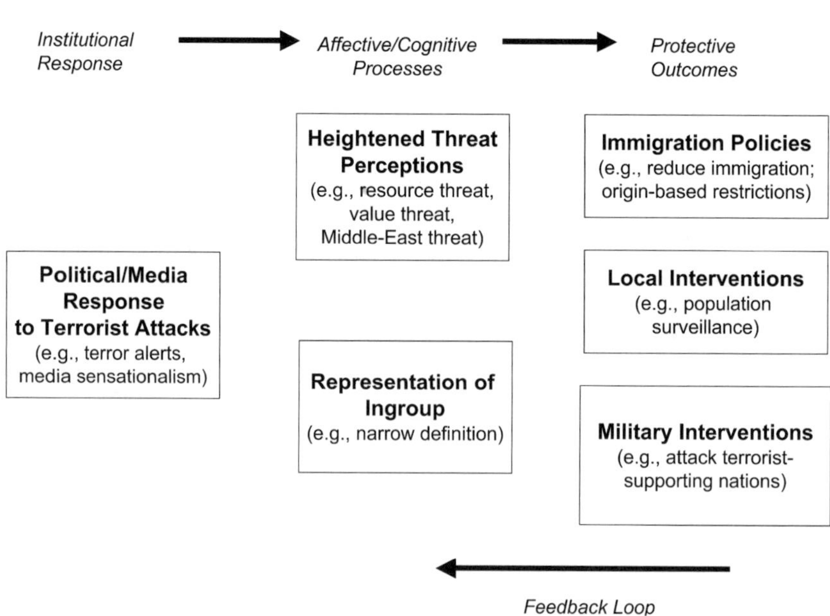

Figure 6.1 A model of predicted response to the threat of terrorism.

alerts by governments and the dramatization of terrorism by the media are likely to result in heightened perceptions of threat and a narrowing representation of the in-group (i.e., what constitutes "us" at a national level). These psychological reactions are likely to be associated with the endorsement of public policy aimed at protecting the national in-group, such as recommendations that immigration be reduced or become based on national origin considerations, the encouragement of intrusive population surveillance at the expense of civil liberties, and support for military action against groups suspected of instigating or supporting attacks on the national group. These processes are likely to reinforce one another as measures to protect the in-group heighten the sense of need for violent and oppressive actions, and this message is communicated through institutions such as the government and the media.

September 11 and Attitudes toward Immigration: An Investigation

To examine the relations between perceptions of threat and representation of the national in-group on the one hand and support for restrictive, aggressive policies and procedures on the other, we collected data at Colgate University in the United States and at the University of Western Ontario in Canada in the months following the September 11, 2001, terrorist attacks. In particular, 76 students at Colgate University and 102 at the University of Western Ontario completed our measures in the autumn of 2001. The relations among threat perceptions, representation of national identity, and support for relevant policies and procedures were then examined. The policies and procedures we focused on were immigration restrictions, increased surveillance of the national population, and military action against suspected terrorist-supporting nations. Although the direction of causality cannot be definitively determined from these relations, as we have argued above, they are likely to be bidirectional.

Affective and Cognitive Measures

The measures analyzed here were part of a larger survey package administered to participants. On most items, participants responded on seven-point rating scales, with higher scores reflecting increased item endorsement. Three measures of perceived threat were included. First, participants were asked to indicate the extent to which people from specific regions of the world pose a threat to their nation in a variety of domains (e.g., safety/security, psychological well-being). Perceived threat by people from Europe, Asia, the Middle East, and Africa were assessed separately. Given our interest in responses to terrorist attacks in the wake of September 11, and the fact that the analyses of perceived threat by people from various regions of the world produced systematic effects only for perceived threat by Middle Easterners, our analyses of threat focuses on the Middle East. Because of our particular interest in relations with immigrants, we also assessed perceived threat from immigrants in two domains: values/culture and economics/power. To do so, we used balanced measures of zero-sum beliefs about relations between immigrants and nonimmigrants.[38–39] An example values/culture item reads: "Allowing immigrant cultures to thrive means that Canadian culture is weakened." An example economics/power item reads: "The more business opportunities are made available for immigrants, the fewer business opportunities are available for Canadians already living here."

In addition, we assessed whether members of the host country and immigrants are considered part of the same group. An example of this type of item is: "The distinction between immigrants and nonimmigrants is artificial. We are all Americans" (reverse coded).[39] In essence, this measure taps the extent to which immigrants and members of the host society do not share a common identity, expressing a narrow and exclusive definition of the national in-group.

Protective Outcomes: Public Policy Recommendations

We examined support for several policies and procedures relevant to protecting the national in-group. In terms of immigration policy, we assessed the extent to which participants supported decreasing or increasing current immigration levels and taking into account the applicant's country of origin. The latter policy has not been present in the United States or Canada since the 1970s, being considered outdated and unfair, but is currently gaining in popularity. For example, a recent poll[30] found that 43 percent of respondents believe that Canada accepts too many immigrants from Arab countries, compared to 16 percent who believe that Canada accepts too many immigrants from Europe.[40] In addition, we assessed degree of support for increased population surveillance within the nation and for taking military action against suspected terrorist-supporting nations. Recent surveys[41] have shown that 42 percent of Canadians support restrictions on civil liberties to curb terrorism, and 33 percent support police searches without warrants. As for military support, in the immediate aftermath of the September 11 attacks, 87 percent of Americans supported President Bush's military reaction to fight terrorism,[42] although support for the war in Iraq has decreased substantially, with 57 percent of Americans recently indicating that it was not worth going to war, and 41 percent believing that going to war was a mistake.[43] This trend suggests that support for retaliatory military invasions and occupations are not only contingent on the salience of terrorism, but also the costs of these activities.

Results and Discussion

Before we compare the groups of respondents presented in Table 6.1, it is worth noting that America was the target of a terrorist attack, whereas Canada, a neighbor and an ally, was not. As can be seen in Table 6.1, the American respondents scored significantly higher than the Canadian respondents in perceptions of Middle East threat and indicated a more narrow representation of the national in-group. As discussed above, this was expected in response to the September 11 terrorist attack against the United States and the portrayal of this attack by media and government. In contrast, the Canadian respondents viewed immigrants as a greater threat to their values than did the American respondents, perhaps due to the greater diversity of immigrant groups in Canada in recent years. In support of this possibility, the 2001 Canadian census found that 18 percent of citizens were foreign-born, compared to only 11 percent in the 2000 U.S. Census.[44] In terms of the endorsement of protective public policies, the American respondents reported significantly more support for reducing immigration, and was significantly more in favor of military interventions against terrorist-supporting nations.

The relations between the affective/cognitive processes and support for protective policies are shown in Tables 6.2 and 6.3. In the American data collected at Colgate University (see Table 6.2), perceived threat by people from the Middle East was significantly related (in the expected direction) to support for all the policies and procedures assessed. That is, increased perceptions of threat from the Middle East were associated with endorsement of restrictive policies to protect the in-group, such as immigration control and military action against terrorists. Similarly, perceived threats from immigrants, assessed in terms of zero-sum beliefs about values/culture and economics/power, were significantly related to support for the restrictive policies and procedures. A narrow representation of the national in-group that excluded immigrants was also significantly related to support for reduced immigration and origin-based immigration policies and to increased surveillance of the population. As discussed earlier, it is likely that the relations between cognitive and affective reactions and public policy support are bidirectional, such that perceptions of threat and tight national boundaries lead to support for protective policies and that support for protective policies are rationalized and lead to increased perceptions of threat from foreigners.

In the Canadian study at University of Western Ontario (see Table 6.3), similar findings were obtained for support of reduced immigration and origin-based immigration policies. That is, perceived threats and a narrow national representation were significantly related to each of the immigration restrictions in the expected direction. They were not consistently related, however, to support for increased population surveillance or military action against suspected terrorist-supporting nations. A positive correlation between zero-sum values and support for military action was the only significant relation between threats and the non–immigration-related policy recommendations. In contrast to the American findings, therefore, Canadian perceptions of threat and a narrow national representation are consistently related

Table 6.1 Comparison of Reactions between the American and Canadian Respondents

	Colgate University (U.S.) sample		University of Western Ontario (Canadian) sample		
	Mean	***SD***	**Mean**	***SD***	***p* value (*t* test)**
Affective/cognitive processes					
Middle East threat	4.94	2.09	3.97	1.80	.001
Zero-sum value threat	2.28	0.92	2.69	1.06	.008
Zero-sum resource threat	3.10	1.07	3.03	1.09	not significant
Narrow national representation	2.43	1.23	1.87	1.52	.009
Protective policy outcomes					
Reduce immigration	−0.59	1.50	−1.19	1.70	.015
Immigration policies taking into account origin	3.89	2.42	4.20	2.89	not significant
Increased surveillance of population	3.81	2.13	3.65	2.71	not significant
Military action against suspected terrorist-supporting nations	6.67	2.37	4.70	2.95	$< .001$

Note: Values of variables range from 1 to 7, with higher scores indicating greater endorsement, except Reduce Immigration which ranges from -4 (strongly oppose) to +4 (strongly support). Colgate respondent *N*s range from 75-76, University of Western Ontario respondent Ns range from 100–102. Two-tailed *t* tests.

only to keeping foreigners out and not to intrusive surveillance of the in-group and military action against out-groups. Thus, in the Canadian study, perceptions of and support for restrictive immigration policies may be mutually reinforcing, although similar effects are not evident for other policies and procedures.

Implications and Recommendations

These data show a relation between psychological perceptions of heightened threat and narrowing representations of the in-group on the one hand and endorsement of public policies that are protective

Table 6.2 Relations between Affective/Cognitive Processes and Protective Policy Outcomes: Colgate University (U.S.) Respondents

	Protective policy outcomes			
Affective/ cognitive immigration	**Reduce immigration**	**Immigration policies taking into account origin**	**Increased surveillance of population**	**Military action against suspected terrorist-supporting nations**
Middle East threat	.35 **	.43 ***	.28 *	.39 ***
Zero-sum value threat	.40 ***	.32 **	.38 ***	.24 *
Zero-sum resource threat	.65 ***	.44 ***	.28 *	.35 **
Narrow national representation	.47 ***	.32 **	.32 **	.08

Note: $N = 75–76$. * $p < .05$, ** $p < .01$, *** $p < .001$.

Table 6.3 Relations between Affective/Cognitive Processes and Protective Policy Outcomes: University of Western Ontario (Canadian) Sample

	Protective policy outcomes			
Affective/ cognitive processes	**Reduce immigration**	**Immigration policies taking into account origin**	**Increased surveillance of population**	**Military action against suspected terrorist-supporting nations**
Middle east threat	.25 *	.36 ***	.15	.10
Zero-sum value threat	.53 ***	.30 **	.19	.22 *
Zero-sum resource threat	.57 ***	.41 ***	.11	.17
Narrow national representation	.35 ***	.39 ***	−.06	.13

Note: $N = 100–102$. * $p < .05$, ** $p < .01$, *** $p < .001$.

of the national in-group on the other. We have argued that threat, heightened differentiation between the in-group and out-group, and out-group exclusion are closely related and may influence each other. In addition, attempts to promote the safety of the in-group against an outside threat, such as the government's regular alerts about the level of terrorist threat and the media's intense coverage of these threats, can intensify the public's psychological reactions with long-term adverse social implications that may reinforce and increase threat perceptions.

Immigration: Beyond Threat

Threat perceptions are associated with negative attitudes toward immigration, at a time when countries such as the United States and Canada are in need of increased immigration to maintain their economies. Clearly, levels of perceived threat need to be managed, even if only for the self-interest of the host societies, not to mention Western ideals of global humanitarianism and egalitarianism. Governments and the media can help by imparting information about the actual level of risk associated with violent actions such as terrorism, rather than exaggerating or sensationalizing threat risk. In the current political climate, heightened perceptions of threat by Arab and Muslim immigrants should be addressed by the media. Just as illusory correlations[45] between blacks and violent crime can exaggerate the perception of black violence beyond its actual level, the high degree of association between Muslims and Arabs and terrorists and terrorism can lead to a false perception that immigrants from these parts of the world are particularly threatening to immigrant-accepting nations. Efforts to de-sensationalize terrorism in the media will serve this purpose with very little effort needed.

In light of the impending need for immigrants,[34] the media and educators are encouraged to emphasize the upcoming economic crisis brought on by an aging North American population that will not adequately replace itself due to low birth rates. In particular, it should be emphasized that immigrants are needed to fill the labor pool. Although such education strategies might encounter resistance, particularly among those who feel that immigrants pose a value/cultural threat, it would overcome the objection that immigrants drain resources from the host society. To the extent that group strife and conflict can be attributed, in part, to competition over resources,[1–4] promoting the perception that immigrants can be a boon to the host economy is a step toward greater acceptance and integration. Yet we suggest this strategy with a caveat: past research demonstrates that prejudiced individuals are likely to reject the notion that immigration is beneficial and that immigrants do not take resources at a cost to the in-group.[38] We suggest that a stronger message may be necessary, that immigrants are *needed* if the host culture is to maintain a foothold in the world economy.

In stressing the role of immigration in promoting national growth and success, educators should be careful to minimize group differences in the process. As noted by Stephan and colleagues:[14]

> Intergroup relations programs that stress group differences, such as multicultural education, diversity training, and intercultural relations training . . . run the risk of creating negative attitudes in their training. This may be particularly true when one of the avowed aims of the program is to strengthen in-group identity, as is often the case with multicultural education. One solution to this dilemma is to be very careful to present information on group differences in a non-evaluative manner and to stress the benefits of group differences.

Such educational strategies for learning about other groups may be fostered by increasing the contact between groups, particularly when such interactions are characterized by equal group status within the situation, the pursuit of common goals, cooperation, and interdependence rather than intergroup competition and institutional support for positive interactions.[46–47] Overall, empirical research supports the Contact Hypothesis under these conditions.[47–49] In terms of our discussion of post-9/11 reactions in the West, educators and policymakers could encourage increased contact between Muslims and non-Muslims, particularly under conditions demonstrated to foster and promote positive intergroup relations. Unfortunately, many preconditions for positive contact listed above are absent or weak in the case of immigration. For instance, newcomers are typically of lower status than members of the host society, particularly in the case of immigrants to North America. A potential first step, therefore, may be to promote increased interaction with second-generation immigrants who tend to be higher in social status than their parents. In addition, the media can play a role in promoting contact with other racial groups at a relatively safe and nonthreatening distance, using television programming to reinforce positive intergroup interaction.[50] By promoting positive norms of intergroup contact, the media can also bolster the perception of institutional support for positive intergroup interaction.

In addition to recommendations that tackle the heightened sense of fear after terrorist attacks, our findings suggest a viable option for promoting positive intergroup relations at a more cognitive level. It appears that a narrow national representation of the in-group is associated with protective policies aimed at excluding the out-group, in this case immigrants, in both of our groups of respondents. There is a growing body of evidence to suggest that strategies to recategorize former out-group members as members of a more inclusive in-group, in keeping with the Common In-group Identity Model,[51] can effectively improve attitudes toward out-group members. In this model, "they" become recategorized as part of "us," and positivity toward in-group members is extended to those formerly conceptualized as part of the out-group.

In the present context of terrorism and the rejection of immigrants, policymakers could emphasize the fact that nations such as the United States and Canada are immigrant nations as part of their national identity and that the distinction between immigrants and members of the host society is largely artificial.[20, 38] This strategy would be particularly efficacious when combined with education programs aimed at promoting the resource benefits of incorporating more immigrants into society. That is, emphasizing the resource/power benefits of including immigrants into the workforce while promoting representations of the national identity that are more inclusive and incorporate immigrants can work hand-in-hand to promote positive attitudes and less aggressive protective outcomes. Tackling threat perceptions and narrow national representations in combination, therefore, represents a strong strategy for improving intergroup relations. Here again the media and government can use their resources to promote these perceptions through public service announcements and education initiatives.

However, as noted earlier, the relationships among threat, in-group solidarity, and bias toward members of other groups is reciprocal and often reinforcing. Thus, how information about threat is communicated can shape public responses in complex ways.

Institutional Delivery of Threat Information

Although most governments use general methods such as press releases and public service announcements to disperse information pertinent to dealing with threats to their citizens, most Western governments have increasingly devoted attention to specific delivery systems to alert for terrorist threats. In the United States, the Department of Homeland Security has developed a color-coded alert system specifically for terrorist threats (see http://www.dhs.gov/interweb/assetlibrary/CitizenGuidanceHSAS2.pdf). Reservations about such emergency announcement systems have been voiced, however. Polls indicate that the public generally finds color-coded terror alert systems confusing,[52] which draws into question the efficacy of this strategy. It has also been argued that terror-relevant warning messages are vague and occur too frequently to be of value, paradoxically serving to exacerbate feelings of terror.[53] In support of this notion, several polls conducted immediately after the September 11 attacks found that 47 to 55 percent of Americans believed that government warnings help people, but 40 to 49 percent felt that such warnings scared people.[42]

Moreover, critics have suggested that the use of terror alerts is driven more by political motivations than by public safety concerns.[52, 54, 55–] In particular, it has been suggested that fear appeals are employed to rush through legislation that limits civil liberties at home and abroad and to boost the profiles of politicians who are seen as "tough on terrorism." As one might expect, government officials are quick to deny such allegations.[56]

Governments constitute only one source of threat information, and they rely heavily on another institution, the media. Many popular commentators such as Michael Moore have questioned the close relations between the media and the U.S. government, suggesting that today in the United States these institutions too often work hand in hand, at times in conjunction with business interests.[57] The relation between objective media coverage and political agendas arguably became blurred, for instance, when influential news anchors such as Dan Rather publicly committed themselves to following the orders of the U.S. president after the September 11 attacks.[58]

The media, of course, have their own interests. The media commercially benefit when headlines speak of terrorism and disaster. As noted by journalist Gwynne Dyer:[59]

> God knows [the media] deserve to be blamed. The greedy sensationalism with which the major Western media greet each new terrorist "outrage" has inflated the danger far beyond its true size in the public's mind, in just the same way as their melodramatic coverage of crime has caused popular anxiety about it to rise steeply in most Western countries even as the actual crime rate has fallen steadily in recent years. Public ignorance about the statistics of risk makes this media manipulation easy: there are heavy smokers who worry about terrorist attacks.

Evidence of sensationalism can be readily observed in daily newspapers. For instance, in the three years following the September 11 attacks, British newspapers made use of the term "dirty bomb" (i.e., crude conventional bombs laced with radioactive material) over 1,000 times, averaging one such reference to a very serious terrorist threat per day.[60] Thus, the media not only report on terrorism, but create and sustain feelings of fear and terror.

Future Directions

Future research could test several issues that are raised in this chapter. First, the link between the government/media and threat perceptions was not directly investigated in our analyses, because we focused more on the perceptions of threat and their relation to restrictive policy endorsement. We have assumed that the link between media presentations and fear perceptions is relatively straightforward, but closer examination of this link is required. As Altheide[61] cautions:

> Students of the mass media and popular culture agree on two basic social facts: (1) Popular culture includes a relatively large amount of information and images pertaining to fear, including crime and violence, and (2) Audience members perceive social life as very dangerous. It is the relationship between these two "social facts" that remains unclear.

Based on such notes of caution, it would be prudent to investigate the link between institutions such as the media and threat perceptions in the population. We may be well served to consider both sociological and psychological approaches in tackling this issue.

Second, the bidirectional nature of the relations between variables proposed in Figure 6.1 could be directly tested. Experimental research now corroborates the correlational relations between threat and attitudes,[1, 14] and future research could examine the reciprocal direction of such influence.

Government, media, and public responses to the September 11 terrorist attacks and subsequent terrorist activities in other parts of the world have included relatively frequent threat alerts, increased nationalism, and policies and procedures to protect the national group. As demonstrated here, perceptions of threat, a narrow definition of the national in-group, and support for restrictive and aggressive policies and procedures tend to be highly related and may be mutually reinforcing. This ensures that the status quo of fear and aggression is maintained. In the current political climate, this can have negative consequences for immigrants to Western nations, particularly those from predominantly Muslim countries. As we have noted, immigrants are often seen as threatening not only access to resources but also the sense of cultural prominence and stability enjoyed by the host society. Dramatic events, such as the September 11 terrorist attacks, clearly evoke an even stronger sense of threat to cultural stability, evidenced from the repeated references to "The Day the World Changed" after the attacks. Unfortunately for immigrants from regions of the world with many terrorist activities, most out-group members are painted with the same brush. The result can be that immigrants from terrorist-supporting nations, many fleeing terrorism themselves, come to represent a source of potential competition and threat to the host society.

There is a growing body of research on the psychological role of threat in attitudes toward other groups. In the present chapter, we argue that threat can impact not only attitudes toward particular groups, but can influence and shape public policy recommendations. How such perceptions of threat are propagated and managed will become an increasingly important issue in the twenty-first century, particularly if immigrant groups are to be successfully integrated when they are needed the most.

References

1. Esses, V.M., Jackson, L.M., & Armstrong, T.L. (1998). Intergroup competition and attitudes toward immigrants and immigration: An instrumental model of group conflict. *Journal of Social Issues, 54*, 699–724.

2. Fiske, S.T., & Ruscher, J.B. (1993). Negative interdependence and prejudice: Whence the affect? In D.M. Mackie & D.L. Hamilton (Eds.), *Affect, cognition and stereotyping: Interactive processes in group perception* (pp. 239–268). San Diego, CA: Academic Press.

3. LeVine, R.A., & Campbell, D.T. (1972). *Ethnocentrism: Theories of conflict, ethnic attitudes, and group behavior.* New York: Wiley.

4. Sherif, M., & Sherif, C.W. (1979). Research on intergroup relations. In W.G. Austin & S. Worchel (Eds.), *The social psychology of intergroup relations* (pp. 7–32). Monterey, CA: Brooks/Cole.

5. At loggerheads: The Canada-U.S. softwood lumber dispute. (2005). Retrieved October 28, 2005, from http://archives.cbc.ca/IDD-1–73-787/politics_economy/softwood/.

6. Bergman, B. (2004, September 20) Here's the beef: Ottawa and Canadian cattlemen battle the U.S. ban. Retrieved October 28, 2005, from http://www.macleans.ca/topstories/canada/article.jsp?content = 20040920_88624_886 24.

7. Chandler, C.R., & Tsai, Y. (2001). Social factors influencing immigration attitudes: An analysis of data from the General Social Survey. *Social Science Journal, 38*, 177–188.

8. Esses, V.M., Haddock, G., & Zanna, M.P. (1993). Values, stereotypes, and emotions as determinants of intergroup attitudes. In D.M. Mackie & D.L. Hamilton (Eds.), *Affect, cognition and stereotyping: Interactive processes in group perception* (pp. 137–166). San Diego, CA: Academic Press.

9. Stephan, W.G., & Stephan, C.W. (2000). An integrated threat theory of prejudice. In S. Oskamp (Ed.), *Claremont symposium on applied social psychology* (pp. 23–46). Hillsdale, NJ: Erlbaum.

10. Struch, N., & Schwartz, S.H. (1989). Intergroup aggression: It predictors and distinctness from in-group bias. *Journal of Personality and Social Psychology, 56*, 364–373.

11. Huntington, S.P. (1996) The clash of civilizations and the remaking of world order. New York: Simon & Schuster.

12. Jackson, L.M., & Esses, V.M. (1997). Of scripture and ascription: The relation between religious fundamentalism and intergroup helping. *Personality and Social Psychology Bulletin, 23*, 893–906.

13. Esses, V. M, Jackson, L.M., Dovidio, J.F., & Hodson, G. (2005). Instrumental relations among groups: Group competition, conflict, and prejudice. In J.F. Dovidio, P. Glick, & L.A. Rudman (Eds.), *On the nature of prejudice: Fifty years after Allport* (pp. 227–243). Oxford, UK: Blackwell.

14. Stephan, W.G., Renfro, C.L., Esses, V.M., Stephan, C.W., & Martin, T. (2005). The effects of feeling threatened on attitudes toward immigrants. *International Journal of Intercultural Relations, 29*, 1–19.

15. Baumeister, R.F., & Boden, J.M. (1998). Aggression and the self: High self-esteem, low self-esteem, and ego threat. In R.G. Geen & E. Donnerstein (Eds.), *Human aggression: Theories, research, and implications for social policy* (pp. 111–137). San Diego, CA: Academic Press.

16. Geen, R.G., Stoner, D., & Kelley, D.R. (1974). Aggression anxiety and cognitive appraisal of aggression-threat stimuli. *Journal of Personality and Social Psychology, 29*, 196–200.

17. Sherif, M., Harvey, O.J., White, B.J., Hood, W.R., & Sherif, C.W. (1961). *Intergroup conflict and cooperation. The Robbers Cave experiment.* Norman: University of Oklahoma Book Exchange.

18. Verkuyten, M., & Nekuee, S. (1999). In-group bias: The effect of self-stereotyping, identification, and group threat. *European Journal of Social Psychology, 29*, 411–418.

19. Citrin, J., Reingold, B., & Green, D.P. (1990). American identity and the politics of ethnic change. *Journal of Politics, 52*, 1124–1154.

20. Esses, V.M., Dovidio, J.F., Jackson, L.M., & Semenya, A.H. (2005). Attitudes toward immigrants and immigration: The role of national and international identities. In D. Abrams, M.A. Hogg, & J.M. Marques (Eds.), *The social psychology of inclusion and exclusion* (pp. 317–338). Philadelphia: Psychology Press.

21. Jaret, C. (1999). Troubled by newcomers: Anti-immigrant attitudes and action during two eras of mass immigration to the United States. *Journal of American Ethnic History, 18*(3), 9–39.

22. Kosterman, R., & Feshbach, S. (1989). Toward a measure of patriotic and nationalistic attitudes. *Political Psychology, 10*, 257–274.

23. Penner, L.A., Brannick, M.T., Webb, S., & Connell, P. (2005). The effects of the September 11, 2001 attacks on volunteering: An archival analysis. *Journal of Applied Social Psychology, 35,* 1333-1360

24. Dovidio, J.F., ten Vergert, M., Stewart, T.L., Gaertner, S.L., Johnson, J.D., Esses, V.M., Riek, B.M., & Pearson, A.R. (2004). Perspective and prejudice: Antecedents and mediating mechanisms. *Personality and Social Psychology Bulletin, 30,* 1537–1549.

25. Doty, R.M., Peterson, B.E., & Winter, D.G. (1991). Threat and authoritarianism in the United States, 1978–1987. *Journal of Personality and Social Psychology, 61,* 629–640.

26. Hewstone, M., Rubin, M., & Willis, H. (2002). *Annual Review of Psychology, 53,* 575–604.

27. Tajfel, H., & Turner, J.C. (1979). An integrative theory of intergroup conflict. In W.G. Austin and S. Worchel (Eds.), *The social psychology of intergroup relations* (pp. 33–47). Monterey, CA: Brooks/Cole.

28. Rothgerber, H. (1997). External intergroup threat as an antecedent to perceptions in in-group and out-group homogeneity. *Journal of Personality and Social Psychology, 73,* 1206–1212.

29. Esses, V.M., Dovidio, J.F., & Hodson, G. (2002). Public attitudes toward immigration in the United States and Canada in response to the September 11, 2001 "Attack on America." *Analyses of Social Issues and Public Policy, 2,* 69–85.

30. Baxter, J. (2002, September 12). Asian, Arab immigrants least favoured: Canadians are more open to accepting newcomers from Europe, Latin America, and Africa. *Ottawa Citizen.*

31. Jones, J.M. (2003, July 10). *Nearly half of Americans say immigration levels should be decreased: Post-9/11 anti-immigrant effect still evident.* Retrieved August 12, 2003, from http://www.gallup.com.

32. Katrina sparks mass US aid giving. (2005, September 9). Retrieved November 4, 2005, from http://news.bbc.co.uk/2/hi/americas/4230334.stm.

33. Reitz, J.G. (2005, October 20). Canada's growing racial divide. Retrieved October 20, 2005, from http://www.thestar.com/NASApp/cs/ContentServer?pagename = thestar/Layout/Article_Type1&c = Article&cid = 1129758429421&call_pageid = 968256290204&col = 9683 50116795.

34. Population report urgent wake up call. (2005). Retrieved October 20, 2005, from http://www.thestar.com/NASApp/cs/ContentServer?pagename = thestar/Layout/Article_Type1&c = Article&cid = 1128031099368&call_pageid = 968256290204&col = 9683 50116795.

35. Cohen, F., Ogilvie, D.M., Solomon, S., Greenberg, J., & Pyszczynski, T. (2005). American roulette: The effect of reminders of death on support for George W. Bush in the 2004 presidential election. *Analyses of Social Issues and Public Policy, 5,* 177-187.

36. Landau, M.J., Solomon, S., Greenberg, J., Cohen, F., Pyszczynski, T., Arndt, J., Miller, C., Ogilvie, D.M., & Cook, A. (2004). Deliver us from evil: The effects of mortality salience and reminders of 9/11 on support for President George W. Bush. *Personality and Social Psychology Bulletin, 30,* 1136–1150.

37. Willer, R. (2004). The effects of government-issued terror warnings on presidential approval ratings. *Current Research in Social Psychology, 10.* Retrieved October 28, 2005, from http://www.uiowa.edu/~grpproc/crisp/crisp.html.

38. Esses, V.M., Dovidio, J.F., Jackson, L.M., & Armstrong, T.L. (2001). The immigration dilemma: The role of perceived group competition, ethnic prejudice, and national identity. In V.M. Esses, J.F. Dovidio, & K.L. Dion (Eds.), *Immigrants and immigration: Journal of Social Issues, 57,* 389–412.

39. Esses, V.M., Hodson, G., & Dovidio, J.F. (2003). Public attitudes toward immigrants and immigration: Determinants and policy implications. In C.M. Beach, A.G. Green, & G.R. Jeffrey (Eds.), *Canadian immigration policy for the 21st century* (pp. 507–535). Kingston, Canada: John Deutsch Institute, Queen's University.

40. Walton, D., & Kennedy, P. (2002, September 7). Muslims feel doubts linger: More Canadians are suspicious of other groups than a year ago, new poll reveals. *Globe and Mail,* A5.

41. CRIC. (2005). Public safety and civil liberties. Retrieved October 28, 2005, from http://www.cric.ca/pdf/cric_poll/portraits/portraits_2005/en_civil_liberties_tb.pdf.

42. USAToday/CNN/Gallup poll. (2001, November 5). USA TODAY/CNN/Gallup Poll results. Retrieved Oct 31, 2005, from http://www.usatoday.com/news/poll001.htm.

43. CNN/USAToday/Gallup poll. (2005, May 4). Poll: Most in U.S. say Iraq war not worthwhile. Retrieved October 31, 2005, from http://edition.cnn.com/2005/US/05/03/iraq.poll/.

44. Statistics Canada. (2003). Canada's ethnocultural portrait: The changing mosaic. Retrieved November 17, 2005, from http://www12.statcan.ca/english/census01/products/analytic/companion/etoimm/canada.cfm#proportion_foreign_born_highest.

45. Hamilton, D.L., & Gifford, R.K. (1976). Illusory correlation in interpersonal perception: A cognitive basis of stereotypic judgments. *Journal of Experimental Social Psychology, 12,* 392–407.

46. Allport G.W. (1954). *The nature of prejudice.* Reading, MA: Addison-Wesley.

47. Pettigrew, T.F., & Tropp, L.R. (2000). Does intergroup contact reduce prejudice? Recent meta-analytic findings. In S. Oskamp (Ed.), *Reducing prejudice and discrimination* (pp. 93–114. Mahwah, NJ: Erlbaum.

48. Dovidio, J.F., Gaertner, S.L., & Kawakami, K. (2003). Intergroup contact: The past, the present, and the future. *Group Processes and Intergroup Relations, 6,* 5–21.

49. Pettigrew, T.F. (1998). Intergroup contact theory. *Annual Review of Psychology, 49*, 65–85.

50. Graves, S.B. (1999). Television and prejudice reduction: When does television as a vicarious experience make a difference? *Journal of Social Issues, 55*, 707–725.

51. Gaertner S.L., & Dovidio J.F. (2000). *Reducing intergroup bias: The common in-group identity mode.* Philadelphia: Psychology Press.

52. Hall, M. (2005). Ridge reveals clashes on alerts. Retrieved October 28, 2005, from http://www.usatoday.com/news/washington/2005–05–10-ridge-alerts_x.htm.

53. Schneier, B. (2004, October). Do terror alerts work? Retrieved October 28, 2005, from http://www.schneier.com/essay-059.html.

54. Blumenthal, S. (2004, August 5). What the terror alerts really tell us. Retrieved October 28, 2005, from http://www.guardian.co.uk/comment/story/0,,1276187,00.html.

55. Vann, B. (2003, February 14). UK/USA employ fear and panic as instruments of war. Retrieved October 29, 2005, from http://www.thetruthseeker.co.uk/print.asp?ID = 518.

56. Borger, J. (2004, August 4). U.S. officials defend terror alert. Retrieved October 28, 2005, from http://www.guardian.co.uk/alqaida/story/0,,1275575,00.html.

57. Herman, E.S., & Chomsky, N. (2002). *Manufacturing consent: The political economy of the mass media.* New York: Pantheon Books.

58. Waisbord, S. (2002). Journalism, risk, and patriotism. In B. Zelizer & S. Allan (Eds.), *Journalism after September 11* (pp. 201–219). London: Routledge.

59. Dyer, G. (2004). *Future tense: The coming world order.* Toronto, Canada: McClelland & Stewart.

60. Beckett, A. (2004, October 15). The making of the terror myth. Retrieved October 28, 2005, from http://www.guardian.co.uk/alqaida/story/0,,1327905,00.html.

61. Altheide, D.L. (1997). The news media, the problem frame, and the production of fear. *Sociological Quarterly*, 38, 647–668.

CHAPTER 7

Efforts To Prevent Terrorism: Impact on Immigrant Groups

Nina K. Thomas

Introduction

All of our lives changed on September 11. No matter where we are, the world is different now. Among these differences are the ways governments' efforts to protect citizens in the post-9/11 world have had significant psychological consequences that must be balanced with the aim of protecting against potential further terrorism. To understand the psychological effect on citizens and residents of the policies and practices begun by the U.S. government in the aftermath of 9/11, we conducted a series of interviews with mental health clinicians. We also interviewed advocates for immigrants, refugees, and undocumented residents in the United States. They repeatedly noted the traumatizing impact of the government's efforts to prevent terrorism, effectively retraumatizing an already psychologically vulnerable population. This chapter reviews some of those policies and practices and considers the psychological implications for Arab American groups in particular, especially the chilling effect on First Amendment freedoms.

> As nightfall does not come all at once, neither does oppression. In both instances, there is a twilight when everything remains seemingly unchanged. And it is in such twilight that we all must be aware of change in the air—however slight—lest we become unwitting victims of the darkness.
>
> —William O. Douglas[1]

"This is how it started." So remarked more than one interviewee when asked to describe how the United States government's actions in the aftermath of September 11 had affected them. In saying, "this is how it started," they were noting the parallel to their experiences in their home countries of being made "other," marked for persecution because of their political beliefs or actions or because they belonged to a particular ethnic or religious group. Being "other," whether in the United States or in their countries of origin, they became the objects of suspicion. In extreme form they feared the possibility of genocide in the United States. The less extreme form was manifest in a more generalized fear of the consequences for speaking out against the U.S. government or, for that matter, speaking at all about government practices. One international student noted that she felt she should "just shut up," as though she were "not allowed to talk at all." She explained that she and her fellow international students were effectively gagged by the new government restrictions on their movements and the threat of detention or worse.

More than one clinician interviewed noted the heightened fearfulness of their clients in the aftermath of September 11. They cited marked increases in symptoms of major depression and of post-traumatic stress disorder (insomnia, isolation, hypervigilance). One refugee counselor remarked that her patients had been speaking much more softly since that date, almost as though they were afraid of being heard. Another telling comment made by a refugee counselor was "nobody protested," referring to a sense of abandonment by the larger population's capitulation to the highly restrictive policies begun in the wake of the attacks. (We discuss this relative silence later in this chapter.)

Government Practices and Policies after September 11

Immediately following the September 11 attacks, the U.S. government arrested approximately 1,200 Arab, Muslim, and South Asian men, 762 of whom the administration detained on immigration violations. Detention meant holding them in Immigration and Naturalization Service (INS) facilities, in some cases in maximum-security prisons. Those the administration labeled security concerns were kept under highly restrictive "lock down," subject to severe restraint, and suffered "exceptionally harsh treatment"[2] at times being held in conditions noted in the Inspector General's investigation as "abusive."[3] The average time from arrest of a September 11 detainee to clearance by the Federal

Bureau of Investigation (FBI) was 80 days, despite directives that called for clearance within 48 hours. For more than a quarter of the 762 detainees, investigations took longer than three months.[4] By June 2002, the administration had deported all but 74 of them.[5]

In November 2001, then Attorney General Ashcroft identified another 5,000 mostly "Middle Eastern" men for questioning. Repeatedly since then the FBI has announced "volunteer" interviewing of Arabs and Muslims. During the elections in November 2004, the FBI announced a plan to interview members of the Arab and Muslim communities. At the time of these elections, the administration had yet to link any of the men questioned to terrorism.

In September 2002, the National Security Entry-Exit Registration System, more commonly known as Special Registration, required noncitizen, nonimmigrant males over the age of 16 from 25 predominantly Muslim countries to register in person with the newly formed Department of Homeland Security's Bureau of Citizenship and Immigration Services. These men check in annually with the government. Hundreds of arrests and detentions have followed from the registration requirement, most for minor visa violations. Repeatedly, reports from immigrant advocates note that INS employees provide conflicting or inaccurate information regarding reporting and filing requirements. Many, if not most, of those arrested and held awaiting deportation had applications pending for permanent residency status. According to Justice Department officials, more than 1 in 10 men under the Special Registration face possible deportation. On May 11, 2003, the Special Registration program had 85,581 men registered; 13,153 were ordered to appear in immigration court; 2,761 were detained; 158 were still in detention; and none were charged with terrorism-related crimes.[6]

In October 2001, Congress passed the United and Strengthening America by Providing Appropriate Tools Required to Intercept and Obstruct Terrorism (USA PATRIOT) Act with virtually no debate, granting the U.S. government new powers to detain noncitizens without charge. This Act authorized Attorney General John Ashcroft to certify any noncitizen as a "suspected terrorist," expanded the definition of terrorist activity, and permitted detention without charges for seven days.

In June 2003, the Migration Policy Institute (a nonprofit, nonpartisan, think tank) issued a policy report titled "America's Challenge: Domestic Security, Civil Liberties and National Unity after September 11."[7] The researchers compiled data profiles of 406 detainees, drawn from media accounts and existing research. They also interviewed detainees, their attorneys, community leaders, policymakers, and government officials across the United States over an 18-month period. These data continue to be the most comprehensive on the individuals detained in the wake of September 11, their experiences, and the government's post–September 11 immigration measures. The advisory panel for the report includes former Manhattan U.S. Attorney Mary Jo White; Vincent Cannistraro, former head of Counterterrorism Operations and Analysis for the CIA; former INS Commissioner James Ziglar; and Doris Meissner, commissioner of the INS during the Clinton Administration. Some of the findings of the investigation are:

- All but 2 of the 19 hijackers had "clean" records (no criminal records and no known terrorist connections) and would probably be admitted in the United States today.
- Most individuals were detained because of so-called profiling by ordinary citizens—for example, a tip from a neighbor who notified the FBI when a box with Arabic writing on it was delivered.
- Not one major terrorism success has come from any of the immigration measures. Any successes are the result of traditional intelligence work.
- Immigration measures and antiterrorism policies effectively alienate the Muslim and Arab communities whose cooperation law enforcement needs most in the war on terror.
- Many Muslims and Arabs have grown more fearful of law enforcement as the administration has detained and deported more people.
- By targeting and alienating Muslim and Arab communities, immigration actions since September 11 have deepened the perception abroad that the United States is anti-Muslim and that its democratic values and principles are hypocritical.
- Immigrants are less likely to report crimes, come forward as witnesses, and provide intelligence information out of fear that they or their families risk detention or deportation.

The post-9/11 measures—the summary arrest and detention of suspected terrorists without access to family or advocates on their behalf[8]—also include severe restrictions on the numbers of refugees accorded entry visas into the United States. Although Congress authorized entry for 70,000 refugees in 2002 (down from 90,000 in 2000), the time required for the heightened security clearances of those held in refugee camps around the world has meant that the administration has granted entry to fewer than 30,000 refugees in any year since 2001.[9] The consequences of such increased restrictions are that many families remain separated for extended periods. This means that children remain apart from their parents, at times languishing in dangerous and debilitating circumstances in countries abroad.

Also, international students have been subjected to significantly heightened scrutiny and restrictions. They have not been allowed to travel outside the state in which they are residents without notifying their International Student Advisor. They must always have their immigration documents with them. If they are found without their papers they can be held in detention. A report by the Arab American Institute found that many Arab international students in the United States on student visas returned home after being singled out for questioning by the FBI in the wake of September 11.[10] These efforts to single out ethnic groups in the wake of 9/11 have reduced the preference for an American education among Arab elites.[11]

Psychological Consequences of Present Antiterrorist Practices

The refugees, asylum-seekers, and undocumented people who are the subject of this chapter are, in some cases, multiply traumatized by the conditions that propelled their coming to the United States. Typically, they have fled persecutory regimes; they may have survived torture, rape, the murder or mutilation of loved ones, and the loss of property and homeland. Besides the pre-immigration stressors they experienced, they face post-immigration ones involving adjustment to an alien culture and environment. Asylum-seekers are in a problematic legal system and are vulnerable, particularly under the terms of the PATRIOT Act, to arbitrary detention without parole for indefinite periods.

A well-researched report by Physicians for Human Rights[12] on the health of asylum-seekers in detention notes the significant incidence of symptoms of depression (86 percent of detainees), anxiety (77 percent), and post-traumatic stress disorder (50 percent). Of particular note is that: "while more than half (58 percent) of the asylum seekers interviewed reported having poor psychological health at the time that they fled their country, 70 percent stated that overall their mental health had worsened substantially while in detention." The report goes on to say that "approximately one quarter of the study participants reported suicidal thoughts while in detention. Two individuals reported having attempted suicide. Even those who won release were burdened with continued symptoms from their INS imprisonment."

Several refugee counselors interviewed for this chapter remarked on the resurgence of symptoms of post-traumatic stress disorder and major depression evidenced by their clients due to the heightened security procedures that were begun after September 11. Many who had been stable before manifested an intensification of depressive symptoms and avoidance, insomnia, and crying. Despite this resurgence, using a psychiatric diagnosis given such demonstrably threatening *real* circumstances is problematic.[13]

Although government antiterrorist practices are unlikely to be the sole cause of their difficulties, the immigrants and refugees did become increasingly isolated, reluctant to leave their homes or narrowly circumscribed communities. Most of them live in economically disadvantaged areas, typically subject to high levels of crime. In the post-9/11 environment, many became even more isolated within their homes, being afraid of going out lest they re-experience the traumas that had occasioned their flight to the United States. One refugee worker likened their isolation to "internal internment, just without the government having to build camps and feed people, because of the fear they have of simply being visibly Muslim in post 9/11 America" (Goldman, personal communication, June 26, 2003).

Hate Crimes

In the aftermath of September 11, immigrants identified as Middle Eastern or Arab (this includes South Asian immigrants as well, because Americans often mistake Hindu Sikhs wearing turbans to be Arabs) faced an increase in the number of hate crimes and other racial violence. The frequency of such incidents increased significantly after international events such as the Achille Lauro hijacking, the Oklahoma City bombing, and the Gulf War. Following September 11, incidents occurred that "were unique in their severity and extent."[14] Arab and Muslim groups reported more than two thousand September 11–related backlash incidents. The Federal Bureau of Investigation reported a 17-fold increase in anti-Muslim crimes nationwide during 2001 compared with the preceding year. A Council on American Islamic Relations poll of 945 Muslim Americans on how September 11 and its aftermath had affected them, found that 48 percent reported that their lives had changed for the worse.[15]

Several clinicians noted ongoing racism toward Middle Easterners marked by an increase in hate crimes, particularly in schools. "Schools have become a very difficult place for many of our clients," remarked one.[16] Schools in several major urban areas reported an increase in the incidence of hate and violence crimes against students perceived as being Muslim. The choice to wear a hijab, for example, did more than express religious identity. It also increased the risk of being subjected to violence.

Many community groups, private charities, faith groups, and government authorities responded with admirable speed to the incidents of racial violence, reflecting significant efforts to establish and nourish relationships with the Arab American community. Even so, immigrants were faced with a confusing scenario. Some local officials responded with compassion to such crimes. Other officials, identifying these immigrants as "suspicious" and "potential terrorists", targeted them with arrests, detentions, deportations, and registration procedures. Whole communities were described as "devastated" by these procedures.[17] In the face of such a climate, creating an atmosphere of anxiety and fear, feeling optimistic about personal safety would be hard for anyone.

Assault on Identity

A patient of mine, citing the political conflict between the government of her country of origin and the United States, feared that her accent and demeanor identify her as being from that country. When confronted with the question: "where are you from?" she is fearful of responding, not knowing the political leanings of the person asking. She noted that the stereotypes by which her ethnic group is identified are not, in substance, so far off from how she knows her own group members. She found herself identifying with the despised aspects of her group. What she describes is typical of the pattern and effect of racism in the United States and elsewhere, including the disavowal of those aspects of the self that are stereotyped. The policies of the U.S. government that promote suspicion of others identified as "different," "other," and "Arab" or "Middle Eastern," actively support this disavowal.

Loss of Safety, Loss of Hope

"If I told you I was going to subject you to terrible things, who knows for how long, perhaps it will last forever, perhaps you'll die here, the situation of uncertainty and the infinity of time, without limits, is very disorganizing mentally."[18]

Hollander was writing here about the situation in Argentina during the Dirty War. Guards in the detention centers for September 11 detainees made similar remarks. In her review of the Inspector General's Report, Wang found that: "[a]ccording to detainees, the verbal abuse included taunts such as 'Bin Laden Junior' or threats such as 'you're going to die here,' 'you're never going to get out of here,' and 'you will be here for 20–25 years like the Cuban people.'"[19] Descriptions of such retraumatizing of refugees because of the post-9/11 practices came up often while gathering data for this report.

Even more abusive was the practice by some authorities at detention centers of denying detainees access to family, lawyers, or other advocates.[20] The Inspector General's investigative report noted that people asking about a specific September 11 detainee were "frequently and mistakenly told" they were not holding that detainee when the opposite was true. Such practices uncannily repeat those to which many refugees were subjected in their home countries. Reportedly, Secretary of State Warren Christopher remarked: "I'll never forget going to Argentina and seeing the mothers marching in the streets asking for the names of those being held by the government. We must be very careful in this country about taking people into custody without revealing their names."[21]

Thus, precisely the same climate of fear they fled in their native lands, was re-created by the U.S. government, one in which they had invested so much hope. The same traumatic conditions that the Physicians for Human Rights report[22] found to be prevalent in the circumstances of detention for many asylum-seekers existed for those detained under the conditions post-9/11. Repeatedly, too, the comment was heard: "there is no place safe any more." America had been a goal of enormous hope: "there are laws," one Burmese asylum-seeker said; "there was a place in the world where you could be safe." The violence of 9/11 shattered that dream for many, not only because terrorism now could occur on American soil but because the response to terrorism could involve many practices undertaken by repressive regimes asylum-seekers had sought to escape.

Asylum-seekers and undocumented people are psychologically an extremely vulnerable population. Being subject to arbitrary processes over which they have little control leaves people feeling helpless and hopeless, promoting an intensification of depressive symptoms. (Refugees from war-torn countries are at much higher risk of physical and psychological health problems than immigrants without a trauma history.)[23] The continuous trauma to which detainees were subjected by virtue of their detention compounded their preexisting traumas. Some chose to return to the countries in which they were subjected to repressive practices rather than to remain in conditions of detention with an uncertain future in the United States.

Positive Outcomes

Even as the situations detailed above paint a bleak picture of the circumstances facing asylum-seekers, refugees, and undocumented persons in post-9/11 America, there have been positive developments as well. Kamel (personal communication) reports that among the immigrants, suffering has promoted an impetus to political action and alliances across communities that have not previously existed. We see some of this in the coordination of efforts of political and faith-based groups, and ethnic associations to bridge the differences among them in creating, for example, Grassroots America Defends the Bill of Rights.

Summary

Ervin Staub's work[24] on the origins of evil and genocide notes that a significant factor lies in the failure of bystanders to oppose reprehensible acts. During the periods of the political repressive regimes in South America, the rationale used to justify the actions of the governments in, for example, Uruguay, Chile, and Argentina was: *Habra hecho algo* (he must have done something). Thus they explained the disappearance of tens of thousands of people. The fear of capricious action by the state propelled and continues to propel people neither to see nor oppose what is going on around them. Interviewees commented that the current practices in the United States effectively replicated for them being singled out for persecution at home. Several noted feeling abandoned by the inaction of the larger population. They described the wide-scale detentions, arrests, and threats of deportation as creating an environment in which they have felt "gagged" from speaking out. Many have been subjected to an atmosphere of hate in which they are identified as the objects of suspicion for potential terrorist threats. Those who have been arrested or detained leave many more thousands of children and families with a loss of income, thereby increasing the economic vulnerability of many households.

Many children who are U.S. citizens by virtue of their birth in the United States, now face deportation because one or both parents has a discrepancy in his or her papers. (As described earlier, many have been subject to detention because of missed deadlines, inaccurate instructions by one or another arm of the immigration service, or some other minor action with major impact.)

The focus of this chapter has been on how the efforts to prevent terrorism in the United States have affected immigrant communities even though the term "immigrant" does not accurately describe the population being addressed. An *immigrant* connotes one who voluntarily chooses to move, typically pursuing a dream. My attention has been on those for whom coming to the United States was occasioned by the trauma of war, genocide, or political repression. They have experienced multiple dislocations, often witnessed inhuman actions against their loved ones, been subjected to torture, and imperiled by starvation and war. They are refugees, asylum-seekers, and undocumented individuals. The psychological circumstances for these groups are very different and include their immigration status; the state of their social and familial supports; the situations in their native country; the family, if any, they have left behind; and the circumstances of U.S. foreign policy toward their country of origin. Their individual psychology is only part of the story.[25] What unites many people I have described is their experience of profound loss in coming to the United States. Trauma compounds the loss caused by the policies and practices undertaken in the aftermath of the September 11 terrorist attacks in the United States.

Recommendations

The United States has a record of ill treatment of immigrant populations during other historical periods of international threat. Our leaders have come to regret and later to apologize for the internment of Japanese Americans and Italian Americans during the Second World War (though not for German Americans during the same period). Again, ethnic origin is compromising the civil liberties of many. Can any of us be secure when that happens to others in our country?

To date, no legislation passed or immigration measure begun since September 11 has aided in the capture of a terrorist. Any antiterrorism success has been the result of traditional intelligence work.[26] The first recommendation from the present study is that government efforts at identifying terrorist threats need to be disentangled from ethnicity. Second, the work on which the present chapter rests is a preliminary examination of issues that demand more substantive consideration from many vantage points, including considerations of public health and policy. The increased isolation, alienation, and experience of discrimination of Arab American, Muslim American, or other Middle Eastern and South Asian communities have significant repercussions for their physical and mental health.[27] Research that studies whether such communities are more isolated now than prior to 9/11, whether community members feel more or less identified with American ideals or values, and the physical and psychological symptomatology in these communities could be valuable in better articulating the consequences of political decision making. Such information is necessary for action that furthers a reparative process. In that regard, government and foundations have a role to play in building on the work of faith-based and voluntary groups' bridges to Arab and South Asian communities. That there may be significant distrust of the dominant culture's intent in those communities would be understandable. And yet, there is a great potential for increasing understanding and cross-communication between these groups. Government efforts to support antibias programs in education, corporations, and the legal system are worth further study, development, and implementation.

Finally, it is difficult to see how the recourse to revenge against immigrant groups, particularly Arab and Muslim, as the current immigration policies wreak, can yield greater security. Too often in the past we have sacrificed democracy in the name of security. When that happens we are left with neither democracy nor security.

Conclusion

While everyone has been influenced by September 11, immigrant and refugee groups have been profoundly affected. The practices of the U.S. government in the aftermath of September 11 have included detentions, interrogations, deportations, and the confiscation of property, directly and indirectly causing a state of fear and a sense of isolation. Moreover, the increase of hate crimes directed against people of Arab and Middle Eastern descent has intensified their communities' sense of anxiety and feelings of "otherness." The basis for some of the action against individuals has been in government-sanctioned regulations or practices, such as detention center personnel denying detainees access to lawyers and family or authorities threatening detainees with verbal abuse. Such government-endorsed practices have contributed to feelings of betrayal and a loss of safety and hope among immigrant, refugee, and undocumented communities. Yet, despite many negative consequences for immigrant, refugee, and undocumented populations arising in the aftermath of September 11, there have also been some positive developments. Alliances across communities have formed, and the attack on immigrants has motivated many to political action. Recommendations are offered to repair the bonds among groups.

Acknowledgments

The author would like to extend sincere thanks for the commentary, editorial assistance, and support in preparing this chapter extended by, among others, Devon Alisa Abdallah of the Arab American Community Coalition and to Amal Sedky Winter of the Arab American Institute, Washington DC. Their generous and thoughtful reading of this work was enormously helpful. Responsibility for what is written rests with the author.

Notes

1. Nat Hentoff, *The War on the Bill of Rights and the Gathering Resistance* (New York: Seven Stories Press, 2003).
2. Muzaffar A. Chishti, Doris Meissner, Demetrios G. Papademetriou, Jay Peterzell, Michael J. Wishnie, and Stephen W. Yale-Loehr. *America's Challenge: Domestic Security, Civil Liberties, and National Unity after September 11* (Washington, DC: Migration Policy Institute, 2003).
3. Office of the Inspector General, U.S. Department of Justice. *The September 11 Detainees: A Review of the Treatment of Aliens Held on Immigration Charges in Connection with the Investigation of the September 11 Attacks.* (Washington, DC: Department of Justice, 2003). Retrieved February 16, 2004 from http://www.usdoj.gov/oig/speial/0306/index.htm.
4. Office of the Inspector General; A. Tova Wang, *The Devil's in the Details: Overlooked Highlights of the Report on 9/11 Detainees* (New York: Century Foundation, 2003).
5. Physicians for Human Rights and Bellevue/NYU Program for Survivors of Torture. *From Persecution to Prison: The Health Consequences of Detention for Asylum Seekers* (Boston: Physicians for Human Rights, 2003).

6. Arab-American Family Support Center, July 15, 2003.

7. Chishti et al.

8. Ibid.

9. United States Department of Homeland Security. Yearbook of Immigration Statistics, Office of Immigration Statistics, 2006. Retrieved May 12, 2006 from http://www.uscis.gov/graphics/shared/statistics/index.htm.

10. Arab American Institute. Civil rights issues in the wake of September 11. In *Healing the nation: The Arab-American experience after September 11* (Washington, DC: Arab American Institute, 2002).

11. Arab American Institute. Delays caused by new visa regulations are behind drop in number of Arab students in the United States. Arab-American Institute, 2002. Retrieved November 18, 2005, from http://www.aaiusa.org/PDF/visa_rpt.pdf.

12. Physicians for Human Rights and Bellevue/NYU Program for Survivors of Torture.

13. Maureen Katz, *Life Gets Harder for Political Trauma Victims and for Those Who Treat Them.* Unpublished manuscript, Berkley, CA, 2003.

14. Hikmet Jamil, Julie Hakim-Larson, Mohammed Farrog, Jalib Kafaji, Laith H. Jamil, and Issa Duqum. "We Are Not the Enemy": Hate Crimes against Arabs, Muslims, and Those Perceived To Be Arab or Muslim after September 11. *Human Rights Watch* 14, no. 6(G) (November 2002).

15. Council on American Islamic Relations. *Poll: Majority of U.S. Muslims Suffered Post September 11 Bias* (Washington, DC, August 21, 2002).

16. Joan Liautaud. Personal communication. October 21, 2003.

17. Dearborn, Michigan, has the largest concentration of Arab American citizens in the United States, approximately 30,000. The more than 13,000 men ordered to appear in Immigration Court as a result of the Special Registration Program amounts to the equivalent of nearly half the Arab American population of Dearborn.

18. Nancy Caro Hollander. *Love in a Time of Hate: Liberation Psychology in Latin America* (New Brunswick, NJ: Rutgers University Press, 1997).

19. Wang.

20. Chishti et al.; Office of the Inspector General.

21. Adam Liptak, Neil A. Lewis, and Benjamin Weiser. "After Sept. 11, a Legal Battle over Limits of Civil Liberty," *New York Times*, August 4, 2002, 1.

22. Physicians for Human Rights and Bellevue/NYU Program for Survivors of Torture.

23. Hikmet Jamil, Julie Hakim-Larson, Mohammed Farrag, Talib Kafaji, Issa Duqum, and Laith H. Jamil. "A Retrospective Study of Arab American Mental Health Clients: Trauma and the Iraqi Refugees." *American Journal of Orthopsychiatry* 72(3) (2002b), 355–361.

24. Ervin Staub, *The Roots of Evil: The Origins of Genocide and Other Group Violence* (New York: Cambridge University Press, 1989).

25. R. Kamel, personal communication, October 21, 2003. Kamel cautions against focusing too heavily on the individual psychology of the immigrant as ignoring the geopolitical realities involved in the situations in the person's home country.

26. Chishti et al.

27. Jamil et al.; Physicians for Human Rights and Bellevue/NYU Program for Survivors of Torture.

CHAPTER 8

Psychological Effects of the Virtual Media Coverage of the Iraq War: A Postmodern Humanistic Perspective

Ilene A. Serlin

Introduction

We usually describe the psychological impact of war in terms of trauma and loss. The media through which news of that shock and loss come is not generally considered a significant psychological influence. However, the war in Iraq introduced a new dimension in war reporting. With round-the-clock and repetitive coverage on major cable networks, the war entered the homes of most Americans at all times and in all places, public and private. The use of embedded reporters and lack of visible blood or death gave the news coverage an immediate and sanitized quality. Minimizing the horrors of the war began inside the White House, where the president's communications advisers devised a strategy to encourage supportive news coverage of the fight against terrorism after September 11, 2001. The idea, they explained to reporters at the time, was to counter charges of U.S. imperialism by generating accounts of the liberation and rebuilding of Afghanistan and Iraq ("Under Bush Administration," 2005). Scenes were staged and reporters were both observers and participants, blurring lines between reality and fantasy. War scenes were repeated in a continuous loop of fragmented images without a coherent narrative or chance to digest them.

The last of the generation of news anchors like Peter Jennings and Dan Rather, who gave Americans a sense of trustworthy coverage and reality, is disappearing. In their place, some of the reporters of the war in Iraq were hired from private advertising agencies. Government agencies also produced news reports that used actors like Karen Ryan to conduct "interviews" with senior administration officials with prescripted questions and answers and no other viewpoints. The changing stories about why we should be in the war, the use of advertising to spin and manipulate reality, and multiple perspectives of this war are characteristic of the shifting realities of a postmodern world in which things are not what they seem (Gergen, 1991; Laing, 1965).

Very little is known about the impact of this new media coverage on the imagination and psyche of Americans. How can we understand impact of the government's unique coverage of the war on terrorism on Americans and what it means to be human? The goal of this chapter is to examine the new role of the media and its impact on psychological issues such as personal integrity, identity, sense of security, reality, trust, and fear.

The impact of the media is explored through interviews with three subjects who were experiencing psychological distress at the beginning of the war in Iraq. I compare their symptoms with reports from the media at that time and suggest how psychologists can better understand the influence of environmental and cultural factors such as media and politics on the psyches of their clients. I recommend that, when appropriate, psychologists be trained to identify and work with such stressors.

The three case histories illustrate psychological themes that emerged during the days preceding and following the beginning of the war in Iraq. Three veterans in psychotherapy with me were interviewed using the narrative/archival research method (Josselson & Lieblich, 1993; McAdams, 1995; Sarbin, 1986; Surlin, 2005). They were Vietnam War veterans who experienced symptoms of post-traumatic stress and depression as the war in Iraq began. I interviewed them twice: once at the beginning of the war and again one year later. I asked open-ended questions about their symptoms and experiences. Since the war was so immediate, it was already present in our sessions. For example, one veteran who was late to a session because an antiwar demonstration blocked the streets came in expressing anger and frustration about the war.

The interviews were coded, and names were changed to protect confidentiality. I read the interviews once to get a general sense of the session, then several times more until clusters of words and phrases relevant to the veterans' psychological health emerged. Phrases that occurred many times were identified in bold type and studied for patterns. These words, phrases, and patterns showed significant amounts of the following symptoms in response to the media coverage of the war: cynicism, distrust, fear, breakdown of reality testing, helplessness/hopelessness, and paranoia. I compare these symptoms with themes from daily newspaper reports in this chapter. Understanding the impact of the media on these veterans will help prepare health professionals to address the current effects of the media's coverage of the Iraq War on American veterans' post-traumatic stress disorder (PTSD) and the effects of future political events on more general issues of mental health.

The Postmodern War: A Perspective from Humanistic Psychology

Why is this a postmodern war? The coverage of the Iraq War is different from past wars in that it mixes the roles of spectator and participant, objective and subjective. This coverage introduces spin and advertising to sell the war on terrorism. Images of the war serve political purposes through an appeal to American values such as the Rumsfeld doctrine that speed and efficiency wins victories over our enemies. Other images show changing rationales for the war in Iraq, decisions marked by unilateralism and secrecy and a sanitized high-technological relationship among combatants. The irony, as noted by Frank Rich, op-ed columnist of the *New York Times*, is that: "Conservatives, who supposedly deplore post-modernism, are now welcoming in a brave new world in which it's a given that there can be non-empirical reality in news, only the reality you want to hear (or they want you to hear)" (Rich, 2005a).

The administration is spinning reality to manage perception consciously. The chief Pentagon spokesperson, Lawrence Di Rita, was quoted as saying, "In the battle of perception management . . . our job is not perception management, but to counter the enemy's perception management." A secret program by Rumsfeld called Information Operations Roadmap was set up to "advance the goal of information operations as a core military competency" (Shanker & Schmitt, 2004). Putting journalists on the administration payroll and hiring an outside public relations firm to create an enemies list of ranking news organizations based on their support for administration policies was documented in the July 2002 Downing Street memos published in the *London Sunday Times* on May 1, 2005. These memos describe how Tony Blair learned about White House efforts to change what was called "the great Watergate cover-up of 2005" (Rich, 2005b). Even the weather reports, used to prove that global warming was not happening, were false. Records from the Environmental Protection Agency show that the Bush administration paid the Weather Channel $40,000 to produce videos about climate change ("Weather Channel," 2005). President Bush told a reporter: "We're an empire now, and when we act, we create our own reality" (Danner, 2005, p. 53).

How does this creation of arbitrary realities affect the psyche? Most basic to the psyche are existential values of security, identity, truth, integrity, and meaning (Bruner, 1986; Bugental, 1989; Frankl, 1959; May, 1975; Murray, 1938). Some people living in a created postmodern reality may experience disorientation, changed identities (deRivera & Sarbin, 1998; Smith, 2002; Turkle, 1995), and an inability to trust their perceptions (Goldberg, 2000). They may feel dehumanized and not know who they are (Fromm, 1941; Serlin, 1995, 2002; Serlin & Cannon, 2004; Shafer, 1992). They may experience a form of disembodiment unique to the age of cyberspace. Philosopher Herbert Dreyfus observed: "It is easy to see the attraction of completing human evolution by leaving behind the animal bodies in which our linguistic and cultural identities are now imprisoned. Who wouldn't wish to become a disembodied being who could be anywhere in the universe and make backup copies of himself to avoid injury and death?" (Dreyfus, 2001, p. 4). In his book, *On the Internet*, Dreyfus warned: "we should remain open to the possibility that, when we enter cyberspace and leave behind our animal-shaped, emotional, intuitive, situated, vulnerable, embodied selves, and thereby gain a remarkable new freedom never before available to human beings, we might, at the same time, necessarily lose some of our crucial capacities: our ability to make sense of things so as to distinguish the relevant from the irrelevant, our sense of the seriousness of success and failure that is necessary for learning, and our need to get a maximum grip on the world that gives us our sense of the reality of things" (Dreyfus, 2001, pp. 6–7).

Philosopher David Abrams notes the absence of relationship in a world that leaves out the senses: "Today we participate almost exclusively with other humans and with our own human-made technologies. It is a precarious situation, given our age-old reciprocity with the many-voiced landscape. We still *need* that which is other than ourselves and our own creations. The simple premise of this book is that we are human only in contact, and conviviality, with what is not human" (p. ix).

Finally, linguist George Lakoff supports the importance of embodied experience to make sense of the world. He describes three main tenets of cognitive science as: "The mind is inherently embodied. Thought is mostly unconscious. Abstract concepts are largely metaphorical" (Lakoff & Johnson, 1999, p. 3). Even rationality requires embodiment, "Reason is not disembodied, as the tradition has largely held, but arises from the nature of our brains, bodies, and bodily experience. . . . Reason is not dispassionate, but emotionally engaged" (Lakoff & Johnson, 1999, p. 4). Thus, we need contact with the world of experience even to reason well.

The experience of dehumanization from created reality may present psychological symptoms of anxiety, depression, loss of identity, derealization, and depersonalization. These are what humanistic psychologist Abraham Maslow called metapathologies (Maslow, 1962) that distort the most fundamental sense of what it means to be human. Coping with these stresses may require a new understanding of what it means to be human that can help us develop a new kind of resiliency (Antonovsky, 1979; Maddi, 1994).

To better understand the stressors created by the war in Iraq, let's listen to the words of the veterans in the following case stories. Their actual words are in quotation marks, and words that describe psychological symptoms are in bold type. Words from media reports from the war later in the chapter are also in bold type to identify similar themes and experiences to which these veterans were exposed.

Case Vignettes

Frank 2003

Frank reports sleep disturbances, early morning awakenings. He asks what triggers these symptoms again. What Frank fears the most is **losing control,** not being able to control his emotions, especially anger, in public. He remembers experiencing surges of anger during the Vietnam War, pounding the table if something didn't come out right. What is he **angry** about now? He is angry that "20 year olds are dying," angry at "the government and society for putting us through this. All that killing and maiming; for what?" At his discharge in 1969, Frank came back and didn't fit into society. He has had a **jaded** view of society ever since. He is **bitter.** The "anger and resentment" he feels now is about war's **depersonalization:** "We're facing the human part now." Frank finds it "distressing to take the human part out of war. The Germans had the perfect machine—but it was the people who were behind those machines who stopped fighting. In Vietnam there was no purpose to being there." He remembers "a suspected Viet Cong, a young woman, shot through the pelvis—the faces of the enemy. An old man shot through the lungs." It "felt **unreal.**" He "didn't feel fear; it seemed a cliché." The message he heard "loud and clear" was: "**The individual is expendable.**" At this point, he feels that his life and thoughts are very different from those of "most people," bringing him "**isolation and loneliness.**" The war in Iraq brought back these thoughts because, "like the Vietcong, because they're Iraqi their lives are not worth as much. And we don't understand why they don't like us. It seems that we are **repeating all the same things over again.** All of this is hyperbole."

Memories return. Frank writes:

> We're in Danang Harbor. Beautiful deep blue water—I watch the sun come up—small Vietnamese fishing boats silhouetted against the rising sun. It's now 10 A.M.—I watch as the life—small, funny looking boat with square bow plowing its way toward the ship—seems out of place in this beautiful harbor. It pulls alongside and there arranged in neat rows—15 body bags. Everyone on deck stops what they're doing and stares. One by one they hoist them onto the deck. Now they're lined up on the deck—I walk up to one of the bags to check the tag—unable to identify neatly typed name. Bags are hoisted down to the morgue—Next!!! . . . Next. After four years—you're done—thanks. After four years of college, you're given a diploma and you have years of wonderful memories; memories that will be shared for many years. After four years of service, you're given a discharge and a head full of **memories that may not be shared.** You've been **trained not to feel,** yet every day those feelings of mourning are with you; those memories of the dead, dying and the suffering. And now after all these years—the feelings grow more intense.

He has been **numb** and now images and feelings tumble back.

Frank 2005

In a follow-up interview in 2005, Frank said:

> Neither of us can remember how long the war has been going. . . . it has been a success because of the election . . . all public relations. They report the dead, but none of the wounded. Some of them are going to be paraplegic, but no one knows how many. It will be staggering. . . . They learned from the war in Vietnam that you cannot let reporters go anywhere they want, like in the famous photo that turned public opinion against Vietnam.

Frank was angry that the war was "no longer on people's minds," that there were "two values—American life and Iraqi life—no wonder they hate us." He knew from his own experience returning from Vietnam that:

> You're not the same person you were when you left. People who are the closest—wives and husbands—will notice it the most. . . . How do you tell someone you've been close to, tender with, that you've killed someone? . . . The glory isn't there—it all seems so hollow . . . all this seems **unreal** . . . it's a new reality. . . . You'll find yourself **isolated**—there's no one to turn to. You'll be **overwhelmed** by thoughts of the past year, yet if you try to explain these thoughts and feelings, you'll be met with stares of disbelief, which will make you withdraw from your friends and family even more. By now you'll find all the happiness and joy you felt when you first returned turn to **disappointment** and even **anger**. . . . I've become very **jaded;** there are more people in Washington whose reputations are at stake. It brought democracy to Iraq, yes, but who paid?

Frank recommended:

> Now's the time to reach out and find someone to talk to. Don't bury yourself into your past. Force yourself to talk about your experiences. Find someone you can trust. Most of all, don't expect people to fully understand what you've been through. You've been through one of the most personal journeys that few people experience. Talk about it. Don't withdraw, that makes things worse. Trust people.

He found it "helpful talking about it in sessions" because it brought "some perspective." "It helps me understand my own feelings about it." As a photographer and birdwatcher, Frank found it healing to "get absorbed" in nature and "create healing images" to counteract those in the media.

Commentary

Frank struggles deeply with the **lack of meaning** in his life, and he sees life as somewhat **surreal and absurd.** He saw that "through war how **human life has so much less value . . . war changes the meaning of life.**" As the war in Iraq triggered memories of a past war, psychotherapy enabled him to talk and work through his anger and cynicism. He describes himself as currently "being more open" to life and its daily pleasures. By confronting his mortality and aloneness, he became less dependent on authority and more self-reliant. He chose to live, and affirmed his own set of values that now anchor and guide him.

Mike 2003

Mike's dramatic response in 2003 to the media coverage of the war in Iraq illustrated its impact:

> The whole thing is orchestrated by some very professional people. Shock and awe showed the superiority of the American forces over selected shots, while destruction was being rained on Iraq. It was almost cartoonish—it avoided showing anyone being directly killed. It was like a theatrical production. It was good theatrics when Bush spoke from the aircraft carrier. I almost threw up. . . . He is master of the art of television; he has embedded people everywhere **(cynicism).** There is someone somewhere in the White House who cranks out these things. The aims of the war changed from being about chemical and biological weapons to freeing the Iraqis, similar to the military in Vietnam. They are blaming the looters and there is always a finger being pointed at someone else. There is not a single word that I believe [**distrust**].
>
> It's **woken me from my lethargy**. . . . Makes me feel a little **ashamed** of being American. I am **fearful** of foreign travel—there is now a vast unknown about your own personal future that pops up. Where is the next target? What's going to happen? [**insecurity**] . . . . People will believe what they see because it's on television" [**reality**].
>
> As the evidence pyramids, I am more than ever convinced that the Bush administration is the most **corrupt,** inept political machine *ever* constructed! I am quickly becoming quite **fearful** of the known and unknown **conspiracies** being concocted at 1600 Pennsylvania Ave.

Mike 2005

Two years later, Mike remained bitter. He said: "As far as the war is concerned, it is highly predictable. . . . Bush has no concept of the average person. He is out of touch with the common, everyday person . . . . Those airplanes that crashed the World Trade Towers were a disaster, but now what they've done is to create a whole new business on airport security, like in the *Wag the Dog* movie." He was afraid: "We have now the right to invade any country. Bush is issuing warnings to China, Syria, Turkey, Iran and Iraq." He thinks that we need "someone to **hate;** brings back the problem of the Jews in Germany."

Mike was still distrustful of the government: "They have a lot of hidden agendas, I don't know what they are. . . . The insurgents are getting worse, it was supposed to be over in a year. We don't want it to end—we are making lots of money." There will be "more of the same in the future, if not worse, because they will be very desperate to maintain the ideology and Shell, Texaco, Phillips are all lined up behind this country waiting for oil to drip in." So are "Bechtel, the construction companies." He reports that his own anger is less: "Day by day I'm getting used to the same song and dance. I have much fewer years ahead of me than behind. I've even thought of Iraq—what would I do? Nothing." He reports a feeling of **helplessness** and **meaninglessness:** "My only complaint is I'm a U.S. citizen sitting here with nothing to do except complain and I don't like to complain."

Commentary

As the war and media coverage intensified, so did Mike's symptoms of **depression, anger, fear,** and **hopelessness.** His report was noteworthy for its expression of **distrust** of the media and the government and feelings of **paranoia** and **powerlessness.** Bringing the political discussion into the therapeutic conversation, however, allowed him to release some of his fear and anger. Therapeutically, it validated his sense of himself as an intelligent human being whose voice mattered.

Charles 2003

Charles focused on the effects of the media coverage and reported feeling **angry, distrustful,** and **depressed.** He noted:

> CNN is almost like the world's news. Everyone tends to watch. What I thought was one of the more **surreal** things was the video phones—everything had a green tint to it. All you'd see at the beginning were explosions in the distance, an eerie color green; a lot of faraway shots; really a **video game**—"Ooh, we blew that up"—almost as though all the other video games prepared us for this.
>
> I turned off a lot. I guess with my age and experience I was very **cynical** about it anyway. But everyone has the urge to know what's going on, so I turned it on anyway. Then I noticed that they kept **repeating** things, so I just changed the channels. During Vietnam we saw reporters talking to people—here I saw mostly reporters talking to other reporters and faraway shots. The female journalists looked like Barbie dolls talking with other journalists about how they felt about being bombed. They were so young, wearing desert fatigues and eye make-up. I was looking to see on their faces little smudges of phony dirt [**link between cynicism, crisis of faith, and depression**].

> It was such a packaged deal. Remember when Bush flew on the aircraft carrier, did they go to Laci Person the day after? It's even scarier if that is such a staged thing. Here is our leader-in-chief in his costume, grand finale and here's Laci Peterson. It made the whole thing seem like a movie. . . . To me what's **scary** is that it all seems like a huge election ploy. Because 60 GIs have been killed since Bush landed on the enemy carrier—when Bush was questioned about those killed, he said "Bring 'em on." The whole John Wayne attitude, none of his kids got killed. It is pretty easy to say things sitting on a couch in Washington. Every time I read in the paper that someone was killed I feel a **pain in my stomach.** I think that's a **desensitization.**
>
> All this stuff around 9/11—CNN, the creation of Homeland Security, orange alerts—doesn't feel **real.** Feels like a political smokescreen. I think the **fear,** threat, is real—but this doesn't help us feel more **secure.** It's a joke—red alert, blue alert—I still have to get on the bus and go to work in the morning. . . . I think my **fear** is that the people in power are using this in such a **cynical** way for their own goals that they are putting us in danger. They're really interested in their political agenda, they're **exploiting** it in ways that don't seem to be helpful for that. . . . It makes me become a combination of **jaded** and **apathetic.** Put me in a bubble and leave me the hell alone! When did the word "**spin**" come into our lexicon? It is not "**lying**" anymore.

Commentary

Charles's statements also showed symptoms of **paranoia, fear,** and **depersonalization** as psychological responses to war trauma. These symptoms appeared in his workplace and home environment. He used psychotherapy to sort through and reality-test his daily experiences. Psychotherapy gave him a safe place to explore his response to the media coverage and develop his own understanding of the political situation and his place in the world.

Media Reports

Media stories from 2003 supported the themes expressed by Frank, Mike, and Charles about truth, reality, trust, fear, and depersonalization.

Truth and Lies

The Associated Press noted that, even in March 2003, the administration knew of **lies:**

> A key piece of evidence linking Iraq to a nuclear weapons program appears to have been fabricated, the United Nations' chief

nuclear inspector said Friday in a report that called into question U.S. and British claims about Iraq's secret nuclear ambitions .... It was deemed "not authentic" after careful scrutiny by U.N. and independent experts, Mohamed El Baradei, director general of the International Atomic Energy Agency (IAEA), told the U.N. Security Council (Kole, 2003).

The *Wall Street Journal* commented:

> Victoria Clarke should take a bow. By embedding more than 500 journalists among U.S. troops, the assistant secretary of defense of public affairs has revolutionized media coverage of war. But has any of this improved our **understanding** of what's really happening in Iraq? As both a consumer and a purveyor of war coverage over the last week, I doubt it. The **fog of war** seems as thick as ever—maybe thicker ... the last Gulf War also was characterized by saturation coverage and a drought of real information ... there's the key point. The military's goal is not to inform the public; it's to win the war and if a little **disinformation** can help along the way, so be it. ... Aeschylus is credited with saying: "**In war, truth is the first casualty.**" Much has changed in this war, but that still holds. (Murray, 2003)

In fact, the whole basis for the war was shown to be shaky. On October 3, 2003, the Bush administration's chief investigator told Congress that, after "searching for nearly six months, U.S. forces and CIA experts have found no chemical or biological weapons in Iraq" (Priest & Pincus, 2003). Since that time, however, the trend toward manufactured infotainment has grown. The *New York Times* reported that a growing number of young people were going to film school to learn how to influence public policy—where the "gruesome execution videos that have surfaced in the Middle East are perhaps only the most extreme face of a complex sort of post-literacy in which cinematic visuals and filmic narrative have become commonplace" (Van Ness, 2005).

Blurring the line between reality and reality television shows, a $200 million partnership between the Army and the private Army Historical Foundation plans to build a museum and entertainment complex two miles south of the Pentagon to show what the life of a soldier is like. In an article called "'Friends' and Enemies: The War as Situation Comedy," we learn that Bochco, who created *L.A. Law* and *NYPD Blue*, plans another pilot series about Iraq ("Friends and Enemies," 2005). "Real" celebrities such as Bobby Brown and Paris Hilton's mother are playing themselves in fictionalized "reality shows" (Rich, 2005c, p. 12).

Psychological and Physical Health

In 2003, the *San Francisco Chronicle* was already warning readers about the toll on their mental health:

> For nearly a week now, the war in Iraq has played on as background noise in countless living rooms across America. . . . But while the constant exposure to the television war—tuned in as we dress for work, get children ready for school and sit down for meals—is keeping us informed, it may also be taking a subtle but real toll on our health. . . . Studies show regular **television exposure to traumatic events can increase risk for stress and depression** and it can even **weaken our immune systems.** Doctors think excessive war viewing before bedtime can cause stress-induced night-time snacking and interfere with sleep. Even young children who seem oblivious to events on the screen may suffer ill effects simply as a result of leaving the television on throughout the day. It's a time of life when kids are really organizing their ability to think forward in time. . . . If the television is going on in the background with competing language, it's quite possible that it **disrupts what may be a very important developmental process**. (Torassa, 2003)

The effect of **depression and stress** was noted in San Francisco. "Staff at adolescent psychiatric unit at St. Mary's Medical Center in SF is seeing an upsurge in calls and requests for admission; in some cases, those feelings are exacerbating or triggering physical symptoms and mental anguish" (Torassa, 2003).

Ironically, new therapies being developed to treat post-traumatic stress disorder use the same technologies of virtual reality that contribute to that stress in the first place. One such new therapy is called tech therapy. It uses virtual reality scenes of conflict and biofeedback through video to help soldiers fight post-traumatic stress disorder (Zimmerman, 2005). A "virtual Fallujah" is being used at the Naval Medical Center in San Diego. This virtual reality was created at the Institute for Creative Technologies at the University of Southern California and uses part of the Full Spectrum Warrior that was originally created to train soldiers for combat. Five million dollars was recently added to the Institute's new PTSD programs as a result of the war in Iraq.

Real and Surreal

Media coverage of the war also confirmed some viewers' **lost sense of reality.** By March 14, 2003, the *New York Times* was reporting:

> And more people than you would think—including a fair number of people in the Treasury Department, the State Department and, yes, the

> Pentagon, don't just question the competence of Mr. Bush and his inner circle; they believe that American's leadership has **lost touch with reality** . . . at this point it is clear that deposing Saddam has become an **obsession, detached from any real rationale** . . . what really has the insiders panicked, however, is the irresponsibility of Mr. Bush and his team with their almost childish unwillingness to face up to problems that they don't feel like dealing with right now . . . the administration's eerie passivity in the face of a stalling economy and an exploding budget deficit: **reality** isn't allowed to intrude on the obsession with long-run tax cuts. (Krugman, 2003)

Commenting on the news spin **a week later,** the *New York Times* said:

> So far the **war itself is selling** like beer on a troopship, thanks in part to compelling news accounts from reporters bunking with frontline units. . . . Like the most sophisticated Madison Avenue marketers, Pentagon planners have also reached out to diverse outlets where public opinion is shaped, by including reporters from MTV, Rolling Stone, People magazine and Men's Health, and foreign journalists running the gamut from Al Jazeera, the Arabic-language television channel, to Russia's Itar-Tass news agency. (Purdum and Rutenberg, 2003)

The *San Francisco Chronicle* echoed Michael Moore's words at the Academy awards: "**We live in fictitious times**" (Wellman, 2003).

The war has been clearly manipulated for political gain. For example, the heroic photos of George Bush **declaring victory in Iraq** were used to sell the war and bring him re-election at the same time. By April 1, 2003, the *New York Times* was already calculating the effect of media coverage on Bush's re-election: "Some Republicans in Washington were clearly jittery about the course and conduct of a war whose outcome they argued was pivotal to Mr. Bush's re-election next year" (Nagourney & Sanger, 2003). Bush's expectations were **unrealistic** and repeated the same mistakes made by previous invaders of Iraq. "And despite evidence that most Iraqis have not welcomed American forces, Mr. Bush cast himself as the country's liberator, telling Iraqis, 'We are coming with a mighty force to end the reign of your oppressors'" (Nagourney & Sanger, 2003). While Bush described his own progress as "brilliant," Saddam Hussein was describing the war as Operation Iraqi Freedom and the "mother of all battles." Heroic images were staged: a fake turkey was supplied by Halliburton for a surprise visit by the president to the troops for Thanksgiving. Bush landed on the carrier U.S.S. *Abraham Lincoln* to the theme from *Top Gun.* Jessica Lynch, who was mythologized as a war heroine, turned out to not have fired a shot. War reporting turned into infotainment. The media glorified war, while sanitizing its depiction.

In March 2003, descriptions in the *New York Times* sounded like Frank's memory:

> This is like "Real World Iraq." In the opening moments of the war, 24-hour cable news shows and network newscasts seemed almost drunk with their access, filling television screens with astonishing images. The mushroom clouds rising from bombed government buildings in Baghdad were shown over and over, as were the tableaus of a marine tearing down a poster of Saddam Hussein surrounded by a handful of cheering Iraqi villagers. . . . What they generally did not see in the first phase of the invasion of Iraq were very many Iraqis . . . . Refugee camps, a staple of war reporting in other conflicts, paled next to the images of high-tech weaponry blazing in real time . . . television also has a way of freeze-framing **the deceptive beauty of war**—the red and gold of burning government buildings along the Tigris river was almost painterly, like a sunset by Sisley. (Stanley, 2003)

Trust and Distrust

The *New York Times* noted: "Where American TV news falls down, without question, is the almost complete lack of anti-war voices or 'in-studio' experts. With paid military advisors dominating maps and thrilling anchors with their battle analysis, there's apparently no room for dissent" (Iovine, 2004). **Paranoia** was justified, as the United States changed its former friends like Saddam Hussein into enemies:

> Washington's policy traces an even longer, more shrouded and fateful history. Forty years ago, the Central Intelligence Agency, under President John F. Kennedy, conducted its own regime change in Baghdad, carried out in collaboration with Saddam Hussein. . . . Washington immediately befriended the successor regime. . . . the United States also sent arms to the new regime, weapons later used against the same Kurdish insurgents the United States had backed against Kassem and then abandoned. Soon Western corporations like Mobil, Bechtel and British Petroleum were doing business with Baghdad. (Morris, 2003)

The *New York Times* noted the relationship of **secrecy** to **trust:**

> While the public was preoccupied with the war, Bush signed an executive order making it easier for government agencies to keep documents classified . . . a reminder that this White House is obsessed with

> **secrecy**. . . . The **value of human life** was **reduced** with the explicit use of assassination. Assassination approved in this war has committed the United States for the first time to public, personalized, open-ended warfare in the classic mode of Middle Eastern violence—an eye for an eye, a life for a life . . . the Bush administration still shrinks from using the word "assassination" and much of the public continues to oppose it as both dangerous and wrong. (Powers, 2003)

Fears and warnings about **retaliation** showed: "the Blair government unleashed a witch hunt against the BBC and anyone in the Blair administration who might have been a source for the news agency's reporting" (Scheer, 2003). Peter Arnett was dismissed for telling an Iraqi interviewer that the coalition battle plans had failed.

Existential Responsibility

Psychological health means **taking responsibility for one's actions** and not projecting it as blame for others. The army manipulated stories about the cost of the war on individual lives, glorifying the deaths of soldiers. For example, Pat Tillman was reported to have died being "gunned down by enemy fire while leading a charge to protect his men," when in fact he was killed by friendly fire by members of his own platoon. His mother said in an interview in the *Washington Post:* "The military let him down . . . the administration let him down. It was a sign of disrespect" (Tucker, 2005).

Summary and Conclusions

Media reports of the war in Iraq have had a significant impact on the mental health of three veterans who were in psychotherapy with me. Themes that emerged from their reports and narratives that were related to the postmodern war media reports were **truth and lies, psychological and physical health, reality and the surreal, trust and distrust,** and **existential responsibility.** Although their symptoms could have been primarily due to post-traumatic stress, their comments closely paralleled reports in the media and pointed to a strong link between the two.

The fact that I was their therapist and interviewer could have biased the results; however, the validity of data from semi-structured interviews depends on the establishment of trust and a safe place in which participants can access nuanced and deeply felt private experiences. In this case, the subjects were already experiencing and expressing their symptoms. The sudden appearance and intensity of their symptoms was remarkable, as I began gathering descriptions of their experiences. This chapter has documented those experiences and analyzed them for themes relevant to understanding the impact of television and newspaper coverage of the war in Iraq on the psychological health of Vietnam veterans.

These clinical implications suggest that current assessments of mental health in veterans should include the impact of media coverage of the war. I found that talking about these media portrayals and their impact has beneficial therapeutic effects. Health care professionals can be sensitized to the therapeutic response to this impact through appropriate psychological training and supervision.

Recommendations

Mental health practitioners should be trained to identify and work with these symptoms of depersonalization, derealization, distrust, and existential fears. This training should include:

1. *A recognition of the effect of external forces such as politics or the media on their clients.* Psychologists are often trained to see psychological events as intrapsychic or rooted in family issues. Instead, cultural factors such as politics and the media have a strong influence and interact with pre-existing conditions, psychological vulnerabilities, and resiliencies.
2. *Allowing clients to talk about this effect in the therapy session.* Clients may need to express, cathart, understand, or struggle with this effect in the session, and often the chance to debrief is in itself healing. Therapists should be trained to work with strong emotions without trying to resolve or fix them. Although the outcome orientation of many managed care companies may push therapists to time-limited treatment goals, symptoms of this intensity might require an in-depth or existential approach.
3. *Clinical assessment* that is focused on the usual symptoms of PTSD, depression, and anxiety and also on the unusual existential ones such as cynicism, paranoia, lack of meaning and purpose, reality, multiple realities and the surreal, identity coherence and identity confusion, and truth and distrust. Clinical assessment should take a thorough client history that looks at patterns and the presence and etiology of such symptoms and identifies particular vulnerabilities that war veterans might have.
4. *Treatment that is contextual and proactive.* Given threats to the basic integrity and sense of security of war veterans, therapists can help

build their clients' resiliency. Healing means providing a safe and caring environment, learning to trust, and finding meaning in the everyday. Healing helps clients become more visible and find their own voices. To do this, they face the existential challenges of mortality, aloneness, play, creativity, suffering, and transcendence.

5. *Research that expands the understanding of PTSD and related conditions.* Psychologists should study the effects of current political and news practices such as embedded reporters and infotainment on the psychological health of veterans with much larger samples and randomized control groups.

References

Abram, D. (1996). *The spell of the sensuous: Perception and language in a more-than human world.* New York: Pantheon Books.

Antonovsky, A. (1979). *Health, stress and coping.* San Francisco: Jossey-Bass.

Bruner, J. (1986). *Actual minds, possible worlds.* Cambridge, MA: Harvard University Press.

Bugental, J. (1989). *The search for existential identity.* San Francisco: Jossey Bass.

Danner, M. (2005, 23 June). What are you going to do with that? *New York Review of Books,* 52–56.

deRivera, J., & Sarbin, T.R. (Eds.). (1998). *Believed-in imaginings: The narrative construction of reality.* Washington, DC: American Psychological Association.

Dreyfus, H. (2001). *On the Internet.* London: Routledge.

Frankl, V. (1959). *Man's search for meaning.* New York: Praeger.

Friends and enemies: The war as situation comedy. (2005, 16 January). *New York Times.*

Fromm, E. (1941) *Escape from freedom.* New York: Holt, Rinehart and Winston.

Gergen, K. (1991). *The saturated self.* New York: Basic Books.

Goldberg, K. (Ed.). (2000). *The robot in the garden: Telerobotics and telepistemology in the age of the Internet.* Cambridge, MA: MIT Press.

Herman, E.S., & Chomsky, N. (2002) *Manufacturing consent: The political economy of the mass media.* New York: Pantheon Books. p. 218.

Iovine, J. (2004, 10 October). The Army wants you for the afternoon. *New York Times,* Section 2, p. 1.

Josselson, R., & Lieblich, A. (Eds). (1993). *The narrative study of lives,* Vol. 1. Thousand Oaks, CA: Sage.

Kole, W.J. (2003, 8 March). U.N. inspectors say U.S. relied on forged reports of Iraq nuclear efforts. Associated Press.

Krugman, P. (2003, 14 March). George W. Zueeg. *New York Times.* p. A29.

Laing, R.D. (1965). *The divided self.* Harmondsworth, England: Penguin.

Lakoff, G., & Johnson, M. (1999). *Philosophy in the flesh: The embodied mind and its challenge to Western thought.* New York: Basic Books.

Maddi, S. (1994). Hardiness and mental health. *Journal of Personality Assessment, 63,* 265–274.

Maslow, A.H. (1962). *Toward a psychology of being.* New York: Van Nostrand.

May, R. (1975). *The courage to create.* New York: Bantam.p.218.

McAdams, D.P. (1995). What do we know when we know a person? *Journal of Personality, 63,* 365–396.

Morris, R. (2003, 14 March) A tyrant 40 years in the making. *New York Times,* p. A29.

Murray, A. (2003, 25 March). Political capital embedding helps, but the fog of war is still very dense, *Wall Street Journal.* p. A4.

Murray, H.A. (1938). *Explorations in personality.* New York: Oxford University Press.

Nagourney, A. and D.E. Sanger (2003, 1 April). A nation at war: Political debate; Bush defends the progress of the war; Privately, republicans fret over uncertainties. *New York Times.* p. B1.

Powers, J. (2003, 13 July) Target practice: When frontier justice becomes foreign policy. *New York Times,* Section 4, p. 1.

Priest, D. and W. Pincus (2003, 3 October) No illegal weapons found in Iraq, U.S. Investigator says: Search draws criticism from many lawmakers. *San Francisco Chronicle* p. A2.

Purdum, J.S. and J. Rutenberg (2003, 23 March) A nation at war: The news-media; Reporters respond eagerly to Pentagon welcome mat. *New York Times* p. B3.

Rich. F. (2005a, 20 February). The White House stages its own "Daily Show." *New York Times.* p. 41.

Rich, F. (2005b, 12 June). Don't follow the money. *New York Times,* 14.

Rich. F. (2005c, 19 June). Two top guns shoot blanks. *New York Times,* 12.

Sarbin, T. (1986). The narrative as a root metaphor for psychology. In T. Sarbin (Ed.), *Narrative psychology: The storied nature of human conduct* (pp. 3–22). New York: Praeger.

Scheer, P. (2003, 23 July). Witch hunt against BBC. *San Francisco Chronicle,* p. A23.

Serlin, I.A. (1995). Year of the whole person. *Psychotherapy Bulletin of Division 29, 40*(1). Washington, DC: American Psychological Association. p. 218.

Serlin, I.A. (2002). Psychologists working with trauma: A humanistic approach. *APA Monitor, 33*(8), 40. p. 216.

Serlin, I.A. (2005). Dancing stories. In G. Yancy & S. Hadley (Eds.), *Narrative identities* (pp. 245–261). Philadelphia: Jessica Kingsley.

Serlin, I.A., & Cannon, J.A. (2004). Humanistic approach to the psychology of trauma. In D. Knafo (Ed.), *Living with terror, working with trauma: A clinician's handbook* (pp. 313–331). Northvale, NJ: Jason Aronson.

Shafer, R. (1992). *Retelling a life.* New York: Basic Books.

Shanker, T., & Schmitt, E. (2004, 13 December). Military debates how to win war of words through disinformation. *New York Times,* A1, A9.

Smith, M. B. (2002) The metaphor and fact of war. *Peace and Conflict: Journal of Peace Psychology, 8*(3), 249–258.

Stanley, A. (2003, 23 March). A nation, a war: TV watch; Show of awe: A thrill ride, but no blood. *New York Times* p. A1.

Torassa, U. (2003, 14 March). The home front battle with depression, stresses are taking their toll. *San Francisco Chronicle.* p. W1.

Tucker, C. (2005, 30 May). No way around it. *San Francisco Chronicle,* B7.

Turkle, S. (1995). *Life on the screen: Identity in the age of the Internet.* New York: Simon & Schuster.

Under Bush administration, a new age of prepackaged television news. (2005, 13 March). *New York Times,* 18–19.

Van Ness, E. (2005, 6 March). Is a cinema studies degree the new M.B.A.? *New York Times,* 1, 15.

Weather Channel, APA climate-report deals. (2005, 19 July). *San Francisco Chronicle,* A3.

Wellman, L. (2003, 26 March) "Consensus reality" in fictitious times. *San Francisco Chronicle,* p. D10.

Zimmerman, E. (2005, 22 June). The game of their lives. *San Francisco Chronicle,* A1, A11.

CHAPTER 9

The Impact of U.S. Antiterrorism Interventions on Terrorist Motivation: Preliminary Research in Afghanistan and Iraq

Michael Wessells

The United States currently combats terrorism through concurrent strategies of coercion, social reconstruction, and public relations. The coercion strategy includes military attacks and intelligence operations against terrorist groups and operations; wars to overthrow regimes shielding terrorists or promoting terrorism and intending to harm the United States; use of tough law-and-order measures to identify and prosecute perpetrators of terrorist activity against the United States; and destruction or seizure of terrorists' financial or military assets. The social reconstruction strategy is to meet basic humanitarian needs and to rebuild for peace formerly totalitarian societies that had harbored or might harbor terrorists. The public relations strategy is to conduct a "hearts and minds" campaign to win over people who live in areas possibly sheltering, supporting, or incubating terrorists. Broadly, the first strategy aims to eliminate or dominate terrorist operatives and prevent future terrorism by showing terrorists that U.S. forces will kill them, or apprehend and severely punish them. The second and third strategies aim to prevent future terrorism by building attitudes and governments supportive of peace and either friendly to the United States or at least not hostile toward it. All three strategies aim to decrease terrorist motivation regarding the United States.

Psychological research stands to contribute to terrorism prevention by doing its share to analyze the efficacy of these strategies. This research, however, should avoid the self-serving and ethnocentric biases visible in official definitions of terrorism and popular attributions about terrorists' sanity and motives. For example, the U.S. State Department defined terrorism as "politically motivated violence perpetrated against noncombatant targets by subnational groups or clandestine agents."[1] This restrictive definition conveniently overlooks the fact that terrorism may also be sponsored, initiated, or implemented by states, including the United States, which has its own long history of using terrorism.[2] Ethnocentrism has also colored analyses of terrorists' sanity and motives. In Western views, it seems incomprehensible that sane people could kill masses of civilians, even killing themselves deliberately in the process. Viewed from the standpoint of individual gains and losses, suicide terrorism seems particularly ineffable, leading to portrayals of terrorist acts as irrational, the work of criminal minds, or deeds of madness. These portrayals find little support in contemporary research showing most terrorists are psychologically normal.[3] In retrospect, ethnocentric biases obscured how the combination of living under conditions of social injustice and humiliation may have interacted with issues of identity, values, and culture to enable people to find meaning through terrorist activities.

Conspicuously absent from research has been an analysis of how people in other countries understand U.S. policies and actions to prevent terrorism and the motives of people who commit or support terrorist acts. Taking empathy as a core value and wanting to avoid ethnocentric bias, I assume that empathizing with people who support political violence and terrorism is vital. We do this not to condone their actions, but to "walk a mile in their shoes" to understand their motives and perspectives. A growing body of literature analyzes people as makers of meaning who, under specifiable conditions, find identity and a sense of purpose in political violence and terrorism, including suicide terrorism.[4] Narrative research lets us learn about the subjective worlds and perceptions of peoples without embracing them as our own.

This chapter presents two preliminary studies of how the war in Iraq and the subsequent occupation affected terrorist motivation in the general population in Iraq and Afghanistan. Examining the general population is crucial since terrorist acts do not occur in a vacuum but often have popular support that may include funding and a ready supply of potential recruits.[5] A narrative research approach probed how young Afghan men and also Iraqi youth and adults interpreted the U.S. operations in Iraq and their likely impact on terrorist motivation. Iraqi and Afghan people might regard the U.S. interventions in Iraq as beneficial because they deposed a repressive dictator and opened the door for religious freedom and democratic governance. This could decrease terrorist motivation against the United States. However, Iraqi and Afghan people might regard the U.S. interventions in Iraq as hostile and harmful, thereby radicalizing Muslim populations and increasing terrorist motivation toward the United States. We conducted the research from July to September 2003, so it affords a window on Afghan and Iraqi perceptions in the early postwar and occupation period.

Each study is presented with an analysis of the sources of the youth radicalization observed. To avoid the narrow focus evident in much of the literature on terrorism, we will make connections with the expanding literature on child soldiers and youth engagement in armed conflict and terrorism. This chapter defines children according to the United Nations (UN) Convention on the Rights of the Child as people under 18 years of age. Youth are defined as people in the age range 13 to 25 years, because, in most societies, people in this age group, even if regarded as adults, are seen as developing into adult roles and making key life choices. Following the presentation of both studies, I'll outline suggestions about how to strengthen efforts to prevent terrorism.

The Narrative Research

A narrative approach is well suited to Afghan and Iraqi societies, which have strong oral traditions and low levels of literacy. The two studies used Afghan and Iraqi interviewers, respectively, since a U.S. interviewer would have aroused suspicion or introduced demand biases. Also, a U.S. interviewer would have missed nuances that a local interviewer could identify and explore. Both the Afghan and Iraqi data collectors said that local people would be more receptive to group discussions, which are appropriate to the local culture and situation, than to individual questioning, which awakens suspicion. Security considerations made it impossible to conduct full-scale, national research projects in Afghanistan and Iraq. Instead, this research aimed to collect pilot data in the capital cities, Kabul and Baghdad, respectively, in hopes of stimulating additional research and informing policy decisions.

The Afghanistan Study

We conducted the Afghanistan study from September 25 to October 5, 2003. I trained and supervised Muhammed Nazeer, an employee of Child Fund Afghanistan (CFA; the Afghan branch of Christian Children's Fund). He is a physician who is fluent in Dari, Pashtun, and English and who is well known and respected at Kabul University, where he received his medical training.

Design and Method

The design included a contrast between current university students who had either opposed or supported the Taliban regime. The focus was on young people because they are often recruits into terrorist networks.[6] We intended the contrast between pro- and anti-Taliban students to bring forward diverse views associated with Kabul's multiethnic composition. In my previous work, key informant interviews with Tajik and Uzbek people in northern provinces (home of the Northern Alliance) had expressed strong opposition to the Taliban and strong support for the U.S. war against the Taliban as part of the war on terrorism. In contrast, the Taliban had consisted mainly of Pashtun peoples of the south and east, and their supporters opposed the U.S. war and humanitarian intervention in Afghanistan. It seemed likely that former Taliban supporters would be more strongly critical of the U.S. interventions in Iraq and might show stronger terrorist motivation. The design also included a third group—young people who were not university students—as a means of identifying differences due to level of education.

The participants were 30 Afghan men between the ages of 18 and 25 years, a time at which educated young Afghans engage in increased political discourse and discussion of world affairs. The male focus, although regrettable, was due to resource constraints. In the Afghan context, a man cannot interview a group of women, and funds were not available to train and support both female and male interviewers. Also, the convening of a group of women is likely to raise suspicions about the real purpose of the research. Nazeer was the only professional available who spoke the necessary languages, understood the focus group method and was in a position to collect the data.

The participants included 10 people from each of the three groups: (1) university students who were anti-Taliban; (2) university students who were pro-Taliban, and (3) young people who were not university students and who were not selected according to their attitudes toward the Taliban. We used a mixture of convenience and snowball selection to construct the first two groups. First, using a process of quiet, local consultation, Nazeer identified people as members of a group according to the stated criteria. Then, he invited them to suggest names of university friends (or people they knew) who were anti- or pro-Taliban, and who might be willing to give an hour of their time for discussion. In each case, he explained he was conducting a group discussion as part of a scientific study of Afghans' personal opinions on the U.S./British war and post-conflict reconstruction activities in Iraq. The modal education level was third year for Groups 1 and 2. Ethnically, Group 1 consisted of six Tajiks and four Pashtuns, whereas Group 2 consisted of six Pashtuns, three Tajiks, and one Hezara.

We used a similar process to identify participants in Group 3. First, Nazeer identified two males who lived in the neighborhood of the CFA office. Then he asked each of them to gather four additional friends for a group discussion as described above. Owing to strong norms of hospitality, paying participants was not necessary.

Consistent with local norms, we obtained informed consent orally. We repeatedly reminded participants that any person was free not to answer particular questions or end his participation at any time. To protect confidentiality, we assured the participants that we would not write down their names, that we would conduct the discussion discreetly, and that we would use the information collected only for scientific purposes and would not share it with local authorities. The latter provision was particularly important for Group 2, because the current Afghan government opposes the Taliban and their ongoing attacks.

The focus group discussions were conducted at Kabul University for Groups 1 and 2 and at the CFA office for Group 3. The one-hour discussions were conducted in either Dari or Pashtun, depending on which language the group felt most comfortable with. For each group, Nazeer opened by explaining the purpose of the study. The focus group discussions were semistructured and addressed five questions:

Q1: Do you personally think the U.S./British attack on Iraq was justified? Why or why not?

Q2: Do you think the U.S./British attack on Iraq has made the United States safer from terrorism. Why or why not?

Q3: Has the war made people more likely or less likely to engage in terrorism? Please explain.

Q4: Do you think the United States has handled postwar reconstruction in Iraq in a constructive manner? Why or why not?

Q5: Do you think the way the United States has handled postwar Iraq has made people more likely or less likely to engage in terrorism? Please explain.

In asking these questions serially, Nazeer emphasized repeatedly that there were no "correct" answers to the questions and encouraged each participant to respond to each question or to what had been said. He also asked frequently for clarification, particularly in regard to the "why or why not?" questions, thereby probing for information about the participants' motives, their personal understanding of the situation, and their attributions regarding U.S. actions. Throughout the discussion, Nazeer tried to create a welcoming environment for diverse opinions. He also took extensive notes, and, immediately following a discussion, he expanded his notes while the discussion was still fresh in his memory.

Results

A high level of agreement occurred in the responses both across and within groups. Overwhelmingly, the participants said the attack on Iraq was unjustified and would make people more likely to engage in terrorism. In addition, there was unanimous, strong agreement that the United States has not handled postwar reconstruction in Iraq well and that this would make people more likely to engage in terrorism. These positions were stated passionately and evoked much head-nodding by other group members. Although Nazeer gave permission repeatedly for people to offer different answers, unity of opinion prevailed; however, as summarized below, participants offered diverse explanations on why they held their views. The only exception to this pattern of strong agreement was the Group 3 response to Question 1. Three members of Group 3 believed the attack on Iraq was justified, whereas seven members of Group 3 said the attack was unjustified.

The following paragraphs summarize the reasons given for the answers to the five questions.

Question 1. Group 1 members emphasized that there was weak, unsubstantiated evidence that Iraq had weapons of mass destruction (WMD). Several members described the WMD issue as a ploy, saying the real U.S. motive for attacking Iraq had been to obtain petroleum. Group 1 members agreed unanimously that on international issues such as how to deal with Iraq, the UN, not the United States, should be the decision maker and main actor. Group 2 members echoed these sentiments, with several members adding that the United States should not have attacked but should have applied harsher diplomatic measures such as suspending diplomatic relations with Iraq or revoking Iraq's UN membership. Group 2 members pointed repeatedly to the failure to have UN Security Council backing for the attack, which indicated that no adequate justification existed for the war. Several members said that, because Saddam Hussein had agreed to full cooperation with weapons inspectors, the war had no justification. In contrast, the three Group 3 members who thought the war was justified pointed to the dictatorship of Saddam, saying he posed a regional threat because he had WMD. The Group 3 members who saw the war as unjustified pointed out that the United States and Britain were supposed to be the "standard bearers" of global democracy but in fact had imposed their will on others. The Group 3 members who opposed the war said it looks as if the United States wants to dominate the Islamic world.

Question 2. Group 1 members said unanimously the war on Iraq could never make the United States safe from terrorism and viewed the poor quality of evidence regarding WMD as indicative of the U.S. intent to occupy Iraq. Group 2 members said the attack would only increase anti-American feeling, especially among Arabs and Muslims. Group 3 members said the attack will not make the United States safe because terrorism is still in effect in different parts of the world, pointing out that the threat of terrorism may grow. Some members of Group 3 spoke of "the genocide of Muslims in Iraq" and said the occupation of Iraq, together with U.S. support for "Israeli terrorism," could move radicals to engage in terrorism.

Question 3. Group 1 members said the war would only increase terrorism, particularly since Iraqis and other Muslims view theft of Iraqi oil as the real motive of the United States. In contrast, Group 2 members offered explanations of why the war made people more likely to engage in terrorism centered on the mistreatment of Palestinians and other Muslims. One member described the problem of Palestine as "a bleeding wound for all the Islamic world," and numerous members said the problem is the continued support by the United States and Britain for "Israel's terrorism." All Group 2 members thought the war will fuel tensions between Islam and the West, sparking more terrorism. Group 3 members said terrorism is spread all over the world and viewed the war on Iraq as making things worse, because people all over the world disagree with the war and see the United States as deceiving people and pursuing its own interest.

Question 4. In animated discussion condemning the U.S. occupation, Group 1 members said the United States has been unable to maintain peace, which is the essential first step in reconstruction. Several participants said only the UN could have maintained peace but had not been given the opportunity. Group 2 members also expressed anger over the sidelining of the UN and identified self-determination as a key issue. Most participants pointed out that the U.S. minority dominates the Iraqi majority, citing this as an example of U.S. and British imperialism. Referring to the experience of their own country in answering this question, Group 3 members said the United States had promised to rebuild Afghanistan for peace but had done nothing or very little. They predicted that the same would happen with Iraq because the United States seeks only its own benefits.

Question 5. Group 1 members often cited themes of Muslim versus Christian and Islam versus the West in responding to this question. Unanimously, they said people will be more likely to engage in terrorism because "they do not like the infidels in their territory." Several members said that, just as Muslims in Palestine and Afghanistan have fought to expel invaders, Muslims in Iraq will do the same. As one participant noted, "when Muslims are fighting for their freedom, the infidels call that terrorism," whereas Israeli bombings and shootings of Palestinians are not called terrorism. Group 2 members said terrorism will be provoked by the way in which the United States has handled Iraq's reconstruction. They pointed out that, because the United States had acted without UN support, everyone would understand that the United States is interested only in its own gains, which strengthens anti-American feelings. Group 3 members appealed to the theme of Islam versus the West, saying the overthrow of Saddam's government and the occupation will intensify anti-West feelings. Group 3 members agreed that to build friendly relations with the Islamic world, the United States should sever its diplomatic relations with Israel. Several Group 3 members noted also that if the United States is serious about reconstruction, "they should work for the prosperity of the Iraqi people and take a place in their hearts . . . if not, people of Iraq will revolt against these infidels and will get their freedom again."

Discussion

Although the small number of respondents and exclusive focus on male students at Kabul University preclude firm generalizations, this study disclosed two important findings, the first of which was a youth radicalization effect. In particular, the U.S. interventions—both the war and the post-Saddam reconstruction activities in Iraq—strongly increased anti-American sentiments among young Afghan men. To some extent, increased anti-American sentiment may reflect Afghans' widespread frustration, evident on the authors' field trips, over the perceived failures of the United States to deliver promised humanitarian aid and development support in a timely manner. Particularly noteworthy was the strong convergence in the views of radical students (pro-Taliban), anti-Taliban students, and non-students. This suggests that, across the political spectrum, the U.S. interventions in Iraq have strengthened anti-American sentiments among young Afghan men and created a relatively uniform base of opposition to the U.S. occupation.

Second, young Afghan men viewed the U.S. interventions in Iraq through the ideological lens of Islam versus the West. This lens, which reflects the Afghan historic experience and culture, creates negative, hostile attributions regarding U.S. actions and enables dismissal of stated U.S. government intentions. It also supports the view that U.S. troops and influences are poisonous and contaminate local Islamic culture, creating a strong need to expunge the "infidel." In this belief system, what is at stake is less about Iraq per se than the preservation of Muslim values and culture. Many participants said the United States wants to dominate Muslim peoples, citing as evidence the U.S. support for Israel and its mistreatment of the Palestinians. In this view, the U.S. government is duplicitous in claiming it sought to free Iraqi people from Saddam's brutal repression, because if that were true, the United States would have opposed or at least not supported Israel.

Regarding the prevention of terrorism against the United States, the prevalence of radical, anti-American views is worrisome because youth radicalization is a known precursor of terrorist engagement in numerous countries.[7] Worldwide, terrorism is part of a globalized system of armed conflict characterized by child soldiering[8] and terrorist activity.[9] In the most recent round of fighting in Liberia, for example, nearly half the soldiers were children.[10] In Sierra Leone, Small Boys Units consisting of boys under 12 years of age committed some of the cruelest atrocities, such as amputating civilians' arms or hands.[11] In Sri Lanka, where the largest numbers of suicide bombings have occurred, the Liberation Tigers of Tamil Eelan recruits and indoctrinates girls for fighting in what they regard as a liberation struggle, and some girls are groomed to become suicide bombers.[12] In Palestine, youth who see themselves as liberating their people from Israeli oppression have committed suicide bombings against Israelis.[13]

Although not all radicalized youth go on to engage in terrorism, extensive damage can be caused even if only a small fraction of youth who harbor anti-American sentiments decide to participate in terrorism. Also, radicalization of local people plays a key role in supporting terrorism, enabling countries to become incubators of terrorism.

Radicalization simultaneously provides a flow of recruits and funding for terrorist activities and creates a climate in which terrorism will galvanize popular support.[14] One of the mechanisms animating terrorist activities such as suicide bombings is competition between radical groups for status, publicity, and the ability to garner attention for one's cause.[15]

Four key processes help to account for the youth radicalization effect reported above: perceptions of injustice, identity threats, extremist ideology, and enemy imaging. Perceptions of injustice owe partly to objective conditions such as social exclusion and oppression. Even more important, however, are perceived deprivations and associated feelings of frustration, shame, and humiliation that spark youth discontent and desire to use violence—including terrorism—as a means of correcting the injustice.[16] Perceived injustices weigh heavily on young people who are at a time in their lives when they are defining their identity, situating themselves in society, and choosing their life course.[17] In Afghanistan, perceptions of injustice relate to (1) the history of invasions from the West and more recently from the Soviet invasion and occupation; (2) the perceived failure of the United States to meet basic humanitarian needs in a timely manner; (3) the high rates of unemployment—80 percent in many areas—among young men; and (4) U.S. policies supporting Israel, which are viewed as part of a wider strategy of U.S. domination of Muslim peoples.

These perceived injustices heighten the threat to collective identity, a factor visible in many ethnopolitical and religious conflicts worldwide.[18] People's social identities help to answer the fundamental psychological issue "Who am I?" and provide a sense of place and meaning in the world.[19] When injustices such as discrimination, deprivation, attack, detainment, or torture are directed toward a member of one's identity group, the members experience a sense of collective threat and victimization. Identity threats also arise from perceived or actual erosion of the group's core values. In the Afghan case, the presence of infidels bringing values antithetical to fervent

Islamic practice. Identity threats at once spark fear and desire to protect oneself and one's group and heighten the sense of victimization warranting action. In many conflicts, the sense of victimization becomes central to group identity, with communities spreading memories of "chosen traumas."[20] Radicalized by a sense of injustice and identity threat, many youth turn to violence—including terrorism—as a means of ending injustice, protecting one's people, and achieving hope for the future. In Afghanistan, as in many developing countries, youth have a strong sense of commitment to their family and people. When Tajik, Uzbek, and other youth of northern Afghanistan felt their people and religious practices were threatened by an unwanted and extremist Taliban regime, large numbers of youth joined the Northern Alliance to fight against the Taliban.[21]

People experiencing identity threats and injustice are frequently drawn to extremist ideologies in an effort to make meaning out of an otherwise confusing situation and to rally with others against external threats. Extremist ideologies, visible in politically reconstructed forms of Islam and Christianity having little to do with religion per se, typically define the world in terms of good and evil, stirring people to fight against perceived or real enemies. Rogue politicians are particularly skilled at manipulating ideologies to convince people that they are victims who have to fight (the Miloševi model) or are the chosen people who deserve to conquer (the Hitler model). Religious leaders, too, may be highly adept at manipulating ideologies and indoctrinating youth for fighting. In Afghanistan under the Taliban, extremist mullahs used the former religious schools, madrassahs, to teach youth that their highest calling was to fight for Allah against Western infidels.[22] Through fighting and acts of terrorism, youth who are caught up in romantic images of martyrs, freedom fighters, and liberation struggles derive a sense of meaning and commitment to a higher cause.[23] If the ideology is religious, youth may view their fighting and terrorism as divinely sanctioned and destined for eternal reward.

Supporting these processes is enemy imaging—the tendency to go beyond objective enmity and portray the adversary as demonic, savage, and inhumane.[24] Psychologically, dehumanized images of the Other stir fear, provide a subjective warrant for fighting lest the evil Other prevail, and rationalize killings and atrocities. Enemy images define identity in part by opposition to the out-group.[25] In Afghanistan, particularly in Taliban-controlled areas of the southeast, many young people learn to view Christian, outside influences as heathen and evil, and to see the United States as eager to dominate the region, making it easier to recruit them into a violent jihad deemed necessary to protect Islamic faith and Muslim autonomy.

Collectively, these processes help to radicalize Afghan youth, increasing their likelihood of supporting or engaging directly in terrorism. A fundamental problem for the United States is how to decrease the prevalence of anti-American sentiments and the lure of radical ideologies.

The Iraq Research

The dangerous situation in Iraq precluded focused questioning about U.S. policies, which could arouse suspicions. Instead, the Iraq research collected information about terrorist motivation in the general population in the context of a situation assessment regarding children. This indirect approach proved feasible, because as Iraqi people talked about the well-being or problems of their children, they naturally spoke also about how they viewed the war, the post-Saddam context, the U.S. government, and the Coalition Provisional Authority that administered the occupation and reconstruction effort at the time.

Method

The Christian Children's Fund (CCF)/Iraq conducted the assessment in the period July 1 to August 9, 2003, as part of an interagency child protection assessment coordinated by UNICEF. The assessment covered Baghdad Governorate, focusing mainly on Baghdad city since it is the main population center and security concerns limited travel outside Baghdad. The assessment covered a wide geographic area within Baghdad, including diverse neighborhoods, ethnic and religious groups, women and men, and children of different ages. The 15 neighborhoods included ethnic groups such as Sunnis, Shiites, Palestinian refugees, and Roma (gypsies). Entry into a neighborhood entailed consultation and dialogue with elders, religious leaders, teachers, and other community influentials to explain the purpose and to gain support and permission to conduct the assessment. The participants, identified through a mixture of purposive, convenience, and criterion-based selection, included 500 Iraqi girls and boys, school-age children and teenagers (youth), and men and women. Approximately half the interviewees were adults or teenagers, the main sources of information regarding terrorist motivation.

Jill Clark, a Canadian child protection expert, led the assessment. Having selected CCF Iraqi staff consisting of six Iraqi men and women who knew the local language, situation, and culture, she provided training on how to conduct focus group discussions with groups such as neighborhood women and parents, teenagers, and street children. Throughout the data collection, she provided extensive supervision and backup support on aspects such as how to collect information about why Iraqi people hold particular views regarding the U.S. occupation and reconstruction effort.

The focus groups were conducted with groups of approximately 10 people. Two CCF staff conducted the discussions, with one staff member leading the discussion while the other took notes. Consistent with Iraqi gender norms, separate focus groups were conducted for men and women, interviewed by male and female staff, respectively. The semistructured interviews included questions designed to identify the main child protection threats, vulnerable groups of children, local sources of support and coping, and key child-related issues.

Consistent with the indirect data collection strategy, the questions regarding terrorism were highly flexible and adapted to the local context. The aim was to find out how Iraqis viewed the war, the post-Saddam U.S. activities, and whether and how the U.S. interventions had influenced sentiments toward the U.S. and terrorist motivation. Because local people were preoccupied with insecurity and lack of electricity, they naturally raised issues such as why is there no security or electricity. Often the discussion turned to questions about U.S. motives, how people feel toward the United States, whether the war had been justified, and how the interventions had affected terrorism. So eager were Iraqis to discuss these issues that CCF staff had only to ask questions such as "Why do you think the United States did X?" or "Does anyone else have a different view?"

Results

Views toward the war were mixed. In some neighborhoods, particularly those consisting mostly of Shiites who had suffered greatly under Saddam's regime, many adults said they were happy to see Saddam gone and grateful for the opportunity to express their religion more freely. However, some people in these same neighborhoods said the war had been a bad thing since it was really a means of the United States gaining control over oil or of dominating Muslim people. In other neighborhoods, strong, uniform opposition to the war prevailed. Many people said whatever positive had come of Saddam's fall had been surpassed by the enormous problems of the post-Saddam era. Many said the United States had used WMD as a pretext and suggested the actual goals of the war had been to obtain oil and to ensure U.S. domination of the region. As evidence, participants pointed to the U.S. support for Israel and disregard for Muslim lives.

In neighborhoods bombed or the sites of fighting during the war, participants were highly critical of the war. Children and adults spoke consistently of the terror experienced during the war, as bombings, door-to-door searches and attacks, and increased prevalence of unexploded ordnance and mines made previously safe neighborhoods in Baghdad highly dangerous environments. Many parents expressed horror and anger at the destruction of their homes, the breaking down of front doors, and confrontations with soldiers pointing weapons at them. In some communities, adults reported strong fear of radiation contamination, as local views held that the United States had used weapons containing uranium in the vicinity. In communities hit hardest by U.S. attacks, many residents said the United States had been committing genocide against Muslims, and some spoke of the need for jihad and retaliation.

Anti-U.S. sentiments also surfaced through means other than interviews. On one occasion, two CCF staff members attempted an unplanned interview with a group of 9- to 13-year-old boys leaving a mosque. Despite their initial interest, the boys soon became rude and were joined by other boys who began to chant "Yes Saddam, Yes Osama, No U.S." When the staff retreated to their vehicle, the boys surrounded it, pounding on the windows. Fortunately, the staff escaped unharmed.

Views regarding the post-Saddam situation and its implications were far more uniform. In a highly consistent manner, adults said that life in the post-Saddam era was far worse than it had been under Saddam's rule. Although many people feared and hated Saddam, most said they would choose living under Saddam over what they have now. The main exception occurred in Saddam City, which has a Shi'ia population that Saddam had brutally repressed. Having been targets of frequent detentions and torture, Saddam City residents said anything was preferable to life under Saddam. However, they also expressed grave reservations about two issues that every group voiced—insecurity and lack of electricity.

The participants spoke repeatedly and passionately about the collapse of law and order in Baghdad, a previously orderly city. Most communities reported a significant increase in lawlessness and crime, including looting, theft, drug use in and near communities, car jacking, and risks of violence toward women. Also, street gangs had increased sharply and committed much of the theft and looting, targeting government buildings and hospitals, schools, and private homes. Due to security concerns, many parents reported keeping their children at home, particularly girls who are severely isolated and live in fear of sexual violence and kidnapping. All the women said rape and sexual violence in the streets were new phenomena, as was the emergence of a large population of street children. Children who live and work on the streets face diverse risks such as attack, abduction, crime, injury by unexploded ordnance, contact with sewage, involvement with street gangs, and drug use. Drug use, mainly in the form of taking valium, drinking alcohol, or sniffing glue, is also a new phenomenon but reportedly was spreading quickly, creating strong concerns about teenagers' safety and the influx of Western problems and values most parents regarded as illicit. Many people linked the widespread insecurity with what they described as the failure of humanitarian assistance to meet their basic needs. Frequently made comments were that without security, people could not go to the hospital, travel to obtain items such as fuel for cooking, or hope to obtain assistance from international agencies, which have curtailed their work due to insecurity.

Nearly all the participants attributed the increased insecurity to deliberate actions by the United States, saying the United States used widespread disorder and insecurity to weaken Iraq or justify continued occupation of Iraq. Many saw this as part of a wider effort to dominate Muslim peoples. Participants expressed great anger over the lack of law and order, refusing to believe it was by accident that the world's superpower could win a war easily and then not provide basic law and order. Many pointed out the Geneva Conventions requirement of occupying powers to ensure the security and protection of the people who live under the occupation. Their anger over the insecurity related also to the nature of daily crimes. Repeatedly, local people expressed disgust and anger that the United States had allowed the rise of drug use and sexual violence, which fervent Muslims see not only as sins but also as forms of contamination likely to spread as the occupation continued.

Further, many participants described the Coalition Forces as major sources of insecurity because they detain young people without stated cause, providing no information about their detention or release date. One family told of having its teenage son detained for 45 days and then released without explanation or apology. Many participants said that under Saddam's rule, they at least had ways of finding out where their sons had been taken, what would happen to them, and how to use bribes and other means of securing their release.

Lack of electricity was the second issue universally eliciting anger, frustration, and condemnation of the United States. Some participants identified this issue as more profound than that of insecurity. Many parents stated with great fervor that lack of electricity has significantly reduced their family income and earning ability, because many businesses have been unable to function. Adults who before the war had lived in poverty expressed strong anger that during the post-Saddam era, their poverty had increased. Parents and children said their families fought more due to inability to sleep in the heat, frustrations over unemployment, and inability to meet basic needs such as clean water, which typically is purified by electrical means. Many children and parents mentioned incidents of family members being hit with gunfire while trying to avoid the stifling heat inside by sleeping outside on roofs and balconies. Parents often noted that the lack of electricity enables lawlessness and crime, since darkness provides cover for illicit activities.

Unanimously, the participants blamed the United States for the lack of electricity. Nearly everyone said the United States had restored power much more quickly following the Gulf War, leading to speculation that the United States was intentionally depriving Baghdad of adequate electricity. Conspiracy theories abounded, as many residents saw the lack of security and electricity as proof of the U.S. government's intent to take Iraqi oil or dominate Islamic societies, including Palestine. Participants often referred derisively to the U.S. support for Israel and the mistreatment of Palestinians as proof that the U.S. plan is to dominate Muslims.

The discussions provided evidence that the pervasive frustration and anger over issues such as security and lack of electricity have radicalized the population. Many participants said even if they had opposed the war, they had hoped that the post-Saddam situation would be better than what they had endured under Saddam's dictatorship. Many had hoped the U.S. presence would improve life and stabilize a dangerous situation. Feeling angry over what they saw as preventable failures of the United States to provide basics such as security and electricity and living in the worst conditions they had experienced, many said they had become active opponents of the United States in Iraq. Among youth, many boys said they had recently joined the jihad because of what the United States had done to their country. As one 15-year-old boy said, "Before the U.S. soldiers came I was not interested in violence. . . . Now, to liberate my people, I have become a jihadi and am willing to die" (Jill Clark, personal communication).

Opinions regarding humanitarian aid such as food and other items were mixed. Some participants, mainly those who lived in unsafe communities, said they were angry over having received little aid. Larger numbers of participants said they had received some items such as food, for which they were grateful. However, nearly all the participants noted the aid delivery made little difference because people lacked basic security and electricity. Further, many said the aid was part of an occupation intended to dominate Muslim people.

Despite the increased opposition to the U.S. presence in Iraq, sentiments were divided in regard to whether the occupation should continue. Approximately half the people said they feared a rapid withdrawal of U.S. troops would create chaos and much fighting. The other half, however, said the occupation had to end very soon because Iraqis need to govern their own country and the continued occupation would only make the situation worse.

Discussion

Caution is required in generalizing these results because Baghdad differs from other regions such as northern, Kurdish areas, where local people demonstrated greater support for the war and postwar intervention. Also, because Baghdad was the source of much fighting, the U.S. military presence there was probably more conspicuous at a neighborhood level than in many other parts of Iraq. Nonetheless, data about Baghdad are important because public sentiments in the capital influence the likely success of any government.

Two key findings of this study were that the U.S. postwar intervention has strongly increased anti-American sentiments, and most Baghdad residents viewed the war and the postwar intervention as part of a malevolent U.S. strategy. Baghdad residents were far more uniform in their criticisms of the postwar reconstruction activities, particularly the occupation, than of the war itself. Many people saw the U.S. failure to meet basic needs for security, electricity, and clean water as inexcusable injustices. The biggest perceived injustice was the occupation, uniformly reviled and interpreted as an effort by the United States to dominate Muslim peoples. The perceptions of U.S.

actions as part of a wider plan to subjugate Muslims resonated with the views of young Afghan men and reflected enemy imaging. An interesting convergence was Iraqi and Afghan perceptions of the mistreatment of Palestinians and U.S. support for Israel as proof of U.S. intent to dominate Muslim peoples.

Identity threats were also visible in Iraqis' fears that the outsider presence contaminated their society and eroded Muslim values. The resulting fear, anger, and hatred created a cauldron of anti-American sentiments ripe for the rise of extremist ideology visible in the subsequent influence of leaders such as Muqtada al Sadr. In fact, many people, including youth, said they had become strong opponents of the United States specifically because of these problems, and some people said they now want to answer the call to jihad as a result. The climate of increased anger, hostility, and frustration toward the United States fuels terrorist motivation, creating conditions conducive to terrorist strikes against Coalition Forces. In short, the U.S. early postwar interventions in Iraq not only lost the hearts and minds campaign, but increased rather than decreased terrorist motivations. Even shortly following the war, negative consequences of the U.S. postwar interventions were highly conspicuous on the ground despite the lack of public discourse about them and the U.S. government's denial of their existence. The de facto conspiracy of silence surrounding these problems made it easy for the United States to continue its course in Iraq without making the serious adjustments early on that might have prevented much of the ongoing radicalization and further destruction that followed.

Recommendations

The results of these two studies, although preliminary, challenge the wisdom of predominantly military "solutions" to terrorism and suggest the need for more comprehensive approaches that address injustices and build pro-U.S. sentiments. The results call attention to the problem of youth radicalization, which military means may inflame rather than reduce. To prevent terrorism, it is vital to decrease radicalism by reducing perceptions of injustice, identity threats, the lure of extremist ideologies, and enemy images. This reduction—difficult to achieve—requires long-term, comprehensive approaches rather than the military approaches easiest to garner public support for. Outlined below are five key recommendations that reflect the learning from this research and guide more comprehensive efforts at terrorism prevention.

1. Avoid wars and occupations not sanctioned by the UN Security Council.

The unilateral execution of the war by the United States and United Kingdom without Security Council approval and against the Security Council's strong objections robbed the war and postwar interventions of international legitimacy and stirred anti-American sentiments among Iraqi and Afghan peoples. Having isolated itself, the United States was unable to obtain significant assistance from the UN or other governments in either the postwar humanitarian operations or military operations needed to establish security. More than any other factor, the U.S.-led occupation triggered strong perceptions of injustice among Iraqis and Afghan men and enabled suspicions of the U.S. humanitarian assistance and cultivation of democratic governance as thinly disguised means of subjugating Iraqis. In the future, the United States should conduct military and humanitarian operations multilaterally or at least with Security Council approval.

2. Limit excessive reliance on military means of addressing terrorism, avoiding the use of torture.

Although military means are necessary for containing and preventing terrorism, they are double-edged swords. They stand to eliminate particular "bad guys" and terrorist leaders, but they also incite anti-American feelings and risk growing terrorism. It is possible that for every terrorist killed by U.S. forces in Iraq, several new terrorists will emerge. The problem is less the "magnet effect" wherein experienced terrorists are drawn to Iraq from neighboring countries than the manufacture of new terrorists, including many youth, due to widespread and impassioned opposition to the occupation. In the context of an occupation already perceived as unjust, military operations against insurgents and terrorists will be regarded as transgressions calling young people to the jihad. Perceptions of the United States as a heavily armed bully or Christian warriors seeking to dominate Muslim peoples will inflame anti-American sentiments and worsen long-term U.S. security. The best antidote for this problem is to limit the application of military force, using it only as a last resort and coupling it with a wide array of nonmilitary measures such as those described below.

When military means are used, they should conform to international law and human rights standards. Although this research was conducted before the revelations about the human rights abuses at Abu Ghraib and other detention sites in Iraq and Guantanamo Bay, Iraqis and Afghan men would no doubt view these abuses as yet additional injustices and identity threats fueling powerful anti-American sentiments. Because the latter sentiments stir terrorism directed against the United States, the United States should prevent the use of torture and abusive treatment as part of efforts to protect human rights and limit terrorism.

3. Systematically plan for and establish quickly security and widespread humanitarian supports following armed conflict.

A cardinal failure of the U.S. government in Iraq was its failure to plan systematically or provide for civilian security as required under the Geneva Conventions. Guided by rosy expectations of Iraqis hailing U.S. troops as liberators, U.S. planners assumed there would be little postwar violence. When widespread looting erupted and then developed into organized crime and insecurity in nearly every neighborhood, the United States failed to react with appropriate security measures. The United States also failed to provide humanitarian support on the vast scale needed, leaving many Iraqis feeling they were deliberately being denied as part of a wider subjugation effort. This feeling is partially due to the humanitarian assistance not being overseen by the UN and the U.S. State Department and nongovernmental organizations (NGOs) that typically steer emergency relief and peace-building operations. It is now being overseen instead by the U.S. Department of Defense (DoD).

The DoD's fitness for such a role was questionable because it was the belligerent, whereas humanitarian aid requires adherence to basic humanitarian principles such as impartiality.[26] Further, the DoD had no experience in or capacity for humanitarian assistance, and the nature of the war sidelined many NGOs and the UN. Although the UN and many NGOs did become involved, they came too late, and the worsening security situation impeded humanitarian action. Following the August 19, 2003, bombing of the Canal Hotel, which killed 18 humanitarian workers, many UN agencies and NGOs sharply curtailed their operations or left Iraq. A significant lesson is that humanitarian assistance must be decoupled from the DoD and provided by well-trained relief and reconstruction professionals in a context made relatively safe by multilateral security forces. Tight linkage of humanitarian assistance with military operations heightens perceptions of humanitarian operations as part of a wider injustice of dominating local people.

4. Establish a wide array of policies and practices supportive of Muslim peoples.

In light of the strong tendency of Iraqis, Afghans, and other Muslims to view events through the prism of the Israeli-Palestinian conflict, a high priority is to change U.S. policies toward Israel and Palestine. Particularly useful are steps such as making U.S. economic aid to Israel contingent on improvements in Israeli adherence to human rights standards, signaling the U.S. intent to protect Muslim people's rights to dignity and protection. Also, U.S. leaders should assiduously avoid statements or actions giving the impression or creating the reality that U.S. foreign policy is part of a war between Christians and Muslims. Through religious education and exchange programs, the United States should embark on a broad effort to increase religious tolerance within its own borders and to show respect for Islamic faith and peoples. This respect should be backed by action such as devoting larger amounts of funding to support Muslim peoples in emergency situations including the woefully underfunded relief effort to support survivors of the Kashmir earthquake of October 2005.

5. Create positive life options and social justice for youth.

The ongoing radicalization of youth in Iraq and other Muslim countries is a national security time bomb for the United States. Reversing this trend of radicalization and ending the lure of extremist ideologies are long-term projects defying singular solutions. In Iraq, Afghanistan, and other Muslim countries, it is vital to end conditions such as chronic poverty, high rates of unemployment, and poor access to education that stimulate feelings of alienation and humiliation, cause a loss of hope in the system, and encourage youth participation in radical groups condoning violence and terror. It is vital also to provide access to skills, jobs, and means of earning a living, enabling youth to achieve meaningful civilian roles rather than find meaning through violence. Although much larger amounts of aid are warranted, the process of delivering humanitarian and peacebuilding supports is equally important. The imposition of outside forms of government or the flooding of countries with large numbers of U.S. ex-patriates who enjoy privileges denied to local people will likely evoke more anti-American sentiment, worsening the situation. More approp riate is a community-based mode of support that builds on local capacities, mobilizes local people and resources, respects local cultural practices and the "do no harm" humanitarian imperative,[27] and engages youth as resources and actors capable of shaping their own future.

To support these changes, there also needs to be increased critical thinking on behalf of U.S. citizens and professions, including psychology. Following 9/11, widespread fear and politicized calls for patriotism had a chilling effect on critical thinking. The new age of globalized terrorism requires more than ever a willingness to challenge dogma, question our ideologies, and empathize with how other peoples see and experience U.S. policies and actions.

Acknowledgment

The author received extensive assistance from Jill Clark on the Iraq portion of this research. Jill died in the tragic bombing of the UN headquarters in Baghdad, August 19, 2003. This chapter is written as a tribute to Jill's courage, work, and spirit.

Notes

1. U.S. State Department, *Patterns of Global Terrorism* (Washington, DC: U.S. State Department, 1999).

2. Richard Falk, "The Terrorist Foundations of Recent US Foreign Policy," in *Western State Terrorism*, ed. A. George (New York: Routledge, 1991), 110–114; Mark Pilisuk and Angela Wong, "State Terrorism: When the Perpetrator Is a Government," in *The Psychology of Terrorism*, Vol. 2, ed. C. Stout (Westport, CT: Praeger, 2002), 122–127.

3. Edward Cairns, *Children and Political Violence* (Oxford, England: Blackwell, 1996), 118; Clark McCauley, "Psychological Issues in Understanding Terrorism and the Response to Terrorism," in *The Psychology of Terrorism*, Vol. 3, ed. C. Stout (Westport, CT: Praeger, 2002), 5–6.

4. Mia Bloom, *Dying To Kill* (New York: Columbia University Press, 2005), 60–75; Farhad Khosrokhavar, *Suicide Bombers* (London: Pluto, 2005); David Rosen, *Armies of the Young: Child Soldiers in War and Terrorism* (New Brunswick, NJ: Rutgers University Press, 2005); Michael Wessells, *Child Soldiers: From Violence to Protection* (Cambridge, MA: Harvard University Press, in press).

5. Martha Crenshaw, "The United States as a Target of Terrorism," in *Global Terrorism after the Iraq War*, ed. J. Klaits (Washington, DC: United States Institute of Peace, 2003), 7.

6. Bloom, 65; Rosen, 91–131; Peter Singer, *Children at War* (New York: Pantheon, 2005), chap. 7; Wessells, *Child Soldiers*, chap. 4.

7. Rosen, passim.

8. Rachel Brett and Irma Specht, *Young Soldiers* (Boulder, CO: Lynne Rienner, 2004); Grace Machel, *The impact of war on children.* Cape Town: David Philip, 2001), passim.

9. Anthony Marsella, "Reflections on International Terrorism: Issues, Concepts, and Directions," in *Understanding Terrorism*, eds. F. Moghaddam and A. Marsella (Washington, DC: American Psychological Association, 2004); Singer, chap. 7; Wessells, *Child Soldiers*, chap. 4.

10. Human Rights Watch, Living in fear (New York: Human Rights Watch, 2004), 1.

11. Human Rights Watch, Sowing terror (New York: Human Rights Watch, 1998), passim.

12. Bloom, 73.

13. Rosen, 91–131.

14. Crenshaw, 7.

15. Bloom, 29–30.

16. Marsella, 29–39; Fathili Moghaddam, "The Staircase to Terrorism," *American Psychologist* 60 (2005): 162–163.

17. Erik Erikson, *Childhood and Society* (New York: Norton, 1963).

18. Ronald Fisher, *Interactive Conflict Resolution* (Syracuse, NY: Syracuse University Press, 1997), 5.

19. Henri Tajfe and J. Turner, "The Social Identity Theory of Intergroup Behavior," in *The Social Psychology of Intergroup Relations*, eds. S. Worchel and G. Austin (Monterey, CA: Brooks/Cole, 1986); Donald Taylor and Winnifred Louis, "Terrorism and the Quest for Identity," in *Understanding Terrorism*, eds. F. Moghaddam and A. Marsella (Washington, DC: American Psychological Association, 2004), 175–178.

20. Vamik Volkan, *Bloodlines* (New York: Farrar, Straus & Giroux, 1997), 48.

21. Ahmed Rashid, *Taliban* (New Haven, CT: Yale University Press, 2005), 22–24.

22. Rashid, 31–33.

23. Brett and Specht; Rosen, passim; Gillian Straker, *Faces in the Revolution* (Cape Town, South Africa: David Philip, 1992); Wessells, *Child Soldiers*, chap. 4.

24. Robert Rieber, *The Psychology of War and Peace* (New York: Plenum, 1991); Brett Silverstein, "Enemy Images: The Psychology of U.S. Attitudes and Cognitions Regarding the Soviet Union," *American Psychologist* 44

(1989); Ralph K. White, *Fearful Warriors: A Psychological Profile of U.S.-Soviet Relations* (New York: Free Press, 1984).

25. Taylor and Louis, 181–184.

26. Michael Wessells, "Negotiating the Shrunken Humanitarian Space: Challenges and Options" in *Handbook of Disaster Psychology*, Vol. 1, 147–164, eds. G. Reyes and G. Jacobs (Westport, CT: Praeger, 2006).

27. Mary Anderson, *Do No Harm* (Boulder, CO: Lynne Rienner, 1999); Michael Wessells, "Culture, Power, and Community: Intercultural Approaches to Psychosocial Assistance and Healing," in *Honoring Differences: Cultural Issues in the Treatment of Trauma and Loss*, eds. K. Nader, N. Dubrow, and B. Stamm (New York: Taylor & Francis, 1999).

CHAPTER 10

Cities of Fear, Cities of Hope: Public Mental Health in the Age of Terrorism

Chris E. Stout and Stevan Weine

Intentions

The terrorist attacks on the World Trade Center and the Pentagon caused a widespread public mental health crisis and led to long-term mental health problems for many Americans, especially in New York City and Washington, DC. The attacks especially frightened many in urban America and caused them to question whether their cities were adequately prepared to face similar attacks. Addressing terrorism requires action on multiple fronts, including facing its causes, consequences, and responses. All are necessary, as reflected in the other chapters in this volume. This chapter focuses on the public mental health consequences of terrorism.

In 2003, the Institute of Medicine issued a landmark report entitled "Preparing for the Psychological Consequences of Terrorism: A Public Health Strategy."[1] It called for a public health approach to the psychological consequences of terrorism. To build and implement this approach in U.S. cities will require systemic changes and new and broader roles for mental health professionals. Federal, state, and city governments and professional and academic organizations are still trying to understand how can it be done.

The faculty of the International Center on Responses to Catastrophes (ICORC) at the University of Illinois at Chicago (UIC) wondered what had been learned since the terrorist attacks of September 11, 2001. How was Chicago preparing to address the public and private mental health consequences of terrorism and bioterrorism? What would community and mental health leaders have to say regarding the perceptions of and responses to the mental health consequences of terrorism in urban America?

To explore these matters, ICORC convened a meeting of a diverse group of leaders for "Cities of Fear, Cities of Hope: America's Public Mental Health in the Age of Terrorism." It was a two-day summit of mental health leaders from Illinois and New York along with representatives from government, academia, community organizations, nongovernmental organizations, public voices, professional societies, religion, and the media. This was a first-of-its-kind dialogue in Chicago and Illinois to explore perceptions of and responses to terrorism in urban America.

The summit involved more than forty participants from various disciplines and representing different sectors of society. The names and affiliations of all participants are listed in the appendix. Three ICORC faculty members led the discussion: Stevan Weine, Professor of Psychiatry; Ralph Cintron, UIC Associate Professor of English; and Chris E. Stout, Clinical Professor of Psychiatry and (then) Chief of Psychology for the Illinois Department of Human Services in the Division of Mental Health. The meeting was supported by a grant to ICORC from the UIC Humanities Lab and also by the UIC Department of Psychiatry, the UIC College of Medicine, and the UIC Office of Vice Chancellor for Research.

On September 11, 2003, ICORC released a white paper containing the findings and recommendations of this summit meeting. This chapter is based on a summary of those proceedings and resultant analyses and recommendations from the ICORC faculty. The overall finding was that, although there is broad agreement that addressing the public mental health consequences of terrorism and bioterrorism should be a priority, there are concerns about how to make it work, concerns that we had not absorbed the more important lessons from New York, and that serious gaps remain in preparedness and response capabilities.

This chapters presents a summary of the key themes that emerged from the dialogues and provides the summit's specific recommendations.

Emergent Themes

The War on Terror

The "war on terror," like the "war on poverty" and the "war on drugs," is government's attempt to define a social problem, causing its institutions and citizens to make policies and programs that offer solutions. But the creation of a term such as a "war" can exacerbate the problem it was created to address. We become focused on military models and move away from the political, social, economic, and psychological initiatives that are more appropriate.

It seems highly unlikely that government itself, acting within the framework of the "war on terrorism," is going to devise strategies, let alone provide solutions, for the problems of mental health as a consequence of terrorism. On the other hand, the concentration of resources and energy mounted by the war on terrorism might allow some good works to occur. In any case, it is important that other individuals, groups, and institutions take the appropriate initiatives without waiting for government direction or funding.

Need for Public and Community Approaches

Since mental health services must be implemented largely through the public sector at the level of affected communities, it is necessary to develop specific public mental health and community-based approaches that respond to the needs and strengths within communities. Yet existing public and community mental health systems are grossly underfunded and overburdened and are basically oriented to serving the severely and persistently mentally ill. Mental health preparedness and response to terrorism requires undertaking a completely new set of functions.

To enhance the state's capacity for public and community approaches to America's mental health needs requires innovative models, methods, policies, programs, collaborations, and research. It is important to remember that whatever is done that is spurred by terrorism's threat should ideally also be a generalizable solution to current non–terrorism-related problems. For example, working to develop better resilience in our children is a beneficial task anytime for any stressor; building better communities is always good work; developing better systems of illness outbreak surveillance and responsive quarantine will be helpful in any public response to SARS, West Nile virus, or other non-bioterrorist contagion outbreaks; increasing better communication in state government and across departments and disciplines will help everyone.

Vulnerable Urban Communities

Cities have pockets. Three specific vulnerable groups in which fear is experienced more intensely were mentioned: Muslims, African

Americans, and women. Muslims in the United States are highly heterogeneous; however, one thing they now have in common is living in fear because of urban terrorism and the "war on terrorism." This is especially true for immigrants, whose communities are not as well equipped to function. Inamul Huq expressed concern for the 10 million Muslim children in the United States, the majority of whom attend public schools, where they are often exposed to threats and lack adequate support. Community interventionists and researchers are challenged to calculate such suffering and marginalization, their limits, and their risks for extremism. They are challenged to document and analyze how some youth survive and thrive with the help of families, teachers, religious communities, and police. They are challenged to devise and test community-based interventions that may help Muslim immigrant children.

African American communities have felt an ambivalent response to terrorism. On the one hand, it was noted that many have long known terror in their daily lives in America. Reverend Smith spoke of the "terror of having to live like you don't matter." As a consequence, for many African Americans, when the United States was attacked, "there was a distance." Many responded with hope, because "terror begets hope in our community." That is, many feel that they have had to deal with the challenges of violence in their communities long before the violence to their country occurred. Thus, there was a baseline of hope they had used already. African Americans who seek help to overcome distress are likely to do so in their churches and through their faith groups.

For the most part, religious leaders are heavily burdened by their parishioners' needs, and there are few, if any, connections between those churches and community mental health services. Some have expressed the need for training and support, but Badonna Reingold noted another concern regarding training: "Will trainings be something used to discriminate against us?" That is, is there a risk of the pathologizing of "rational anxiety" for consumers of mental health care services?

Judith Gardiner raised the following concerns and questions regarding gender:

> Fear, terror, terrorism, responses to terrorism, and manipulations of fear and the fear of terrorism are all gendered and these gender connotations are not trivial or incidental but may be significant aspects of the psychologies that undergo and that perpetuate fear. How then is terrorism gendered and how are responses to it gendered? How do anxieties

about masculinity and about changing gender and sexual roles fuel terrorism? How are responses to terrorism manipulated to increase anxieties or to allay them, and how are these responses then used to justify a more compassionate or more destructive treatment of others?

Sources of Fear and Sources of Hope

Most city dwellers would agree with experts that terrorism generates fear. The common definition of terrorism is "the illegal use or threatened use of force or violence, and an intent to coerce societies or government by inducing fear in their populations."[2] In the new era of terrorism and bioterrorism, governmental and nongovernmental organizations are responsible for managing these fears. These include fears generated by the aggressors, but also by the government's counter-responses to actual or anticipated aggression. The public considers the government and media as the messengers and, to a certain extent, the sources of fear. Participants expressed concern that mainstream media was uncritically conveying the message of the Bush administration and that terrorism and the war on terrorism were being promoted to reap political benefits and as an impetus for cultural change.

Bill Campbell said that the media could be either a source of fear or a source of hope. The media educate through providing information. The media have an obligation to depict hope, not just fear. Stevan Weine questioned whether it is realistic to expect that hope is going to come from the institutions obligated to manage fear. There was much discussion around the exact sources of hope. People discover hope in many places: in culture, families, communities, and in faith traditions. African American community representatives noted that hope is a result of interactivity and openness. One impact of fear is to limit communal interaction and promote seclusion and "closed-mindedness," all of which diminish hope.

Collaborative Efforts

To be relevant, let alone effective, mental health and social science professionals need to pursue more assertively collaborative relationships with multiple partners. Kelly Ryan said that mental health is systematically excluded from the table at preparedness discussions. Mental health professionals have to become better at knowing their role and "selling" their services to government, funding sources, and agencies. There is a need to define mental health's role with respect to the community. Mental health services tend be identified with "rushing to the scene" rather than being essential in indirect or longer-term roles; however, their role need not, and perhaps should not, be primarily "restricted" to debriefing at disaster sites. Other roles include consulting on organizational effectiveness, conducting and evaluating training, preparing to evaluate responses when events occur, coordination and support of services, risk communication, and community resilience.

Collaborations between media and mental health are needed to better address the representations of terrorism and its consequences in the media, and the effects on journalists and others as a result of the repeated telling of traumatic stories. The Dart Center for Journalism and Trauma at the University of Washington (Seattle) has done pioneering work in this area (see www.dartcenter.org). Steve Jones said that studies of the media ecology of peoples' lives have demonstrated an overall decrease in news consumption through traditional channels and an increase in people finding ways to get information in a manner that best fits them. In the moment of crisis, organizations did not rely on the Internet to communicate; they used the formal and informal structures they were already familiar with.

Vaughn Fayle said that this is an important time to think of new collaborations between clergy and mental health professionals. There is very little collaboration and no literature or research to guide such efforts. Most persons in distress go to clergy or chaplains. After 9/11, more religious leaders were sought out than mental health care professionals. But many faith leaders did not feel adequately equipped to deal with the mental health issues often posed to them.

Faith communities are important before, during, and after a terrorist event, but more work needs to be done to enhance these communities' capabilities to be more effective in the aftermath of such an event. There is also the problem/risk of enigmatic religious leaders who may exploit their congregation's fears in the context of community tensions or divisions for their own purposes. A truly ecumenical, "apolitical" model that blends pastoral and clinical services would provide the ideal approach and avoid the proverbial "cult of the personality" issues associated with Machiavellian charismatic leaders.

Another important area of collaboration is between mental health professionals and employee assistance program professionals. The workplace can be a very feasible and fertile site for delivering preventive and responsive mental health services, disaster planning, response, and resilience development.

Training

The era of bioterrorism introduces problems, priorities, and needs that are not being addressed in the current training of psychiatry residents and other mental health professionals. Psychiatry residents and residency trainers report a need for new paradigms and curricula for the training at local and national levels. Training often does not prepare trainees sufficiently for preventive or community-based work.

Training of current mental health professionals and paraprofessionals (i.e., clergy, seminarians, and ministers) in skills and knowledge that would support mental health responses to terrorism is needed. However, there are important challenges to make training sessions more relevant and useful to developing these services. The Task Force on International Trauma Training published consensus-based guidelines for trauma training that should be consulted to guide training initiatives (these are available via www.ichrsc.org and www.istss.org).

Emergency Responses

The differences in emergency response to a man-made disaster (e.g., terrorist attack) versus a natural disaster are marked. Terrorist attacks often occur as more than one "event," thus putting first responders at greater risk than would generally be the case in an accident or natural disaster situation. For example, following an initial bombing, there may be a second bombing in the same location with the intent of killing the first responders. A man-made disaster is also a crime scene, requiring different evidentiary procedures and the interface of investigative law enforcement officials with emergency procedures and personnel. This results in delays in surviving family members' receiving the loved one's remains and thus increases the psychological trauma of a man-made disaster as compared to the aftermath of a natural disaster.

The research in terms of psychological first-aid in a terrorist attack is not mature, and thus approaches such as Critical Incident Stress Debriefing—"techniques designed to assist others in dealing with the physical or psychological symptoms that are generally associated with traumatic exposure"[3]—may not be as helpful or scalable and generalizable as once thought.[4] Also, so-called spontaneous volunteers can be more problem than help as they bring with them the problems of maintenance (e.g., their need for food and housing), issues of ability (expertise that is relevant to the situation), and questions of liability (malpractice).

Short- versus Long-Term Response

Mental health issues in a crisis or disaster situation are normal reactions to abnormal situations. The role for the Red Cross in such abnormal situations is to provide basic needs: food, shelter, clothes, security, and information. "Shelter-in-place" (the practice of not relocating to a public place, like a local school gymnasium, and instead staying put at home, work, etc.) is a concept that parallels a local quarantine and may be of use for post-terrorist events. The primary focus of response efforts has been on the emergency phase and on short-term individual pathological consequences of terrorism. This is necessary, but it is also necessary to move beyond this. Chip Felton reported that one of the biggest challenges in the New York response was getting providers and organizations to organize support services for addressing longer-term needs. In Illinois, there are no preparations for such longer-term responses.

Response versus Preparedness Public Education

In New York, media outreach was initially done though public service announcements. Later a public education campaign was developed. The Project Liberty campaign was developed by professional advertising agencies using high-quality television advertisements, posters, and billboards. Chip Felton said that the campaign reached a large proportion of New Yorkers and made them aware of social, medical, financial, and mental health services that were available and how to access them. In New York, mental health is now integrated with public health. It overlaps with all aspects of disaster preparedness. Mental health is managed by both professionals and paraprofessionals. Other human service agencies came in after the attack to play critical roles in helping with housing, child care, and job loss—all of which caused psychological stresses as well. To publicize available services in New York, a professional public relations campaign and agency was successfully used.

Communication is critical in preparation for, and resilience during and after disasters and crises. However, there remain important questions regarding the New York experience. How effective was the content of the messages, for instance? How did they fare among diverse communities? At the time of the conference, Project Liberty was preparing to shut down. The Project Liberty staff were working to preserve public education materials and to understand what could be learned from their experiences. Models they found worth employing were more related to public health than mental health. The primary lesson, Chip Felton said, was that "mental health should get into the public health business" because it had rarely been involved in preparedness for disasters and crises.

State-Sponsored Mental Health Services

In New York, the state department of mental health had to accommodate a services program focused on care for the healthy but traumatized, in addition to caring for the chronically mentally ill. In Illinois, the guiding philosophy of the state program is that responses and resources have to be crafted locally. Mental health clinics are institutional bases of the state's disaster response efforts. Staff, whose primary responsibility is focused on the care of the chronically mentally ill, can now complete training in disaster mental health. The current focus of the community mental health system on the chronically mentally ill is vastly different from a focus on community mental health needs following a terrorist attack. Lisa Razanno noted that 500 persons are trained as part of the Assertive Community Treatment (ACT) teams in Illinois (as in many other states). These clinicians can devote time to helping those in crisis as a result of a natural or man-made disaster.

Training for mental health responses to terrorism and bioterrorism could be added to ACT teams to address post-traumatic events for institutional-based providers through state mental health facilities. Such an enhancement is absent from traditional ACT trainings. One limiting factor in the development of community-based approaches is that the predominant focus has been centered on "crisis response." Little attention has been paid to long-term outcomes and to issues of mental health infrastructure and resilience, especially in preparation for a terrorist incident.

Resources

In the immediate aftermath of a disaster, federal funding for preparedness and community resilience is a challenge. Kelly Ryan said that prevention money might be found in federal preparedness funds. Concerns and questions were raised about how much of federal and state resources are currently devoted to preparedness in the state of Illinois and the city of Chicago. In Illinois, one senior administrator spends approximately 20 percent of his time on terrorism-related issues. The fundamental question framed by one state official was,

"How much as a society do we wish to invest in changing our way of life for an event that we are not clear will happen?" The process of obtaining money after a disaster was also discussed. The current system, in which an application must be made within two weeks, is biased toward emergency and short-term interventions, making it harder to address preventive community resilience and longer-term issues.

Learning from New York

It is important to learn from New York leaders and professionals involved in mental health response efforts. Their experience provides important lessons and specific recommendations. These include less focus on emergency response; less emphasis on post-traumatic stress disorder (PTSD) and more on community resilience; collaboration with media and religious leaders; increasing mental health advocacy in the government; and updating and improving mental health service delivery to address long-term needs. Risk communication that effectively reduced anxiety and minimized the likelihood of panic had the following characteristics: it was credible and endorsed by trustworthy leadership; it provided specific information about risk and efforts to reduce risk; it contained a clearly defined set of steps citizens could take; and it acknowledged apprehension.[5]

These points were carefully considered in formulating the following recommendations.

Recommendations

Clarify Mental Health Roles in a Catastrophe

Given that the number one morbidity associated with terrorism is mental health, it is important for mental health professionals and organizations to better understand their roles. Before an event, the role of mental health professionals is to help build a suitable level of preparedness. This could be in community resilience training, integration with schools and businesses, and establishing working relationships with local first responders and community authorities *before* an untoward event occurs. After an event, their aim would be to participate in various short- and long-term responses. Mental health professionals should be careful not to pathologize normal stress responses. They should build and coordinate clinical services with community-based services (e.g., disaster relief, local houses of worship); conduct and evaluate trainings before an event (e.g., with first responders, emergency department personnel at local hospitals, local county health departments, schools/faculty, Medical Service Corps volunteers); provide public information; and conduct assessments and research on a community's service offerings, identifying gaps and recommending solutions.

Advocate for Mental Health Resources within Government

Mental health is too often excluded from terrorism-/bioterrorism-related government initiatives. When bureaucrats think of terrorism, they think of communication systems, push-packs of medications and supplies, and so on. It is easier to think of concrete needs and then plan for distribution of materials. There is nothing wrong with this approach, but it offers an incomplete solution because it ignores a critical aspect of human behavior and emotions—panic. Available federal funds for mental health preparedness are not necessarily being used for those purposes, perhaps because there are no programs available or perhaps there are not adequate state, county, or community-based mechanisms to administer the funding. To improve mental health's role in disaster response, it is important to have effective mental health lobbyists and advocates working with state and local governments. Very few state leaders consider themselves to be in the health care "business," let alone the behavioral health care business, despite having departments or divisions devoted to treating those with mental health needs. Professional and consumer organizations could support such lobbying and advocacy efforts, but their focus tends to be limited to advocacy for those with severe, chronic mental illnesses rather than terrorism preparedness or response. Thus, it is equally important to communicate the message of prevention planning and resiliency follow-up to these advocates.

Build and Enhance Multisectoral Collaborations

Instead of unproductive competitiveness among mental health organizations and other sectors, mental health professionals need to establish new forms of collaboration among themselves. A first step toward the goal of being part of an organically built, integrated, cross-disciplinary system of care would be greater consultation and collaboration among mental health organizations. One nascent example is the development of a Disaster Response Committee in Illinois. It represents a mutual collaboration between clinicians (psychologists, addictions specialists, pastoral counselors, nurses, psychiatrists, and professional counselors); consumers and family members; academics (medical schools, emergency department faculty); and public and private organizations and associations (Illinois Division of Mental Health, Illinois Psychological Association, Illinois Mental Health Association, Illinois Chapter of the Alliance for the Mentally Ill, Illinois Psychiatric Society, Red Cross, Illinois Emergency Management Authority, and others).

Other important areas of collaboration include working with the media, community leaders, and chaplains and religious leaders. Mental health professionals could give talks on resilience and stress management at churches, local businesses, area libraries, chambers of commerce and service organization (e.g., Rotary, Lions, YMCA) meetings. Free materials on resilience and on warning signs of unaddressed stress could be placed in public venues such as restaurants, schools, and libraries. Other communication opportunities include guest appearances on radio programs, cable television interviews, newspaper op-ed and informative pieces, Web sites and blogs, and community listservs.

Build Collaborations with Chaplains, Religious Leaders, and Mental Health Professionals

Collaborations between mental health professionals and institutions and chaplains and religious organizations are needed to link vulnerable persons to mental health services, provide support for chaplains, and better integrate faith-based and clinical science approaches. In this way more culturally and socially appropriate interventions can be offered to trauma-affected persons who would not typically seek mental health services. These interventions could be advertised via guest speaking opportunities during a service or other meeting times, and materials could be made available for reprinting and distributing in mailings, bulletins, and in the libraries of places of worship. Information could be sent to members via e-mail and posted on the organizations' Web sites. Links between mental health professionals and chaplains and religious leaders could also include collaborative dialogue and training and establishing referral systems.

Build Collaborations between Journalists and the Media and Mental Health Professionals

Concerns to be addressed include how to report mental health issues associated with terrorism and bioterrorism and how to spread public information regarding mental health concerns. The Dart Center for

Journalism and Trauma at Washington University in Seattle (see www.dartcenter.org) is a model of such collaboration (see also chapter 9 in this volume).

Address the Psychological Needs of Those Affected by the War on Terrorism

Several U.S. subpopulations experience especially adverse consequences of the war on terrorism, such as Muslim youth, who may require clinical and preventive interventions. It is necessary to assess collaboratively the needs and perspectives of these communities. The next step would be to develop and implement community-based programs to address the most pressing needs and concerns. These programs could include supportive groups and facilitated conversations conducted in a group format in homes, places of worship, community centers, or schools (see also chapter 8 in this volume).

Promote Community Resilience

The concept of community resilience should be used as a framework for developing preparedness and response initiatives. It offers a necessary alternative to the medical and crisis focus of the PTSD framework. Developing and implementing a community resilience framework can be done through academic-public-community partnerships. Along these lines, the American Psychological Association (APA) has developed a set of materials known as The Road to Resilience. It emerged from the results of focus groups conducted after the September 11, 2001, terrorist attacks. This initiative is designed to provide the public with tools and information to help them develop and build resilience. The overarching messages are that: resilience can be learned; resilience is a journey, not a single event or point in time; and each individual's journey is different. As part of The Road to Resilience initiative, APA members may request easy-to-use tools and information to make personal connections in their communities and carry out grassroots activities around the theme of resilience.[6]

Train Students and Professionals

The next generation of mental health professionals needs to learn new concepts, methods, and practices to become capable of addressing the mental health consequences of terrorism and bioterrorism. There is a need for change in educational programs and individual teaching centers and a need for articulating guidelines, curricula, and materials for use nationally. The issue is one of folding the guidelines that exist into the curricula of medical schools and graduate schools. There is a related, budding literature that can be used and built upon, such as the trauma training guidelines published by the International Society for Traumatic Stress Studies.[7]

Conduct Multidisciplinary Research

Finally, more research is needed to develop an empirical basis for clinical and preventive responses to the mental health consequences of terrorism. Specifically, research should be conducted that: (1) addresses long-term processes; (2) goes beyond survey research and includes ethnography and qualitative methods; (3) addresses community resilience and strength; (4) understands help-seeking and how to enhance it; (5) investigates how to develop mental health services; (6) focuses on family-, community-, and societal-level phenomena; and (7) examines the interaction of mental health issues with social, economic, political, and cultural processes.

Appendix: The Participants

Religious, Community, and Media Representatives: Rev. Bob Bossie (Eighth Day Center for Justice); Bill Campbell (Host and Presenter, ABC-Channel 7 "Chicagoing"); Rebecca Ephraim (Editor, *Conscious Choice Weekly*); Inamul Haq (Islamic Studies, Benedictine University); Bill Purcell (Office of Peace and Justice, Archdiocese of Chicago); Sr. Barbara Sheehan (Director, Urban Clinical Pastoral Education, Chicago Theological Schools); Rev. Ozzie Smith (Pastor, Covenant United Church of Christ); Rev. Michael Sykes (Associate Pastor, Trinity United Church of Christ and Chaplain, Michael Reese Hospital).

New York Officials: Kelly Ryan (New York City Department of Health); Chip Felton (New York State Department of Mental Health).

Illinois Officials: J.W. Holcomb (Disaster Coordinator, Illinois Department of Human Services, Division of Mental Health); Tom Simpatico (Chicago Bureau Chief, Illinois Department of Human Services, Division of Mental Health); Chris E. Stout (Chief of Psychology, Illinois Department of Human Services, Division of Mental Health).

Professional and Consumer Groups: Mary Halpin (President-elect, Illinois Psychological Association); Ken Busch (President, Illinois Psychiatric Society); Janice Hodge (President, Coalition of

Illinois Counselor Organizations); Michael Delgatto (Association of Employee Assistance Professionals); Jan Holcomb (Director, Mental Health Association of Illinois); Badonna Reingold (Chicago Community Mental Health Board).

Academic: Ala Albazzar (Psychiatry Research, UIC); Joan Meyer Anzia (Psychiatry and Veterans Administration, UIC); Pavil Cherian (Psychiatry Resident, UIC); Ralph Cintron (English Department, UIC); Judith Cook (Professor of Psychiatry, UIC); Peter Czarnkowski (Psychiatry Resident, UIC); Vaughn Fayle (ICORC Center, Psychiatry, UIC); Joe Flaherty (Chair, Psychiatry Department, UIC); Judith Gardner (English, Gender and Women's Studies, UIC); Steve Jones (Head of the Department of Communications, UIC); Daniel Kim (Psychiatry Resident, UIC); Navid Rashid (Psychiatry Resident, UIC); Lisa Razanno (Associate Professor of Psychology, Psychiatry, UIC); Amer Smajkic (Psychiatry Resident, UIC); Stevan M. Weine (Director, ICORC, Associate Professor of Psychiatry, UIC).

Notes

1. L. R. Goldfrank, Chair, Committee on Responding to the Psychological Consequences of Terrorism, Institute of Medicine, *Preparing for the Psychological Consequences of Terrorism: A Public Health Strategy* (Washington, DC: National Academies Press, 2003).

2. Ibid.

3. J. A. Davis, *Providing Critical Incident Stress Debriefing (CISD) to Individuals and Communities in Situational Crisis*, http://www.aaets.org/article54.htm (accessed February 3, 2006).

4. "Two Studies Raise Doubts on Trauma Counseling's Value," *Washington Post*, 6 September, 2002, http://www.washingtonpost.com.

5. M. Heldring, "Mental Health and Primary Care in a Time of Terrorism: The Psychological Effect of Public Communication about Risk," in Kimmel (2005) The Report of the Task Force on the Psychological Effects of Efforts to Prevent Terrorism. Unpublished.

6. Road to Resilience Campaign, http://www.apapractice.org/apo/insider/pec/resilience.html# (accessed December 13, 2005).

7. S. Weine et al., "Guidelines for International Training in Mental Health and Psychological Interventions for Trauma Exposed Populations in Clinical and Community Settings," *Psychiatry* 65 no. 2 (2002), 156–164.

Afterword

Chris E. Stout

When the topic of terrorism comes up, it seems to spur many responses—fear, curiosity, and opinions. I have been in many preparedness planning meetings over the last four years, and without exception have found that psychology was at best an afterthought vis-à-vis planning. Maybe some people thought of post-event mental health response, but in 2001 and 2002, very few people thought psychology was relevant to planning for terrorism. In one meeting, the official responsible for local emergency planning for a very large urban setting admitted that they had not included any psychological aspects in their operations. Because of our meeting (see chapter 10 in this volume), he now would.

This book explores the meta-impacts of the "war on terrorism." As Stevan Weine and I note in chapter 10, the war on terror, like the "war on poverty" and the "war on drugs," defines a social problem, thereafter expecting its institutions and citizens to make policies and programs that offer a solution. The creation of a term such as a "war" creates a rubric that can exacerbate the problem it was created to address. We become focused on a military model and move away from the political, economic, and psychological initiatives that are more appropriate.

Zimbardo notes in the foreword that contemporary psychological research can instruct us how to provide successful public alarms. Beyond his example of the color-coded alerts, there is much more that psychology has to offer—across its various areas—social, political, clinical, experimental, forensic, cultural, personality, behavioral, systems theory, cognitive organizational and more. There is a fine line of knowing how much and what type of information is optimal for keeping the public up to date without causing panic or information fatigue. Perhaps psychology's guidance about issuing general alarms that make people more paranoid and less alert will help officials understand that "accurate risk-assessment when combined with appropriate preparation can go a long way in mitigating fears and anxieties."[1]

"Anthrax is not contagious, fear is!" This is one of my favorite quotes. It was made by Rear Admiral Brian W. Flynn, former Assistant Surgeon General of the U.S. Public Health Service, during his presentation "Terrorism and Mental Health" at the National Health Policy Forum. Again, I think it speaks to the importance of message management and the communication disconnect to which Zimbardo refers.

At the time of this writing, there has been a new controversy regarding domestic spying—from the revelation that the National Security Agency has been tapping phone conversations without warrants. Stephen Flynn from the Council on Foreign Relations, said "I believe that when it comes to protecting and safeguarding the American people, we must not only focus on the dangers posed by terrorists and their weapons, but we must be mindful of the need to protect ourselves from ourselves." Ironically, while many contributors to this volume stress the dangers of negative biases toward those of Islamic faith or Middle Eastern appearance, the FBI considers the worst domestic terrorist threats to be ecoterrorist and radical animal rights groups. These groups are responsible for more than 1,450 criminal acts in the past 29 years resulting in $110 million in damages.[2]

There are serious questions from observers of all political perspectives about the efficacy of the Department of Homeland Security. Constructive criticisms should not be summarily dismissed as anti-American or seditious. Instead, constructive dialogues need to be conducted among policymakers and advisors with the benefit of psychologically informed, scientific input. Psychologists can contribute to both the process and the success of dealing with terrorism while mitigating or avoiding any iatrogenic effects and unintended consequences.

Notes

1. Chris E. Stout, "Using Psychology To Counter Terrorism at the Personal and Community Level," in *The Psychology of Terrorism*, condensed edition, ed. C. E. Stout (Westport, CT: Praeger, 2004), p. 1.

2. "How Safe Is the Homeland?" *Wall Street Journal*, January 1, 2006, p. A7.

Index

About the Series Advisory Board

BRUCE BONECUTTER, Ph.D., is Director of Behavioral Services at the Elgin Community Mental Health Center, the Illinois Department of Human Services state hospital serving adults in greater Chicago. He is also a clinical assistant professor of psychology at the University of Illinois at Chicago. A clinical psychologist specializing in health, consulting, and forensic psychology, Bonecutter is a longtime member of the American Psychological Association Task Force on Children and the Family. He is a member of the Association for the Treatment of Sexual Abusers, International, the Alliance for the Mentally Ill, and the Mental Health Association of Illinois.

JOSEPH FLAHERTY, M.D., is chief of psychiatry at the University of Illinois Hospital, a professor of psychiatry at the University of Illinois College of Medicine, and a professor of community health science at the UIC College of Public Health. He is a founding member of the Society for the Study of Culture and Psychiatry. Flaherty has been a consultant to the World Health Organization, the National Institute of Mental Health, and the Falk Institute in Jerusalem. He's been director of undergraduate education and graduate education in the Department of Psychiatry at the University of Illinois. Flaherty has also been staff psychiatrist and chief of psychiatry at Veterans Administration West Side Hospital in Chicago.

MICHAEL HOROWITZ, Ph.D., is president and professor of clinical psychology at the Chicago School of Professional Psychology, one of the nation's leading not-for-profit graduate schools of psychology. Earlier, he served as dean and professor of the Arizona School of Professional Psychology. A clinical psychologist practicing independently since 1987, his work has focused on psychoanalysis, intensive individual therapy, and couples therapy. He has provided disaster mental health services to the American Red Cross. Horowitz's special interests include the study of fatherhood.

SHELDON I. MILLER, M.D., is a professor of psychiatry at Northwestern University, and director of the Stone Institute of Psychiatry at Northwestern Memorial Hospital. He is also director of the American Board of Psychiatry and Neurology, director of the American Board of Emergency Medicine, and director of the Accreditation Council for Graduate Medical Education. Miller is also an examiner for the American Board of Psychiatry and Neurology. He is founding editor of the *American Journal of Addictions* and founding chairman of the American Psychiatric Association's Committee on Alcoholism. Miller has also been a lieutenant commander in the military, serving as psychiatric consultant to the Navajo Area Indian Health Service at Window Rock, Arizona. He is a member and past president of the Executive Committee for the American Academy of Psychiatrists in Alcoholism and Addictions.

DENNIS P. MORRISON, Ph.D., is chief executive officer at the Center for Behavioral Health in Indiana, the first behavioral health company ever to win the Joint Commission on Accreditation of Health Care Organizations Codman Award for excellence in the use of outcomes management to achieve health care quality improvement. He is president of the board of directors for the Community Healthcare Foundation in Bloomington and has been a member of the board of directors for the American College of Sports Psychology. He has served as a consultant to agencies including the Ohio Department of Mental Health, Tennessee Association of Mental Health Organizations, Oklahoma Psychological Association, North Carolina Council of Community Mental Health Centers, and the National Center for Health Promotion in Michigan.

WILLIAM H. REID, M.D., is a clinical and forensic psychiatrist and a consultant to attorneys and courts throughout the United States. He is a clinical professor of psychiatry at the University of Texas Health Science Center. Reid is also an adjunct professor of psychiatry at Texas A&M College of Medicine and Texas Tech University School of Medicine, as well as a clinical faculty member at the Austin Psychiatry Residency Program. He is chairman of the Scientific Advisory Board and medical advisor to the Texas Depressive & Manic Depressive Association as well as an examiner for the American Board of Psychiatry and Neurology. He has served as president of the American Academy of Psychiatry and the Law, chairman of the research section for an International Conference on the Psychiatric Aspects of Terrorism, and medical director for the Texas Department of Mental Health and Mental Retardation. Reid earned an Exemplary Psychiatrist Award from the National Alliance for the Mentally Ill. He has been cited on the Best Doctors in America listing since 1998.

About the Editors and Contributors

PAUL R. KIMMEL is chair of the APA Task Force on the Psychological Effects of Efforts To Prevent Terrorism. As the first public policy fellow at the American Psychological Association, Kimmel influenced the APA to join a legislative effort to establish the U.S. Institute of Peace. He was one of the first peace fellows at the Institute. He has served as an evaluator of State Department and Agency for International Development international education programs, a trainer of international business people going abroad, and a professor at several universities culminating in his contributions to the Peace Studies program at Saybrook Graduate School and Research Center. He is also a past president of the APA Division of Peace Psychology and of Psychologists for Social Responsibility.

CHRIS E. STOUT is series editor for the Praeger series Contemporary Psychology. Stout is a licensed clinical psychologist and is a clinical full professor at the University of Illinois College of Medicine's Department of Psychiatry. He served as an NGO special representative to the United Nations. He was appointed to the World Economic Forum's Global Leaders of Tomorrow and he has served as an invited faculty at the annual meeting in Davos, Switzerland. He is the founding director of the Center for Global Initiatives. Stout is a fellow of the American Psychological Association, past president of the Illinois Psychological Association, and is a distinguished practitioner in the

National Academies of Practice. Stout has published or presented over 300 papers and 30 books and manuals on various topics in psychology. His works have been translated into six languages. He has lectured across the nation and internationally in 19 countries and has visited 6 continents and almost 70 countries. He was noted as being "one of the most frequently cited psychologists in the scientific literature" in a study by Hartwick College. He is the recipient of the American Psychological Association's International Humanitarian Award.

DANIEL J. CHRISTIE is professor of psychology at Ohio State University, has served as president of the Society for the Psychological Study of Peace, Conflict, and Violence, the Peace Psychology Division of the American Psychological Association. Christie edited, with Richard Wagner and Deborah Winter, *Peace, Conflict, and Violence: Peace Psychology for the 21st Century* (2001), and *Journal of Social Issues* (2006, Vol. 62, no. 1) on the topic, Peace Psychology since the Cold War: More Differentiated, More Integrated Systemically.

JOHN F. DOVIDIO is professor of psychology at the University of Connecticut. He is editor of the *Journal of Personality and Social Psychology—Interpersonal Relations and Group Processes.* Dovidio's research interests are in stereotyping, prejudice, and discrimination; nonverbal communication; and altruism and helping. He received the Gordon Allport Intergroup Relations Prize in 1985, 1998, and 2001 and the Kurt Lewin Award in 2004 (with S. L. Gaertner) for his work on prejudice and discrimination.

VICTORIA M. ESSES is professor of psychology at the University of Western Ontario, Canada. She has served as associate editor of *Personality and Social Psychology Bulletin* and of *Group Processes and Intergroup Relations.* She has also served as council member and publication chair of the Society for the Psychological Study of Social Issues. Her research interests include intergroup relations, prejudice, and discrimination, with a particular interest in group competition, and attitudes toward immigrants and refugees.

STEPHEN FABICK is a clinical and consulting psychologist in Birmingham, Michigan. He has been president of Psychologists for Social Responsibility and written two manuals used by that organization, *US & THEM: The Challenge of Diversity* and *US &*

THEM: Moderating Group Conflict. He has been editor of *Enemy Images: A Resource Manual on Reducing Enmity.* He leads workshops on conflict and prejudice reduction.

GORDON HODSON is an assistant professor at Brock University, Canada. His research interests include prejudice and discrimination, individual differences, perceptions of intergroup threat, and group contact.

BERNICE LOTT is professor emerita of psychology and women's studies at the University of Rhode Island. She received her university's Excellence Award for scholarly achievement, served as president of the APA's Division 35 (the Psychology of Women), and has been honored for scholarly, teaching, mentoring, and social policy contributions by the APA's Committee on Women, Division 35, the Association for Women in Psychology, and the National Multicultural Conference and Summit. In 1999, the University of Rhode Island awarded her the honorary degree of doctor of humane letters. She is a fellow of APA and of Divisions 1, 8, 9, and 35. Her areas of interest are interpersonal discrimination; the intersections among gender, ethnicity, and social class; the social psychology of poverty; and multicultural issues. Currently, she represents Division 9 on the APA's Council of Representatives; is a member of an Interdivisional Minority Pipeline Project working on strategies to increase the recruitment and retention of graduate students of color; and has represented Divisions 9 and 35 on the coalition of Divisions for Social Justice.

CLARK MCCAULEY is professor of psychology at Bryn Mawr College, Director of the Solomon Asch Center for Study of Ethnopolitical Conflict at the University of Pennsylvania, and Codirector of the National Consortium for Study of Terrorism and Responses to Terrorism. He is co-editor of *The Psychology of Ethnic and Cultural Conflict* (Praeger, 2004), and with Dan Chirot authored *Why Not Kill Them All? The Logic of Mass Political Murder and Finding Ways of Avoiding it* (2006).

ILENE A. SERLIN is a fellow of the American Psychological Association, where she served on the Presidential Task Force on the Psychological Effects of Efforts To Prevent Terrorism. She is past president and council representative from Division 32

(Humanistic Psychology), and wrote "Psychologists Working with Trauma: A Humanistic Approach" in the *APA Monitor* and (with Cannon) "A Humanistic Approach to the Psychology of Trauma" in *Living with Terror, Working with Trauma: A Clinician's Handbook* (ed. D. Knafo; 2005). She received a citation from the American Red Cross for work during the San Francisco earthquake and has served on the San Francisco and Marin County Psychological Association Disaster Committee and wrote "Reconstructing Lives" in the *San Francisco Examiner.*

NINA K. THOMAS is a psychologist/psychoanalyst in private practice in New York City and Morristown, New Jersey. She is co-chair of the Relational Orientation of the New York University postdoctoral program in psychotherapy and psychoanalysis, and co-coordinator of the Trauma Specialization Project of the NYU postdoctoral program. She is the author of: "An Eye for an Eye: Fantasies of Revenge in the Aftermath of Trauma" *Living withTerror, Working with Trauma: A Clinician's Handbook* (ed. D. Knafo; 2005) and "The Use of the Hero" in *On the Ground after September 11: Mental Health Responses and Practical Knowledge Gained* (eds. Y. Danieli and R.L. Dingman; 2005).

RHODA UNGER is a professor emerita of psychology at Montclair State University and a resident scholar at the Women's Studies Research Center at Brandeis University. She has been president of the Society for the Psychology of Women and, more recently, president of the Society for the Psychological Study of Social Issues (SPSSI). She was the inaugural editor of SPSSI's electronic and print journal *Analyses of Social Issues and Public Policy.* In that capacity she edited the special issue on Terrorism and Its Consequences, which appeared on the Internet just two months after September 11, 2001. She has recently co-edited a special issue of *Feminism & Psychology* on the relationship between feminism and political psychology.

STEVAN WEINE is a psychiatrist, researcher, writer, teacher, and clinician in the Department of Psychiatry of the University of Illinois at Chicago. He is director of the International Center of Responses to Catastrophes at the University of Illinois at Chicago. He was co-founder and co-director of the Project on Genocide, Psychiatry and Witnessing, which provides family-focused community-based mental health services to Bosnians, conducts interdisciplinary research on survivors, and engages in mental health reform in postwar countries. He is principal investigator of a National Institute of Mental Health–funded research study investigating the Coffee and Family Education and Support intervention with Bosnian and Kosovar families in Chicago. In 2001, he was awarded a Career Scientist Award from the National Institute of Mental Health. Weine is author of a book of survivor's oral histories called *When History Is a Nightmare: Lives and Memories of Ethnic Cleansing in Bosnia-Herzegovina* (1999). Another book is in press, *Testimony and Catastrophe: The Traumas of Political Violence and Mikhai Bakhtin.* Weine is also chair of the Task Force on International Trauma Training of the International Society for Traumatic Stress Studies. He is co-founder of the Kosovar Family Professional Education Collaborative and Services and scientific director of the Services Based Training for Kosovar Community Mental Health and Prevention.

MICHAEL WESSELLS is senior child protection specialist for the Christian Children's Fund and professor of psychology at Randolph-Macon College. He has served as president of the Division of Peace Psychology of the American Psychological Association and of Psychologists for Social Responsibility. His research on children and armed conflict examines child soldiers, psychosocial assistance in emergencies, and postconflict reconstruction for peace. He regularly advises UN agencies, donors, and governments on the situation of children in armed conflict and issues regarding child protection and well-being. He has extensive experience in postconflict reconstruction in countries such as Afghanistan and East Timor. In countries such as Afghanistan, Angola, Sierra Leone, East Timor, Kosova, and Afghanistan, he helps to develop community-based, culturally grounded programs that assist children, families, and communities affected by armed conflict.

PHILIP G. ZIMBARDO is internationally recognized as the "voice and face of contemporary psychology" through the PBS-TV series, *Discovering Psychology,* his media appearances, best-selling trade books on shyness, and his classic research, The Stanford Prison Experiment. Zimbardo has been a Stanford University professor since 1968, having taught previously at Yale University, New York University, and Columbia University. He is now an emeritus professor but still teaches undergraduate courses. He has been given numerous awards and honors as an educator, researcher, writer, and for service to the profession. Among his more than 350 professional publications and 50 books is the oldest current textbook in psychology, *Psychology and Life* going into its 18th edition. Zimbardo is enmeshed in his major opus detailing the chronology of the Stanford Prison Experiment, its links to the Abu Ghraib abuses that is to appear in 2007, *The Lucifer Effect: Understanding How Good People Turn Evil.* Zimbardo has been a social-political activist, challenging the government's wars in Vietnam and Iraq, and the American correctional system. Zimbardo was president of the Western Psychological Association; president of the American Psychological Association; chair of the Council of Scientific Society Presidents, representing 63 scientific, math, and technical associations; and is now chair of the Western Psychological Foundation and president of the Philip Zimbardo Foundation. He is also director of a new terrorism center co-sponsored by Stanford University and the Naval Postgraduate School, and the Interdisciplinary Center for Policy, Education, and Research on Terrorism.